3-22-06

THE
BROTHERS
BULGER

How They Terrorized
and Corrupted Boston
for a Quarter Century

HOWIE CARR

WARNER BOOKS

NEW YORK   BOSTON

Warner Books

Time Warner Book Group
1271 Avenue of the Americas, New York, NY 10020
Visit our Web site at www.twbookmark.com.

Printed in the United States of America

First Edition: February 2006
10   9   8   7   6   5   4   3

Library of Congress Cataloging-in-Publication Data
Carr, Howie.
     The brothers Bulger : how they terrorized and corrupted Boston for a quarter century /
Howie Carr.— 1st ed.
       p. cm.
     Summary: "A portrait of Boston's infamous Bulger brothers, Whitey and Billy—one as
the city's most feared mobster, the other as a power in the Massachusetts State Senate."—
Provided by publisher.
     Includes index.
     ISBN-13: 978-0-446-57651-2
     ISBN-10: 0-446-57651-4
  1. Bulger, Whitey, 1929– 2. Bulger, William. 3. Gangsters—Massachusetts—Boston—
Biography. 4. Murderers—Massachusetts—Boston Region—Biography. 5. Politicians—
Massachusetts—Boston—Biography. 6. Organized crime—Massachusetts—Boston—Case
studies. 7. Political corruption—Massachusetts. I. Title.
     HV6452.M4C37 2006
     364.1'092'27461—dc22   2005023524

Book design by Giorgetta Bell McRee

For Kathy and my father

ACKNOWLEDGMENTS

First, I'd like to thank my beautiful wife, Kathy, and our three lovely daughters: Carolyn, Charlotte, and Christina.

Without the help of everyone at the *Boston Herald*, where I have worked for so many years, I could never have written this book. Thanks especially to publisher Patrick Purcell, editorial director Ken Chandler, former editors Andy Costello and Andrew Gully, and to all the reporters, photographers, columnists, and editors going back to the days of Hearst, especially Joe Heaney. My gratitude as well to the *Herald*'s peerless library staff, especially, in recent years, Al Thibeault, John Cronin, and Chris Donnelly.

Thanks to my literary agents, Larry Moulter and Helen Rees, and to my editors at Warner Books, first Rick Horgan, now at Crown, and later Les Pockell. Also, thanks to my "book doctor," Jeff, whose assistance was invaluable. My researcher, Stuart Horwitz, also did fine work, obtaining interviews from people who might not have spoken to me, and he always persevered, despite the occasional brush-off.

Also, I owe much to some reporters at the *Boston Globe* with whom I have worked (and competed against), although I won't name them for fear of damaging their future prospects. But I must single out two people who no longer work on Morrissey

Boulevard—former *Globe* staffers Dick Lehr and Gerard O'Neill. In many ways their 1999 book *Black Mass* lit the path for others to follow. In particular, their work on the 75 State Street scandal, first for the newspaper and then in their book, cannot be overpraised.

The information provided to me in the preparation of this book came from more people than I could ever hope to list, even if they wanted me to, which I believe most of them don't. They know who they are, and they know how much I am in their debt. Thanks to one and all, especially to the survivors, and that is not too melodramatic a word to use when considering what so many people involved in this sordid story have endured over the past forty or so years.

I would also like to express my appreciation to, in no particular order, and for various reasons: Chris Lydon, Nancy Shack, Larry Bruce, Michael Goldman, and Jon Keller, and among those who are now gone, Jerry Williams, Paul Corsetti, Jackie McDermott, and Fred Langone.

If I have neglected to mention anyone by name who wanted to be so identified, I apologize. Better safe than sorry, even now.

PREFACE

THIS BOOK WAS WRITTEN based upon material gathered from both the public record and interviews I have conducted and documents I have procured during the last twenty-five-plus years, working as a reporter and columnist for the *Boston Herald*, a reporter for several Boston TV stations, and as a radio talk show host.

None of the incidents or dialogue in this book are imagined. This is a work of nonfiction. Much of the information came from bugs and wiretaps, among them the 1981 FBI recordings of the Angiulo brothers' conversations with their associates at the gang's headquarters at 98 Prince Street in the North End. Another source of material came from the FBI recording of the Mafia initiation ceremonies in Medford in 1989. Other material came from various criminal trials and filings in court cases. Large portions of this book are based on testimony during U.S. District Court Judge Mark Wolf's hearings in 1998 in the case of *U.S. v. Francis P. Salemme et al.* Other material comes from earlier books that have been written about some of these events, and I have tried to cite those works in this book whenever it was appropriate.

During Judge Wolf's hearings, hundreds of previously classified FBI documents were turned over to the defendants and/or made public, and these were made available to me during the writing of this book. I have also had access to previously unreleased documents, including videotapes, police reports, Whitey Bulger's military records, and his complete writings on the LSD experiments in which he took part at the Atlanta Federal Penitentiary in the late 1950s.

Some of the dialogue comes from the St. Patrick's Day breakfasts that William M. Bulger hosted every March through 1996. I have also read most of the *Boston Herald*'s newspaper clipping files on the major characters in this account. Those files include reports from both major daily newspapers in Boston, as well as, in earlier years, stories in such now defunct newspapers as the *Record American*, the *Sunday Advertiser*, the *Traveler*, and the *Evening Globe*.

I was present at both congressional committee hearings to which William M. Bulger was subpoenaed to testify in 2002–03.

Full disclosure: The lawyer at various points for both William M. Bulger and corrupt FBI agent John "Zip" Connolly was R. Robert Popeo, who has also represented me in two investigations of my tax returns, one by the Internal Revenue Service and the other by the Massachusetts Department of Revenue. I have always maintained, and continue to do so, that both probes were politically motivated, and no charges were ever filed.

Harvard Law School Professor Alan Dershowitz, who is mentioned here in connection with the appointment of William Bulger's aide Paul Mahoney as a district court judge in 1990, represented my wife in a 1998 libel action against two broadcast networks and radio talk show host Don Imus. That lawsuit was settled out of court.

When Steven "Stippo" Rakes, whose story is told in chapter 13, was convicted of perjury in U.S. District Court, at his request I, along with many others, including the late Congressman J. Joseph Moakley, wrote to his judge before sentencing. I asked the judge to consider the unusual circumstances of Rakes's action, and urged him to impose a lenient sentence. I would write the same letter again. (Rakes received probation.)

During the heyday of the Bulger gang, I was indirectly threatened several times by Whitey's minions. At one point in the late 1980s I worked at a TV station in Dorchester near the South Boston Liquor Mart, Whitey's store. One of my co-workers, the son of a former mayor of Boston, often stopped in at the store. A store employee once inquired of my colleague why, although I drove by the store almost daily and often saw Whitey and Stevie Flemmi conducting business outside, I had never once pulled into the parking lot, let alone entered the store. My friend nervously said he had no idea why I preferred to patronize the package store in Andrew Square.

"Tell him we got a Dumpster out back waiting for him," the unidentified gang member told my colleague. "It'll be another Robin Benedict."

Robin Benedict was a prostitute in Boston's red-light district, the Combat Zone, who was murdered by an infatuated Tufts University professor; her body was never found.

After Whitey's flight, a photographer for the *Herald* ran into Kevin Weeks at a tanning salon in Framingham, and Weeks informed him that the gang had once known where I lived—next to a graveyard in Acton.

On another organized crime wiretap, a gang associate was recorded as saying Whitey was "henshit" at me after *Boston* magazine, for which I freelanced at the time, estimated his net worth at $50 million. Whitey, according to the associate, concluded (erroneously) that I was trying to set him up for a "snatch" by Italian gangsters.

Billy Bulger did not like my coverage of him either at the State House or later during his tenure as president of the University of Massachusetts. At the State House, he referred to me

publicly at least once as "the savage," and during his sworn testimony in 2003 described stories I had written as "savaging"
the daughter of his brother's girlfriend, who was on a public
payroll. At the hearing, he blamed many of his problems on
"the tabloid talk show stuff in Boston." I work for both a
tabloid and a talk show.

During the televised congressional hearings in 2003 I sat
two rows directly behind Billy during the morning session. In
full view of the C-SPAN camera, I periodically grimaced, made
faces, stuck out my tongue, rolled my eyes, and grabbed my
throat when I thought Billy was being less than forthcoming
in his testimony.

For this performance I was criticized in some quarters, and
applauded in others.

In the summer of 2003, I was approached, informally, by a
representative of Governor Mitt Romney about becoming a
member of the board of trustees of the University of Massachusetts, along with, according to press reports, Professor Dershowitz and retired judge E. George Daher, the first man to
refer to Billy Bulger as a "corrupt midget." I immediately said
that if offered the position of trustee, I would accept it.

Shortly after he was informed of the likely appointments of
the three of us to his board, Billy resigned as president of the
university. Others were then appointed to the UMass board of
trustees.

Finally, I am in no way related to Howard T. "Howie" Winter, who preceded Whitey Bulger as boss of the Winter Hill
Gang. Winter and I do share the same first name and nickname
and at different times Winter and I did live one street apart in
the Spring Hill section of the city of Somerville. My home was
on Montrose Street and he resided on Madison Street, but that
is the only connection between us.

Boston is a small town. Somerville is smaller yet.

PROLOGUE

BILLY BULGER WAS ON THE spot. This time he couldn't take the Fifth Amendment when a congressman asked him if he knew where his fugitive gangster brother was hiding out, with a $1 million bounty on his head.

It was June 19, 2003, and the sixty-nine-year-old president of the University of Massachusetts was sitting in a packed hearing room in the basement of the Rayburn Office Building in Washington, D.C. For six months, ever since he'd stonewalled the House Committee on Government Reform in Boston, William Michael Bulger had called in every chit, pulled every string, to prevent this moment from arriving.

But the reality was that despite his $359,000-a-year salary, Billy Bulger was no longer the most powerful man in Massachusetts politics, and he could not defy Congress.

His brother James—better known by his nickname of Whitey—had been on the lam for more than nine years now. He was on the FBI's Ten Most Wanted List, charged with nineteen murders, and two years earlier his wanted poster had appeared briefly in the film *Hannibal*. But Whitey hadn't actually been seen in the United States since 1996, and he was slowly making his way into the pantheon of vanished legends—Ambrose Bierce, D. B. Cooper, Jimmy Hoffa, Judge Crater . . .

Billy had bought a new suit for his appearance before Congress. It was from Brooks Brothers on Newbury Street, to Billy the epitome of upper-crust Yankee respectability. Everyone back in Boston would be watching the C-SPAN feed that was being broadcast on every major TV station in the city.

The committee chairman was Tom Davis, a Virginia Republican, Amherst College '71, and Billy had tried to play the Amherst card with him—hey, can't we work something out? In Boston, they had negotiated over a closed-door hearing—no cameras, no damnable reporters. But word had leaked, and now Davis was gaveling the public hearing to order.

The chairman asked Billy if he wished to make a statement before the questioning began. Billy looked down at a prepared text, which had already been distributed to the press.

"I now recognize," Billy said of his brother, hesitantly, without a trace of his fabled cockiness, "that I didn't fully grasp the dimensions of his life."

It was a far cry from what he'd proudly told newspaper reporters of his brother in 1988: "There is much to admire."

Billy was now immunized—nothing he said could be used against him, unless he lied. But he could no longer invoke his Fifth Amendment privilege against self-incrimination. He was faced with a Clintonian dilemma, and there was only one way out. He would have to . . . not remember.

"I am particularly sorry," Billy continued, "to think that he may have been guilty of some of the horrible things of which he is accused."

About the allegations made against his older brother, Billy had written in his memoirs seven years earlier: "I am confident much of it has been circulated as an oblique political attack on me. I know some of the allegations and much of the innuendo to be absolutely false."

But that was before the Massachusetts State Police recovered six bodies, including those of two twenty-six-year-old women, from the shallow graves Whitey and his underworld partner, another serial killer named Stevie Flemmi, had dug on public property in and around Boston. In his memoirs, Billy had never mentioned that Stevie Flemmi was a pedophile, or that Flemmi's parents had lived next door to him since 1980. Nor did he inform his readers that Flemmi often spent the night at his parents' house, across the courtyard from Billy, and that most Sundays, Whitey and Stevie huddled at the Flemmis' house with the FBI agents they had bribed with cash, jewelry, and wine.

"I do still live in the hope that the worst of the charges against him will prove groundless," Billy Bulger read. "It is my hope."

But the congressmen would have none of it. Although the committee was ostensibly investigating almost forty years of corruption in the Boston FBI office, today's hearing was about the Bulger brothers—Whitey and Billy. Even the Massachusetts Democrats on the committee, playing to the vast television audiences watching in New England, would take their shots. But the most relentless congressman was Republican Dan Burton, the former committee chairman who had pursued Billy for more than a year. Dan Burton was from Indiana—a "jerkwater state," as Billy would have described it at one of his annual St. Patrick's Day breakfasts in South Boston. This was Dan Burton's show, and he couldn't be cajoled or threatened. If Burton had been from Massachusetts, Billy would have known which buttons to push. But he was from Indianapolis, and Billy Bulger was now under oath.

"Mr. Bulger," Burton began, "what did you think your brother did for a living?"

Gone was the glib, gavel-wielding boss of Massachusetts politics. "Well, I know that he was for the most part," Billy stammered, speaking uncharacteristically in sentence fragments. "I had the feeling that he was uh in the business of gaming and and uh . . ." He paused. "Whatever. It was vague to me but I didn't think, uh—for a long while he had some jobs but uh ultimately uh it was clear that he was not uh um being um uh you know he wasn't doing what I'd like him to do."

Billy's biggest problem was a phone call he'd received from Whitey in January 1995, just after he'd fled Boston. Though Billy was an attorney, an officer of the court, he had told no one in law enforcement about the conversation until 2000, after one of Whitey's underlings had disappeared into the Witness Protection Program. The feds had called Billy before a grand jury, laying a perjury trap, but much to the feds' chagrin, he'd admitted receiving the call. Angry and frustrated, someone in the U.S. Attorney's Office had leaked his testimony to the newspapers.

"I expected I would receive a call," Billy said, tentatively, mixing tenses. "That was his request. I am sure he would like a private conversation."

Billy had had six months to prepare his answers, but he still couldn't come up with the witty, cutting responses that had so long been his trademark in state politics. In fact, Billy sounded as tongue-tied as one of his majority leaders.

"I never thought we'd still be—that there would not have been a resolution of it. Ordinarily in these cases—"

—the cops catch the guy. Billy stopped himself before he actually said it. The only other time Whitey had been a fugitive, from a bank robbery indictment in 1955, he'd lasted only three months on the lam before the FBI collared him. But in 1994, Whitey was forty years wiser, and perhaps $40 million richer.

"So the tone of it," Billy said, "was something like this: He told me, uh, don't believe everything that's being said about me. It's not true."

But of course it was true. All of it.

"I think," Billy said, slowly, "he was trying to give me some comfort on that level and he—I don't know . . ." Billy paused, as everyone stared at him. "I think he asked me to tell everybody he was okay and, uh, and then I told him, well, we care very much for you and um, we're very hopeful. I think I said I hoped this will have a happy ending. At the time there was no talk of the more terrible crimes."

It was December 23, 1994, the day that Whitey Bulger vanished. He had always assumed that it would come to this, so in 1977 he had begun constructing a new identity for himself. The most powerful organized crime figure in New England was about to turn into "Thomas F. Baxter."

When the cops got around to searching his condo, and his girlfriends' houses, they would find an Irish passport, as well as how-to books about living on the lam. There were almost as many of them as there were World War II books and videotapes. Whitey was obsessed with Nazis, so much so that in 2004 the feds would consider staking out the sixtieth anniversary commemorations of D-day in Normandy, hoping to catch him traveling on a European Union passport.

The cops would also find his diaries. He'd begun putting his thoughts down on paper a lot just before he left. He would sit at the kitchen table in his condo in Quincy, where he'd replaced the sliding glass door that led to his back patio with a bulletproof steel plate. Night after night, he'd write in his old-fashioned Palmer-style longhand about the LSD experiments he'd taken part in while in prison in Atlanta in the late 1950s.

"It's 3 a.m. and years later, I'm still effected [sic] by L.S.D. in that I fear sleep—the horrible nightmares that I fight to escape by waking, the taste of adrenalin[e], gasping for breath. Often I'm woken by a scream and find it's me screaming. I later read while still in prison that LSD can cause chromosome damage and birth defects—that one article determined for me that having children was too risky."

Would a jury buy it? That Whitey Bulger cared about children? Whitey hoped he never had to find out.

It was late afternoon, and as he drove toward downtown Boston, the Christmas lights twinkled in the projects and the three-decker houses of South Boston where he'd spent his entire life, except for a few years in the air force, and later almost a decade in federal prison, in Lewisburg, Atlanta, Leavenworth, and Alcatraz.

About to be indicted again, for the first time in thirty-eight years, Whitey would disappear, until he could put the fix in, the way he always had. Something always seemed to happen when the law got too close to Whitey—wiretaps would be compromised, bugs discovered. Cops hot on his trail would find themselves demoted or transferred. Witnesses would disappear, or recant, or forget. Or Whitey would receive a phone call moments before the police raided a warehouse stuffed with marijuana that just happened not to be under his protection.

Surely something could be worked out this time too. And if not, "Tom Baxter" would enjoy his golden years, another retired gentleman on the road with his lady friend.

Beside him in the front seat of the Grand Marquis was his most trusted underling, Kevin Weeks, age thirty-seven. Weeks had been with Whitey almost from the day he graduated high school in 1974. Like all of Whitey's closest associates, Weeks called him "Jim." Over the years he'd helped Whitey plan his eventual flight. They had beepers, and code words, and now Kevin would be Whitey's eyes and ears in the Town, as they referred to South Boston.

In the back seat sat Theresa Stanley. At fifty-seven, she was the oldest of Whitey's girlfriends, and she preferred a more traditional, lace-curtain Irish phrase to describe their relationship. She "went with him," and had since 1965 when he was a thirty-six-year-old ex-con, fresh out of Leavenworth, and she was a single mother of four young children.

Theresa had been looking forward to Christmas this year. She and Whitey had just returned to Boston after a lengthy trip to Europe, a dry run for the journey they were about to embark upon. Whitey had made good use of his time, renting safe-deposit boxes in banks in Dublin, London, and Venice, before they finally returned home, at Theresa's behest, after Thanksgiving.

On this day, Whitey and Theresa had been planning to drive to Copley Square and finish their Christmas shopping at Neiman Marcus. But around 4:00 p.m., dusk on one of the shortest days of the year, Kevin Weeks had beeped Whitey and asked where he was.

"Theresa's," Whitey said. "We're just going out."

"We need to talk," Kevin Weeks said. This was one of Whitey's rules: Never talk on the phone if you didn't have to, and if you had to, always keep it vague.

Weeks had gotten a tip from John Connolly—"Zip," as Whitey called him—about an hour earlier. Zip, a retired FBI agent who'd been raised in the same public housing project as the Bulgers, had been feeding Whitey information for years—about informants, indictments, investigations, and wiretaps. And now, in addition to his FBI pension, Zip had a six-figure job at Boston Edison, compliments of Billy, Zip would always tell his friends while he and Billy both denied it publicly.

Five minutes after Weeks's call, Whitey's Grand Marquis pulled up in front of the South Boston Liquor Mart at the rotary on Old Colony Avenue, the gang's headquarters for the last decade or so.

Weeks hopped in, but said nothing. That was another one of the rules. You didn't talk in the car, not since the Drug Enforcement Administration had put the new door on Whitey's car back in 1985 as part of Operation Beans. It had been yet another attempt to bring down Whitey that had failed after he received a propitiously timed tip.

At sixty-five, Whitey was not the stereotypical elderly driver. Years later, on the witness stand, Weeks was asked how they could get from South Boston to the Back Bay so quickly during rush hour two days before Christmas. Could Whitey make cars magically move and disappear?

"Jim Bulger could make a lot of things magically move and disappear."

Whitey pulled the Mercury into the tow zone in front of Neiman Marcus. Then all three of them—Whitey, Kevin, and Theresa—got out of the car and Whitey told Theresa he'd be right with her. She waited at the entrance to Neiman Marcus, eyeing them nervously, as Kevin Weeks passed on the information he'd received from Connolly, that the indictments had come down, that they were sealed, and that the feds were planning to round up everybody over the holidays—including Whitey, his partner Stevie Flemmi, and Frank Salemme, the boss of the local Mafia.

"Have you told Stevie yet?" Whitey asked.

"I haven't seen him," Weeks said.

"Make sure you tell Stevie."

Whitey called Theresa back over to the car and told her, "We're going away again."

Their first night on the road, Whitey and Theresa checked into a hotel in Selden, Long Island. They would be visiting a cousin of Kevin Weeks's named Nadine, and her husband. Later Nadine and her husband would tell the FBI that they had no idea that they were entertaining a powerful, well-connected mobster. To them, they said, he was just Tom Baxter.

Theresa and "Tom" stayed in Selden for four days, then drove to New Orleans for New Year's, where Whitey registered at a

French Quarter hotel using his real name. No need to become "Tom Baxter" if this was all just a false alarm. By January 5, almost two weeks had passed since Whitey had been warned about the indictments, and still nothing had happened. Whitey told Theresa they were going home.

That night Stevie Flemmi pulled away from Schooner's, his son's new restaurant in Quincy Market, with his latest girlfriend, an attractive Asian thirty-five years his junior. Two Crown Vics cut Flemmi's car off and blocked its escape.

A DEA agent dragged Stevie out of the car and put a gun to his head.

"What is this?" Stevie said in disgust. "A grandstand play?"

A few minutes later, Stevie's younger brother, Michael, a Boston cop, walked quickly into the L Street Tavern, which would soon become famous in the movie *Good Will Hunting*. Officer Flemmi saw Kevin Weeks playing cards at a table and asked him if he could have a word with him outside. Weeks threw in his hand, grabbed his coat, and walked outside with Flemmi. The cop told him about his brother's arrest, and Weeks quickly paged Whitey. As usual, Whitey was one step ahead.

"I just heard it on the radio," Whitey said. "I'm turning around."

This time they drove back to Manhattan, where he and Theresa checked into a hotel and Whitey spent the night thinking things over. In the morning they headed west, driving aimlessly—the Grand Canyon, Los Angeles, San Francisco—two aging tourists with an old-fashioned reliance on cash, rather than credit cards. Two weeks later Theresa Stanley told Whitey she'd had enough. She wanted to go home. Or so she testified later.

Whitey drove to Clearwater, Florida, withdrew his "Tom Baxter" documents from yet another safe-deposit box, and drove back to Selden. There "Tom Baxter" traded in his old

Grand Marquis for a new one. He needed a new traveling companion too, and he had one in mind. Her name was Catherine Greig, age forty-two, and he'd had her on the string for close to twenty years. She was a twin, divorced from a Boston firefighter, an old-time Southie broad like Theresa who knew better than to ask questions, even about her ex-brother-in-law, whom Whitey had murdered twenty years earlier and buried on Tenean Beach in Dorchester.

The feds knew who Catherine Greig was. They'd tapped her phone at least once. They had surveillance shots of her and Whitey, walking her two black miniature poodles, Nikki and Gigi. Whitey was always complaining about those damn dogs, even though he had taken them to obedience school in Clearwater. Kevin Weeks had made it clear to her that she could not bring them along. Not on this trip.

But "Tom Baxter" and Theresa would spend one final night together. On their way back to Boston, they checked into a hotel in downtown Manhattan, and in the room, Whitey turned on one of his favorite shows—*America's Most Wanted*. He watched, silently, as John Walsh introduced him as the Fugitive of the Week, and ran the blurry 1991 surveillance video of himself at the Massachusetts State Lottery Commission headquarters in Braintree.

The pictures were almost four years old now. Whitey was wearing sunglasses and a white Red Sox cap as he claimed his "share" of a $14.3 million Mass Millions ticket that he had received under murky circumstances.

At the time, strolling into Lottery headquarters had seemed like a lark, but now Whitey saw it for the hubris that it was. For the first time, the cops had video of him. Not that it would matter much—during the next nine years, *America's Most Wanted* would feature Whitey twelve times, to no avail.

The next day, Whitey and Theresa returned to Massachusetts. Just after dark, he pulled into a restaurant parking lot in Hingham.

As Theresa got out of the car, Whitey told her he was headed for Fields Corner in Dorchester, to meet Kevin Weeks. In fact he was about to drive to Malibu Beach, where Kevin Weeks would deliver Catherine Greig to him.

As for Theresa, she had some nice diamond jewelry she could hock, if times got tough. Or she could go back to being a banquet waitress, if her varicose veins didn't act up. Sooner or later, Whitey knew, the cops would come calling, and she'd give up "Tom Baxter." But then she'd feel guilty, and call Kevin, and Kevin would beep him. With any luck, all this would be straightened out by then, and if it wasn't, he would have a new alias, or two, or three. For that, he was counting on his old friends from Alcatraz.

But right now, he wanted to talk to his brother Billy. In case the feds already had a pen register on Billy's phone, they would use Eddie Phillips's house in Quincy. Eddie worked for Billy at the State House, and the joke was that his most important qualification was that he was one of the few guys in the building shorter than Billy.

Once Whitey talked to Billy, he could get back on the road. Whitey wanted to drive and drive and drive. That's what he'd done when he'd gone on the lam in 1955, and that was still the plan. A year later, when the feds recovered "Tom Baxter's" Grand Marquis, in Yonkers, New York, it would have 65,000 miles on its odometer.

Whitey watched as Theresa got out of the car in front of the restaurant in Hingham, clutching her single suitcase.

"I'll call you," he said.

She never saw him again.

Nine years later, his brother Billy was still being questioned, under oath, about the phone call, by one of the few congressmen of either party on the committee who seemed even slightly sympathetic, Representative Henry Waxman of Los Angeles.

"Where were you," Waxman asked Billy, "when you received the telephone call from James Bulger?" He pronounced the last name incorrectly, as "Bul-gar," rather than "Bul-ger," with a soft *g*.

"I was in a friend's, an, an employee's home," he said. "I was asked where I would be and I received a call there."

Waxman: "Who asked you where you would be?"

"I don't have a specific recollection," he said. "But the only person it possibly would have been would be his friend, Kevin Weeks."

His ex-friend, now. Weeks had been arrested, finally, in 1999. After less than a month in the federal holding pen in Central Falls, Rhode Island, he had flipped. Overnight his nickname in Southie went from "Kevin Squeaks" to "Two Weeks."

All-powerful a decade earlier, the Bulger gang had scattered to the winds—they were either dead, in prison, on the lam, or under house arrest. Even the youngest Bulger brother, Jackie, had just pleaded guilty to federal perjury and obstruction-of-justice charges involving Whitey's safe-deposit box in Clearwater, Florida. The conviction cost Jackie four months in prison and, at least temporarily, his $3,778-a-month state pension.

Zip Connolly, the Bulger family's personal FBI agent, was in a federal prison in Lexington, Kentucky, until June 2011, unless, perhaps, he could serve up someone else, the way Kevin Weeks had delivered Connolly with his testimony in U.S. District Court.

Now Dan Burton was asking Billy what he discussed with his brother, the serial killer. Billy's response was gibberish.

"I'm his brother," Billy said. "He sought to call me. Or he sought to call me and I told his friend where I'd be and I received the call and it seems to me, um, that is in no way inconsistent with my devotion to my own responsibilities, my public responsibilities as a, well, at that time, uh, president of the Senate. I believe that I have always taken those as my first, my first obligation."

Burton asked Billy if he had offered Whitey any advice.

"My brother's an older brother," Billy said. "He doesn't—he didn't—come to me looking for advice."

Four Massachusetts congressmen watched anxiously, awaiting their turns to question Billy. Not so long ago, when he had controlled congressional redistricting, many of these same politicians had flattered him, attending his St. Patrick's Day breakfasts and laughing at his ancient jokes, donating more than generously to his campaign committee. Now they couldn't wait to throw him overboard.

Representative Marty Meehan of Lowell took the microphone now. Before Marty had first run for Congress he had been solicitous enough of Billy's blessing to arrange a formal introduction from one of Billy's dearest friends, a lobbyist. Like everyone else on Beacon Hill, Meehan had considered it imperative to have the imprimatur of Mr. President before he embarked on any endeavor, political or otherwise.

Not that any of that mattered now. Meehan was ambitious, he wanted to run for the U.S. Senate someday, and as a former prosecutor he knew how to draw blood. He asked Billy about the proximity of his house to the Flemmi residence, which the feds had lately taken to calling a "clubhouse" for Whitey's Winter Hill Gang.

"How much distance," Meehan asked, "is there between your house and the Flemmis'?"

"Perhaps from here to the first desk." About fifteen feet, in other words.

"Nothing ever looked suspicious over there?"

"No."

"You're aware Debra Davis was murdered next door?"

"Yes." Debra Davis, one of Stevie's girlfriends, had been twenty-six when Whitey strangled her.

Next up was John Tierney, from the North Shore of Massachusetts. He had more questions about Zip Connolly.

"Did you encourage Connolly to attend Boston College?"

There was a pause, followed by a sigh. "I may have," Billy said. "I honestly don't recall. I would, um, I was a little older of course and Connolly would be, uh, around, and I, I could very well have."

Tierney: "Did you write a letter of recommendation for him to attend graduate school?"

"I don't believe so." Then Billy's lawyer leaned over and whispered something in his ear.

"Oh," Billy said, nodding. "About the Kennedy School of Government, I am reminded I think I did send a letter over to the Kennedy School."

Tierney: "Mr. Connolly worked on some of your campaigns?"

"I believe he probably did."

The committee counsel brought up the subject of one of Whitey's hitmen, John Martorano, who had already pleaded guilty to twenty murders between 1965 and 1982. Martorano had testified under oath that Whitey once told him that Billy had ordered Zip Connolly to keep Whitey out of trouble.

"He said that?" Billy asked. "And was Mr. Martorano there when I did? Was he present?"

"He understood," the lawyer said, "that you had done that at some point."

"I see," said Billy. "Well, if I ever did say something like that uh, influence him to stay on the straight and narrow, if that's what's meant by it I could well have said it. . . . I think it's a pretty innocent comment, if in fact I made it. I have no recollection but I don't want to quarrel with that source."

When Billy was asked about his relationship with Kevin Weeks, he looked weary. He mentioned how he knew Kevin's brother, a onetime advance man for Governor Mike Dukakis.

And how Kevin would sometimes stop by Billy's home on East Third Street, unannounced, and they would talk.

"I think I was inflicting my advice upon him," Billy said. "He seems very young to me. His brother is in Chicago and I know I told him that he should go to Chicago and that he should take his wife and family and go to Chicago."

Instead, he pleaded guilty to being an accessory to five of Whitey's murders and his testimony sent Zip Connolly to prison for nine years. He wasn't so young anymore either. He was forty-seven.

Then it was Burton's turn again, and this time he came at Billy from out of left field. Had Billy ever tried to arrange for Zip Connolly, the convicted-felon FBI agent, to be appointed police commissioner of the city of Boston? The crowd murmured at this new information.

"Can you give me an idea of the year of that?" Billy said, and Burton instantly deduced that Billy was stalling for time to come up with an answer that wouldn't cost him his job as president of the University of Massachusetts.

"Did you recommend him?" Burton repeated.

"Excuse me, who's the mayor at that time?" It was Ray Flynn, Billy's neighbor from South Boston, a political rival whose popularity Bulger had often envied, and whose intellect he had always disparaged.

Burton stared at him, waiting for Billy to respond, and Billy stared back.

"Maybe way back," Billy finally said. "Many years before, there was a neighbor of ours who was mayor, and I may have suggested John to Raymond Flynn . . . I may have suggested him as a candidate, somebody that might be looked at."

As the morning wore on into the afternoon, Billy delivered more and more of his answers in the same vague manner—in the passive voice, always prefaced with a claim of inability to recall anything of substance. No one would ever be able to prove he'd lied, at least not beyond a reasonable doubt.

Did Billy know a crooked state cop convicted of leaking information to him through Kevin Weeks?

"I don't recall him but I've been told that I know him."

Did the FBI ever visit his home?

"I'm told they did but I do not recall it."

Whitey's bank safe-deposit box in London—the one the bank called Billy at home about because Whitey had listed him as the contact person—when, Mr. Bulger, did you learn about that bank account in Piccadilly?

"Whenever it appeared in the newspaper."

Did you know that your brother and his crew had stored the largest criminal arsenal ever confiscated in New England in their clubhouse fifteen feet from your home?

"I didn't know. Whoever put them there didn't tell me."

Were you responsible for the smears of Dan Burton in the Boston papers?

"If there were any ad hominems they didn't come from me."

They touched on allegation after allegation in which a state employee had gone after Whitey, only to be transferred, or have his pay frozen, or his staff cut. Billy said he knew nothing about any of it.

He even claimed he had nothing to do with the hiring policies at the Massachusetts Convention Center Authority, which he'd personally set up and then handed over to a former mailman from Southie named Francis Xavier Joyce. Franny Joyce had been Billy's top aide at the State House, as well as the tin whistle player in Billy's band, the Irish Volunteers.

"I told Joyce, do the best you can."

Joyce had immediately hired the daughter of one of Whitey's hitmen. He kept on one of Stevie Flemmi's old Mob associates as a garage cashier. Both quickly began stealing large amounts of cash. Then Joyce hired Theresa Stanley's daughter, Nancy.

"She was a very good worker," Billy told Burton.

But mostly, the questions were about Whitey.

Burton: "Did you know he was involved in narcotics trafficking?"

Bulger: "No."

"Did you know anything about the Winter Hill Mob?"

"The what?"

"The gang he was connected to."

"No, I didn't." Pause. "I don't think I met anybody from that."

"You didn't know Flemmi?" Burton asked.

"I did know Steve Flemmi, yes."

"Well, he was part of that gang. You didn't know he was part of that gang?"

"No."

"Did you know what Steve Flemmi did for a living?"

"I thought he had a restaurant somewhere. And I thought he had a club, or something like that."

It was the Marconi Club, in Roxbury. The Boston police eventually dug up its basement floor, looking for more bodies.

"Any indication your brother was involved in murder?"

"Someplace. I saw it in the paper."

Most of the reviews of Billy's testimony would not be kind. In a poll that morning, one TV station found that 52 percent of Massachusetts residents wanted Bulger removed as president of UMass. By that evening, the percentage of people in favor of his firing had risen to 63.

Burton questioned Billy Bulger about yet another legislative attempt to punish honest police who had gone after Whitey. In 1982, a rider was anonymously added to the state budget that would have forced the retirement of several senior State Police, one of whom had authorized the bugging of a West End garage that Whitey was using as his headquarters.

"Did you talk to anybody about that investigation?" Burton asked.

"I don't think so," Billy answered again, much to Burton's annoyance.

"The point is," Burton said, "you're saying, 'I don't think so.' You know, we've had a lot of people testify before the committee who've had what I call convenient memory loss and what I want to know is, can you categorically say that you did not talk to anybody about that investigation?"

Billy considered his words carefully before replying.

"My preference is to say that categorically I cannot recall ever talking with anybody."

Burton sighed and reiterated how odd it seemed that the president of the state Senate, a renowned micromanager, could forget a no-fingerprints amendment to the state budget that was aimed solely at destroying the careers of a handful of police officers, including one who was causing "heartburn," as Burton put it, for the Senate president's gangster brother.

Burton: "Did you speak to anyone about the investigation?"

"I don't believe so, no."

"You don't believe so? Categorically, can you say you didn't?"

Billy started to make a point about the nuances of legislation, and how surely the congressmen questioning him must understand. But as he studied their faces, he realized that this was one sneaker he couldn't put a shine on. So he reverted to form.

"There is," he told Burton, "a tendency to forget."

CHAPTER 1

IT WAS AN AVERAGE-SIZED family by pre–World War II South Boston standards—six children. And the Bulgers, like most families, harbored a secret. A seventh child, born soon after Jimmy, on September 3, 1929, and before Billy, on February 3, 1934, had died almost immediately after his birth in 1931. Infant mortality was not unknown in those grim Depression days. But the tight-lipped Bulgers told so few of their neighbors about the brief life of their seventh sibling that as late as 2004, it was one of the few facts that the FBI's task force hunting Whitey across Europe refused to reveal to the public.

"If Whitey ever calls," one agent explained, "the one way I can know positively that it's him is if I ask him some questions about his dead sibling, and he knows the right answers, the ones only a Bulger could know."

In almost every other way, the Bulger family did not stand out among their neighbors in South Boston. Although Whitey and Billy would later become the faces of South Boston, and of the last days of the Irish-American hegemony in Boston, they themselves were not natives of the city's most Irish neighborhood.

Their father, James, was raised in Boston's North End, where many of the city's Irish immigrants initially settled, among them the Fitzgeralds, whose daughter Rose would someday marry Joseph P. Kennedy, JFK's father. Jim Bulger's wife, Jean, was twenty years younger than her husband. She was from Charlestown, just across the bridge from the North End, a neighborhood that remained Irish throughout the twentieth century.

Like most of their neighbors, the Bulgers were poor. As they grew up, all of them, even Whitey, would seek jobs with the government. The Bulgers distrusted all types of private enterprise, perhaps because of a railyard accident in which their father, a third-generation laborer, caught his arm between two boxcars and had to have it amputated.

As Billy would explain bitterly in his memoirs: "A straw boss explained that a one-armed laborer was of no further use and fired him. The railroad calculated the wages due him—up to the time he had fallen, mangled, to the cinder bed—paid him, and forgot him. He acquired a prosthetic arm, crude by today's standards, which he fruitlessly tried to conceal by keeping the wooden hand in a pocket."

James Bulger Sr.'s predicament was a common-enough occurrence in those days. Many Irish politicians were raised in homes where the father was either dead or maimed after an industrial accident. Jean McCarthy Bulger's father—the grandfather of Whitey and Billy—had been killed in a shipyard accident in Charlestown.

At that time, there were no disability pensions, no workmen's comp, no doles of any sort. Life insurance was for the wealthy. If you were unable to work, your family was consigned to a life of poverty.

After the accident, the Bulgers drifted from one apartment to another in Dorchester until 1938, when they heard about a new public housing project in South Boston called Old Colony Harbor, the second such public housing project in the nation. It was the brainchild of Congressman John McCormack, who

hoped that a plentiful source of inexpensive housing might de-
fuse the class tensions that had boiled over during the 1936
elections in Southie, when third-party candidates backed by
the radical anti-Semitic radio priest Father Charles Coughlin
had done unexpectedly well.

The projects were a boon for the Bulger family. Jim Bulger
was fifty-two, and jobs for a one-armed man weren't easy to
come by. The Bulgers were among the first families to move in.
At the time, there were three surviving children—Jean, the
oldest, born in 1927, and Whitey and Billy. Three more children would quickly follow—Carol, Jackie, and Sheila—although the older siblings would always dominate the family.
In the projects, the Bulgers had three bedrooms—one for the
parents, one for the boys, and one for the girls.

The address was 41 Logan Way, Apartment 756. It was on
the top floor, the third. The rent was $29 a month.

There had been Irish in Boston almost since the beginning.
But they did not begin arriving en masse until the 1840s,
when the Irish Potato Famine began. Between 1850 and 1855,
the Irish population of Boston tripled. Most were from the
west, beyond the Pale as it was known. They were tolerated,
briefly, but as they continued swarming into Boston's slum districts, the native Protestant population galvanized into what
became known as the Know-Nothing Party. In 1854, the
Know-Nothings took over the state government in an electoral
landslide unprecedented in state history.

The Know-Nothing governor, Henry J. Gardner, in his in-
augural address, vowed to "Americanize America." He proposed, among other things, an amendment to the state
constitution prohibiting public aid to parochial schools, which
140 years later Billy Bulger would unsuccessfully attempt to
repeal.

The Know-Nothings vanished just as completely in the next

election, sinking under the weight of their own scandals—including one legislative chairman who charged the state for the services of two prostitutes in Lowell and also made "suggestive remarks" to a pair of nuns in Roxbury.

It was an early lesson in "reform" for the Irish immigrants, and Billy was nothing if not a student of history. As Billy Bulger would say at his annual St. Patrick's Day breakfast all those years later, "Show me a reformer, and I'll show you someone who won't be back."

By 1874, when James Michael Curley was born in a Roxbury tenement to a young Irish couple from County Galway, the Irish were almost the majority in Boston. But they were still treated with contempt by the ruling Protestant classes in the Athens of America. In the view of many of the Yankee natives, they had forever ruined "the once orderly and peaceful city of the Pilgrims," as the Brahmin Ephraim Peabody put it.

As far as the proper Bostonians of the day were concerned, James Michael Curley would come to be the most vexatious Irishman of them all. Almost a half-century after his death, for Bostonians, if not for the nation as a whole, it is Curley, not John F. Kennedy, who is the quintessential Boston Irish politician. And it is Curley who was truly Billy Bulger's political model.

For the first half of the twentieth century, all politics in Boston, and sometimes in the entire state, seemed to revolve around Curley. At the turn of the century, Curley went to jail briefly for taking a civil service examination for a constituent. That stretch produced one of his first electoral slogans: "He did it for a friend." Ideology mattered little, at least when compared to jobs.

For Curley, as for Billy Bulger two generations later, politics was the only way out. As the fictional Curley says in Edwin O'Connor's novel *The Last Hurrah*: "I wanted a job with a suit that didn't come equipped with a chauffeur's cap."

He got his wish, but the price was steep. He was elected governor once, a congressman twice, and mayor four times, and went to jail twice, the last time to the federal penitentiary in Danbury, Connecticut, after a mail fraud conviction in 1946. He outlived all but two of his nine children.

Whether he won or lost, though, Southie remained one of Curley's strongholds to the day he died in 1958, even though on occasion he would deride the residents of Southie as he campaigned from the back of a flatbed truck.

"You are nothing but a pack of pickpockets and second-story workers," he bellowed at a crowd of hecklers on Broadway one night. "You are a bunch of milk-bottle robbers and doormat thieves."

The Southie voters ate it up. South Boston was Curley country.

In the Bulger boys' youth, the avenues out of poverty and into the middle class were few. One was the church. There was always a need for more priests—in Southie alone there were seven parishes, and each of them had at least two priests, not to mention a full complement of nuns who taught at the parochial schools. Another accepted career path was the police department, though it didn't pay particularly well, not since Governor Calvin Coolidge broke the Boston Police Strike of 1919. In Southie when people said they wanted a job with "no heavy lifting," it was a literal as well as a figurative expression.

Other than running funeral homes and saloons, virtually no opportunities existed for the Irish in business above the level of clerk. The signs that are still sold at the John F. Kennedy Library at Columbia Point—No Irish Need Apply—did in fact exist. When the Irish began arriving in the 1840s, they brought with them no native entrepreneurial skills. They were subsistence farmers in a one-crop economy. Generations after the potato blight, successful businessmen like Joseph P.

Kennedy were few and far between, and Kennedy himself felt so ostracized as a millionaire Irishman in Boston that he moved his growing family to New York. As a Harvard graduate, he was also an outsider; in the Irish districts, if a promising high school student was by some strange quirk admitted to the quintessential Yankee institution across the Charles River, he might expect to be lectured from the pulpit by his local parish priest about the "duty" of Roman Catholics to attend a school more in line with the teachings of Holy Mother the Church. In 1937, when one of Jim Curley's sons was admitted to Harvard, Curley intercepted the acceptance letter and destroyed it, forcing George Curley to matriculate at Holy Cross.

This was the world into which Billy and Whitey were born— a clannish, suspicious society that viewed success as somehow un-Catholic, un-Irish. The Boston Irish distrusted outsiders; few even had bank accounts. Those who dreamed of rising above their station were derided as "two-toilet" Irish. It was a world of small-timers, and that was what the Bulgers were, even in their heyday. It was their legacy, that of a parochial upbringing in a parochial city.

People who knew James Bulger Sr. remember him as a taciturn sort. Like his sons, and unlike so many others in Southie, he wasn't a heavy drinker. But as he grew older, James Bulger became morose, self-pitying. Jim Bulger's wife, Jean, it is said, was the one in the family with a personality more like Billy's, relying on quick wit and pointed barbs. Unlike her husband, who seemed resigned to his fate, she dreamed of something more for her children.

Whitey was more his father's son, always keeping to himself on those rare occasions when he was with the rest of the family, stand-offish to the point of surliness. Whitey was seldom at home in the evenings, even as a boy. Billy retired to his room at the prescribed time, but always took a flashlight to bed with him so that he could read after lights out. Walking by outside, passersby could see the light in the boys' darkened bedroom. Soon, in recognition of the flashlight, Billy became known in some circles as "the Beam."

The projects then weren't what they have since become. The families were intact, and almost everyone had employment of some sort. There were no drugs, no unwed mothers, and next to no welfare. And in "the Town," everyone seemed connected to everyone else in one way or another. Just down the street from the Bulgers, at 51 Logan Way, lived young Joe Moakley, a year older than Whitey. Moakley would lie his way into the merchant marine at age fifteen during World War II. Later Billy would succeed him in the state House of Representatives, and ten years later, the state Senate.

On the other side of Logan Way, at number 38, lived a young boy named Francis "Buddy" Leonard, the same age as Jackie Bulger. Buddy's family would later move to the D Street projects, and Whitey would shoot him twice in the head as he consolidated his control over the Southie rackets in 1975.

Another resident was John "Zip" Connolly, born in 1940, son of an Irish immigrant known as "Galway John." Whitey had nicknames for everyone—besides Zip, the future FBI agent and gangster would eventually answer to "Elvis," because of his thick black hair, and also to "Neighbor," because of his early years in the project. Decades later, Connolly loved to recount for reporters his first memory of Whitey, when he used some of his ill-gotten gains to buy ice-cream cones for all the young boys swarming around him in adoration. Kevin Weeks's family would move in later, and his two brothers would go to Harvard, without having to endure the reproaches of their local parish priest.

No one in the projects had a lot of money, but with living expenses so low, not much was needed. Turnover was next to nothing. The projects in those days were considered a godsend, not a blight.

* * *

South Boston was a place not much thought of, one way or the other, by the rest of the city. It was a peninsula, but it may as well have been an island. There were pockets of Lithuanians and Poles here and there, as well as the occasional Italian, like Joe Moakley's mother, for instance. Almost everybody was Catholic. A handful of Protestants survived, unmolested, but there were virtually no Jews, though by age twelve Billy had a job working at a grocery store owned by a family of Russian Jews, the Karps. For many years, people in Southie bragged that their neighborhood had the lowest crime rate in the city, and in those days, before Whitey turned cocaine distribution into an industry, it did. It was old-fashioned—a writer for *GQ* magazine said that even in the early 1990s, crossing the Broadway bridge was like going back a generation in time. As recently as the late 1960s, Southie boys who had impregnated their underage girlfriends were often given a choice by the local judges—marry her or join the marines. An abortion, of course, was unthinkable. Everyone went to Mass on Sunday, and if you didn't, you would be noticed, and watched henceforward.

It was Whitey rather than Billy who first went to Catholic school, before the family moved to South Boston. Whitey attended St. Mark's in Dorchester for the first grade, then switched over to St. Margaret's for three years. It wasn't until the family moved to Southie in 1938 that he entered the public schools.

According to his fifth grade transcript, in 1939–40, Whitey's conduct marks dropped from month to month, from C to C– to D, and then, it appears, someone changed his E ("Very Poor") in March-April into an A ("Best Work").

Billy started first grade in public school. By the fourth grade, Billy was an above-average student, but his report card

was not dotted with straight As. His only A for the year came
in spelling.

Even as a youth, Whitey was always in trouble. The first notation on his police record comes in 1943, at age thirteen, for larceny. Quickly he advanced to assault and battery and then
robbery, but was never packed off to reform school. In those
days, if the cops "liked" you for a crime but couldn't prove it,
they might just give you a beating at the station house. The
Boston cops "liked" Whitey a lot in those days.

"He was just a bad kid, always spoiling for trouble," said one
retired cop. "But there were a lot of bad kids around back then.
No one ever could have predicted what happened, at least I
hope not."

There were two main youth gangs—the Mullens, named
after Mullen Square, where they congregated, and the Sham-
rocks. Whitey was a Shamrock, or at least hung out with them.
In his book, Billy paints a fanciful picture of Whitey's youthful escapades that reads like something out of a novel, a movie,
or both.

According to Billy, Whitey acquired an ocelot, a story not
unlike the lion-in-the-basement tale of Jimmy Breslin's novel
about the Brooklyn mob and Crazy Joey Gallo's crew, *The Gang
That Couldn't Shoot Straight*. He supposedly dated a stripper he
met at the old Howard burlesque house in Scollay Square, who
shocked Jean when she later wrote letters to Whitey after her
return to Chicago. She signed them Tiger Lil.

Or so Billy wrote.

Billy may have been the more studious of the brothers, but
he couldn't always avoid getting involved with Whitey. Will
McDonough, the late *Boston Globe* sportswriter who was Billy's
lifelong friend, used to tell the story of the day he and Billy
were walking home from the beach. They were about thirteen.
Suddenly, Whitey pulled over to the curb. He was driving a

Cadillac convertible neither McDonough nor Billy had ever seen before. He was bare-chested and wearing a fedora, and he told the two younger boys to get in the car. They climbed in and Whitey took off toward Broadway.

As they drove along, Billy spotted another kid his age pedaling one of those old bicycles with an ice-cream chest attached to the handle bars. His name was O'Hara, and he was trying to make a few extra dollars for the summer.

"I never liked that kid," Billy said, and Whitey just nodded. He slowed down the Cadillac and pulled behind O'Hara. Then he tapped the back of the bike with the front fender. O'Hara, alarmed, turned around long enough to see who was behind him, and when he saw the Bulgers, he took off as quickly as he could, toward Broadway. Whitey inched up behind him again and tapped the bike. O'Hara sped up even more, and so did Whitey.

"Jimmy," said Billy, "I just said I didn't like him. I didn't say kill him."

Whitey looked over and smiled at his younger brother as O'Hara sped through a stoplight, not even paying attention to the oncoming traffic as he tried to flee.

"We're not going to kill him," Whitey said. "When he gets to Broadway and barrels out into the street, the bus'll kill him."

Even in his youthful pranks, Whitey preferred someone else to do his dirty work for him.

Other parts of Whitey's youth are mentioned less frequently. He was a handsome boy, blond, and as a teenager he found himself hanging around the Third Street Café, a real shabeen— the Gaelic word for a bar of low repute. It was a sort of neighborhood version of the bars that dotted Dover Street, across the bridge in the South End's skid row district. Even in the immediate postwar era, Boston had a flourishing homosexual scene.

The size of the homosexual community in those days is sug-

gested by the police manpower devoted not so much to the enforcement of the anti-sodomy laws, but to the shakedowns of
those who broke the unenforceable three-hundred-year-old
statutes. According to the book *Improper Bostonians*, compiled
by the History Project, at the time Whitey began turning homosexual tricks in the late 1940s, one of the most lucrative police assignments in Boston was to the Rest Room Squad, which
patrolled the bathrooms that were still open in many of the
MTA subway stations. The homosexuals would be given a
choice: Pay off or be arrested. In the bars of Bay Village, which
on certain nights of the week catered to lesbians, the cops took
out their shakedowns in trade. Many of the lesbians were blue
bloods from Beacon Hill. The prospect of public scandal terrified them enough to accept the cops' smirking offer of a trip
out to the prowl car for a quick blow job rather than an arrest
that would be picked up, if not by the dailies, then at least by
the local weekly scandal sheet, the *Mid-Town Journal*.

According to survivors of the era, Whitey worked out of a
couple of gay bars on Stuart Street, primarily a joint called
Mario's, which was also known as the Sail Aweigh. As a young
male hustler, he quickly became adept at rolling his tricks—
his police record indicates an arrest for "unarmed robbery" on
March 18, 1947. Another of his favorite pickup spots was the
Punch Bowl, which was frequently raided by the Vice Squad.
According to one patron quoted in *Improper Bostonians*, the bartender would flash the "emergency lights" to warn everyone
that the police had arrived.

"You had to stop dancing with your boyfriend," he recalled,
"since it was illegal back then. You could dance with a lesbian,
or you could sit down."

Whitey may have been hustling to raise some spending
money, but he was never exclusively homosexual. On January
6, 1948, he was arrested by Boston police and charged with assault with intent to rape. The charge was later reduced to as-

sault and battery, and Whitey eventually pleaded guilty to simple assault and paid a fine.

Whitey joined the air force at the end of 1948, but he was not cut out for military life. His records indicate he was finger-printed on January 3, 1949, although the charges against him, if any, are not listed. A year later he was arrested for being AWOL. In June 1951, he was arrested on suspicion of rape, a charge that was later reduced to assault.

His records also indicate a serious problem with discipline. By June 1949, his commanding officer at Smoky Hill Air Force Base in Salina, Kansas, was trying to get Whitey thrown out of the air force on the grounds of "fraudulent enlistment," since he had not mentioned his earlier robbery and rape arrests in Boston. But the base's personnel officer wrote a memo to the CO, noting that there were no grounds for a discharge, since the felony charges against Whitey had been dropped.

Whitey's disciplinary problems persisted even after he was transferred to Great Falls, Montana. A few transcripts of his disciplinary hearings have survived, and one details how, out on the parade ground, his CO told him he didn't deserve to be a corporal.

"Well, then bust me if I don't deserve it," Whitey retorted.

On June 24, 1952, with his term of enlistment about to expire, another disciplinary hearing, just one step short of a court-martial, was held in the matter of James J. Bulger Jr. The surviving records are sketchy, but it seems that Whitey asked for it himself, apparently because of the threat of a less-than-honorable discharge that was hanging over his head. He must have been somewhat concerned, because he told the hearing panel that if he wasn't treated fairly, he would write his con-gressman. This was the first recorded instance of John McCor-mack's name being dropped by a member of the Bulger family or gang.

"You know," the captain told Whitey, "you could get a dishonorable discharge, and if that happens, you'll never get a good job on the outside."

According to his records, Whitey had a prophetic, classic response: "I could go back to the work I used to do, no matter what kind of discharge I get."

On August 16, 1952, Whitey received an honorable discharge from the United States Air Force.

Back in Boston, Whitey did indeed go back to the work he used to do. He was soon again turning occasional tricks in Bay Village, and that was where he met a twenty-six-year-old FBI agent named H. Paul Rico. Rico, a Belmont native and Boston College graduate, had joined the bureau in 1951, and could justify his sojourns to the Bay Village gay clubs as reaching out to new "sources." But Whitey was now less interested in rolling gays than he was in the big money, and he was soon an apprentice wiseguy, a hoodlum wannabe. After Whitey's conviction on bank robbery charges in February 1956, H. Paul Rico wrote in his pre-sentencing report to the judge that the Boston office of the FBI had long followed Bulger "because of his suspected implication in tailgate thefts. We knew of his extremely dangerous character, his remarkable agility, his reckless daring in driving vehicles, and his unstable, vicious characteristics."

Or, as Billy put it in his book, "He had an abundance of good humor and a wildly creative talent for impish mischief."

In 1948, at age fourteen, Billy worried that his life already seemed to be slipping away from him. He had finished the ninth grade at South Boston High, and he could already see where that led—down to the docks for the morning shape-up, or, if you were lucky, or connected, to the electric company— "the Edison." And after work, to the corner tavern for a wee small taste of the creature—Green River whiskey washed down with a Pickwick Ale chaser—waiting for the Payoff Edition of the *Record* to hit the streets so you could see if you hit the "nigger-pool" lottery number. Or you could stay at Southie High and get into the sheet metal training program. Or play a varsity sport, go into the army after graduation, then come back home and take the civil service exam.

Billy wanted something more. He looked up to his Logan Way neighbor, Joe Moakley, back from the war and already at BC. Joe Moakley was going places, and Billy Bulger wanted to go places too.

But he needed to get into a good high school, one that would provide him a way out. There were only two choices: Boston Latin, the public exam school or Boston College High. Latin was tough for a Southie kid, especially one from public school and the projects. Everything came down to your score on the exam.

That left BC High. Billy put on his Sunday suit—his only suit—and walked straight to the school, unannounced. In the front lobby sat the school registrar, Charles Doherty.

"[I] explained that I wanted to go to BC High," Billy recalled, "but that my family couldn't afford it and I wasn't qualified."

He wasn't kidding about his lack of academic credentials, so he offered to repeat the ninth grade, and pay the tuition himself. Doherty decided to take a chance on Billy, and that fall he entered as a ninth-grader. He had financial help from his older sister, Jean, who was working and engaged to be married. Plus, he still made money from his various "odd jobs," as he put it. He occasionally worked for the Karps at the local grocery store, and in the winter the "snow button" was available from Knocko McCormack, the congressman's brother and the biggest bookie in South Boston. If you got a "button" after a snowstorm, the city would give you a day's pay for shoveling out the streets. The really big money was down on the docks.

When Billy got lucky, he could sometimes make $3.50 an hour. In the summer, he had another public sector job, as a lifeguard at the L Street Bathhouse.

In his later high school years, he also began dating, if a bit tentatively. Jimmy Condon, the state rep whom Billy would someday join in the House, had somehow secured hundreds of passes for a day trip to Provincetown on the SS *Steel Pier*, and was passing them out to his constituents, even if they weren't quite yet of voting age. On the dance floor that day Billy would meet his future wife, Mary Foley, who lived on Pacific Street. Once the ship docked, they walked the streets of the old fishing community together, chuckling at the eccentric locals. Billy recalled having 70 cents in his pocket, with which he bought fried clams.

The next spring, he took her to his BC High School senior prom. The next year, with Billy a freshman at Boston College, she invited him to her prom at Gate of Heaven High School. But by then, Billy had come to the conclusion that he couldn't afford BC. The Jesuit fathers had waived the hefty $400 tuition for his freshman year, but now that he was finishing up his first year at the Heights, there was, as usual, no money in the till. Jean was now a brokenhearted widow—her young husband had been killed in the Korean War. With few alternatives open to him, Billy took what was then the common way out: He enlisted in the U.S. Army. There would be no OCS—Officer Candidate School—for Billy. He just wanted to do his two years, qualify for the GI Bill, and return to his old life—Southie, BC, and Mary. It was an uneventful twenty-four months, basic training at Fort Dix and then a routine assignment in the Cold War army at Fort Bliss, Texas.

Billy was discharged in August 1955, three months after Whitey had begun his new career—robbing banks.

Billy would later blame Whitey's criminal career on falling in with "an older group." But Whitey had been looking to hook up with a gang, because his solo life of crime was going nowhere. Almost immediately after his discharge from the air force in 1952, he'd been arrested in the Back Bay on charges of attempting to steal a beer truck—the "tailgating" referred to in the FBI memo of 1956.

In those days, much of Southie's crime involved pilferage from trucks. An aspiring thief would either steal something off the back of a truck, or, more profitably, hijack an entire load. The hijacks were almost always inside jobs—a Teamster would be paid to turn over his load of, say, Gillette razors, to someone else from the neighborhood. Violence was rare, and the only ones who lost money in the flourishing trade were the insurance companies, and the honest policyholders who subsidized this informal redistribution of wealth with their higher premiums.

The problem for Whitey was, a few of his fellow tailgaters got set up. They might mention something about a future score to Whitey, just in passing, and sure enough, when they showed up to grab the truck, the FBI or the local cops would be there waiting. H. Paul Rico's personnel file soon included commendations from the director, J. Edgar Hoover. At the time, no one suspected Whitey—it was inconceivable that one of Southie's own would become a rat. Squealing might be grudgingly tolerated in some neighborhoods, but not in Southie.

But the fact was, whoever Whitey took up with usually wasn't around very long. Whitey Bulger, his associates came to believe, was a jinx, and the tailgate jobs soon dried up.

In early 1955, at the age of twenty-five, Whitey fell in with an older con, a jailhouse lawyer named Carl G. Smith Jr. Smith had been serving a term at the state prison in Charlestown when he convinced the Massachusetts Supreme Judicial Court to overturn his burglary conviction on a technicality. It was his third such victory before an appeals court.

Released, Smith took up with Whitey and several other younger hoodlums, and they began organizing a bank-robbing gang. Smith and Bulger added a second-generation Cambridge hoodlum, Ronald Dermody, who would later die in the Irish Gang War. Their first score came in May 1955, when they robbed a bank in Pawtucket, Rhode Island, of $42,000. Whitey carried a .22-caliber revolver and ordered two bank employees to the floor. The three escaped in a stolen car. With $14,000 in his pocket, Whitey was finally a big shot back in South Boston. In September, he and a new girlfriend from Dorchester left Boston and journeyed to Florida, where he "registered at various motels under his true name," according to the report the FBI would later send to his first penitentiary, in Atlanta.

In October 1955, at Smith's behest, Whitey drove to Indiana "and there participated in the casing of the Mercantile National Bank, Hammond, Indiana," along with Smith and a new member of the gang named Richard Barchard. The plan was to rob the bank, and they even stole a car in a nearby shopping center. But when they reached the bank, they noticed a police officer inside and immediately abandoned their plan. They returned the vehicle to the shopping center they'd stolen it from, and there they noticed that another bank "looked like a soft touch."

A few days later, Whitey and Barchard returned to Hammond to rob the "soft touch." With them were two women—Whitey's Dorchester girlfriend and Barchard's twenty-nine-year-old wife, Dorothy, who would be connected with several gangland figures in the coming years. In Hammond, they stole a '55 Oldsmobile and headed straight to the bank.

According to the statement the FBI sent to the federal penitentiary in Atlanta in 1956, "BULGER, carrying two sidearms, and BARCHARD, unarmed, entered the victim bank. BULGER covered the employees and customers in the bank by mounting the counter. BARCHARD vaulted the counter and scooped the money from the tellers' cages. They were unmasked during the robbery and both issued commands while in the bank. During the course of the robbery, the customers and bank employees were forced to lie on the floor."

They wore identical sport shirts and hunting caps with ear flaps.

The take was $12,612.28. They split it, and then Whitey and his girlfriend headed to Florida for a vacation. Whitey and his female companion returned to Boston for Christmas, but he didn't stay long. On January 4, 1956, a warrant was issued for his arrest. In a scenario very much like the one he would employ thirty-eight years later, he first fled to California, then returned a couple of weeks later to pick up his girlfriend, after which he headed to Wilmington, Delaware.

Then the couple took off across the country. They stopped in Reno, San Francisco, Salt Lake City, New Mexico, and Chicago before heading back to Boston. Among his aliases: Martin Kelley, Paul John Rose, and Leo McLaughlin.

"In a further effort to avoid apprehension," the FBI report states, "BULGER dyed his hair black, adopted the wearing of horn-rimmed glasses, changed the style and color of his clothing, and assumed the practice of carrying a cigar in his mouth to distort his facial features."

On March 4, 1956, Rico received a tip that Whitey had been hanging out at a nightclub in Revere. The FBI agents staked it out for a couple of nights, and finally, on the evening of March 6, they arrested Whitey as he walked out. He was unarmed and in the company of an ex-con named John DeFeo.

The next morning, at his arraignment, the prosecutor described Whitey as "a vicious person, known to carry guns, and [who] by his own admittance has an intense dislike for police and law enforcement officers."

Bail was set at $50,000. For the Bulger family, it might as well have been $50 million.

The Bulgers managed to find a politically connected lawyer for Whitey, a former state rep who would eventually become a judge. But the case was hopeless, and on June 21, 1956, after being described by the U.S. attorney as a "habitual criminal," Whitey was sentenced to twenty years in federal prison by U.S. District Court Judge George C. Sweeney.

"I went to court the day Jim was sentenced," Billy wrote, leaving it at that. He had just completed his sophomore year at BC.

Whitey would not return to Boston for nine years.

Back at college, money was no longer such a pressing problem for Billy, thanks to the GI Bill. Billy's plan, in the fall of 1955, was to finish up at BC, then go on to BC Law School, after which he would enter politics. By now he and Mary were "courting," and often they walked to Castle Island, where they'd stand in line at Kelly's Landing to buy a box of fried clams. Billy supplemented his income by working, not just as a lifeguard, but also as a master of ceremonies at parties held at McLaughlin & Gormley's, a banquet hall in Dorchester.

He had returned from the army just in time to witness his hero James Michael Curley's final campaign for mayor. In his book, Billy recalls the night of the preliminary election in 1955. He has Curley finishing second, although it was actually fourth. Billy then recounts Curley's final concession speech, in the ballroom of the old Brunswick Hotel, quoting John Paul Jones at the end of his sixty-year political career.

"I have not yet begun to fight."

In 1960 Representative Joe Moakley ran for the state Senate seat held by John E. Powers. Only two years earlier, Powers had become the first Democratic president of the state Senate since before the Civil War, but he was wounded. After John B. Hynes decided not to seek a fourth term as mayor in 1959, Powers had been a heavy favorite to succeed him at City Hall, but had been defeated after Boston police raided an East Boston bookie joint in a building that just happened to have a large "Powers for Mayor" sign above it. Photos had appeared on all of the front pages, and Powers lost, the victim of a classic dirty trick.

But no one had time to mourn. All that mattered in the jungle of Southie politics was that Powers was now vulnerable. Never one to stand on ceremony, Moakley sensed an opportunity, and he took it. He would not succeed in ousting Powers this time, but his decision to oppose Powers was a boon for Billy; there was now an open House seat in South Boston. Billy hadn't expected to run so soon; he still had a year left in law school. And he was also planning to ask Mary Foley to marry him. But open House seats didn't come along often, especially in South Boston, where service in the legislature was considered an opportunity, not a duty. But Billy's father, growing ever more timid in his dotage, tried to talk him out of both the race and the marriage.

"You can't support her," Billy recounts him saying in his book. "For God's sake don't tell anybody about this."

Billy and Mary were married nonetheless, at St. Margaret's in Dorchester, where Whitey had attended parochial school twenty-five years earlier. The couple soon settled into an apartment, in Southie of course. Mary was almost immediately pregnant with Bill Jr.

Billy's major source of income was the summer lifeguarding job, but he plunged ahead with his plans to run for Moakley's open seat in a crowded field of sixteen candidates.

His skeptical father told Billy his opponents would use Whitey against him. For once, his father was right. In one incident, which he mentioned in his congressional testimony, one man snarled at him, "You belong in prison with your brother."

Billy's campaign manager was Will McDonough, his oldest friend, by now a sportswriter for the *Globe*. Another campaign worker was Roger Gill, whom Billy would reward with jobs on various state payrolls for the rest of his life. They envisioned themselves as street urchins, going up against what Billy called the F.I.F.'s—the First Irish Families of Southie.

Of necessity, Billy ran a low-budget campaign. He had a single blue suit, and his clever opponents quickly nicknamed him "One Suit" Bulger. He recalled running into Mary when she got off the subway at Andrew Square, returning from her job at the State House, and telling her he'd dipped into their rent money to buy bumper stickers. He looked chagrined, he recalled, and she smiled and offered to buy him some fried clams.

One of his most formidable opponents was Gerry O'Leary, a high school football hero who would later go to prison for an attempted $650,000 shakedown of a school bus company in 1980 while he was serving on the Boston School Committee. Another tough foe was James Collins Jr., son of a well-heeled bookmaker who would later move out of Boston and be elected treasurer of Norfolk County. Collins too would end up in prison, in 1985, for embezzling county pension funds. The Collins family's most memorable contribution to Bulger lore would be to spread the rumor that he was actually part Polish or Lithuanian—a believable enough falsehood, given his light hair.

By most accounts, Billy and his crew simply outworked everyone else, and on primary day they prevailed. On election night, he stopped in at the parties of all his major opponents. Where they had called him "One Suit" Bulger, Billy later recalled, he told them he owed his victory to his lucky suit. When he ran into Collins's father, he told him it was the Polish and Lithuanian votes that had put him over the top. All the while Billy kept smiling. In January he would be a state rep. Finally, a male member of the Bulger family would have a real job.

CHAPTER 2

BILLY BULGER WAS SWORN in as a member of the Massachusetts House of Representatives on January 5, 1961. Senator John F. Kennedy would succeed Dwight Eisenhower as president in just over two weeks.

A new era might have been about to dawn nationally, but back on Beacon Hill it was business as usual. Politics was still an overwhelmingly Irish game, so much so that an Irish name, it sometimes appeared, was all you needed in politics to succeed.

Everyone seemed to be named Hynes, or Hines, or Craven, or McDonough, or McCormack. There were Tierneys and Kearneys and Connollys galore. Both the president-elect and the state treasurer of Massachusetts were named John F. Kennedy. John E. Kerrigan would soon be joined on the Boston City Council by John J. Kerrigan.

Billy Bulger took office as one of 240 members of the House of Representatives. There were few actual offices at the State House for most of the legislators. All but about forty—the leadership and the chairmen of the more important committees—operated out of the House chambers, from their desks, which were more like open carrels in a public library. The reps had no direct phone lines; calls were taken at the bank of telephones just outside the chambers.

White flight out of the city of Boston was just beginning, and the city delegation still represented one-sixth of the House—forty of the 240 members. Twenty-three of the forty were Irish, seven were Italian, five were Yankee Republicans, and four were Jews. Of the three blacks in the delegation, two had been elected for the first time in 1960—an indication of the continuing black migration into Roxbury, which was starting to spill into North Dorchester.

The rules of life at the State House in 1961 boiled down to three points:

1. Nothing on the level.
2. Everything is a deal.
3. No deal too small.

The Boston reps lived and died by that credo. Of the forty House members from Boston who were sworn in with Billy in January 1961, at least five ended up in prison—two for income tax evasion, one for bribery, one for assaulting a federal narcotics agent, and another for larceny in connection with a state sidewalk-construction project. Another of the 1961–62 reps was eventually indicted, but acquitted, and two others, including Billy, made appearances before grand juries.

That was how Massachusetts politics operated. Edwin O'Connor, the author of *The Last Hurrah*, summed up the era in his final novel, *All in the Family*: "Corruption here had a shoddy, penny ante quality it did not have in other states. . . . Here everything was up for grabs and nothing was too small to steal. . . . In our politics there seemed to be a depthless cushion of street-corner cynicism, a special kind of tainted, small-time fellowship which sent out a complex of vines and shoots so interconnected that even the sleaziest poolroom bookie managed, in some way, however obscure, to be in touch with the mayor's office or the governor's chair."

Or both.

The police, by and large, were just as compromised as the politicians. As in most large urban areas, many of the cops had grown up on the same street corners with future Mob kingpins. Long before Whitey Bulger perfected the use of law enforcement as both witting and unwitting tools of organized crime, gangsters in Boston had been using them in similar ways.

Anything could be fixed—absolutely anything. Frank Salemme, Stevie Flemmi's early partner, recalled for a congressional committee in 2003 a time when two Boston cops witnessed one of Stevie's brothers, "Jimmy the Bear," murder another man in a car.

"Jimmy Flemmi got out of the car and left, and they [the police] took the car and pushed it out of their division so it would be in another division and they wouldn't have to investigate it."

Then the cops returned to the South End, hunted down Stevie Flemmi, and demanded $2,500 in return for not turning in his brother. Stevie didn't quibble over the amount.

"That's the era it was, anything for money, even murder," Salemme said. "It wasn't considered illegal to do that kind of thing, as crazy as that may sound today."

If, by some unimaginable bit of bad luck, you were arrested by an honest cop, and you couldn't fix the case in the district attorney's office, or bribe a juror, other options remained even after you were in jail.

You could buy a pardon or a commutation from the Governor's Council, the way Raymond Patriarca, the first boss of the Mafia in New England, had done back in 1938, when a governor's councilor even composed a letter from a nonexistent priest, attesting to Patriarca's stellar character.

The council had been around since colonial times, and consisted of eight members whose primary responsibility was confirming the governor's judicial nominations, as well as his commutations and pardons. Their only real power was their ability to stop someone from getting something he had already paid someone else, either the governor or a legislator, to obtain. Therefore, in order to keep business, and payoffs, flowing smoothly, the governor needed to have a majority of the eight councilors permanently on his side. Whoever the governor was, Democrat or Republican, rogue or reformer, he would almost always be willing to toss a few bones their way—judgeships and clerkships, as well as the occasional pardon.

When Billy arrived at the State House, the governor's councilors were making the real money rubber-stamping pardons. A couple of the councilors had even printed up what amounted to rate cards—a pardon for, say, manslaughter, naturally cost more than one for an armed robbery, with rapes the second most expensive pardon to purchase, behind only murder.

The prime shopping season for pardons was Christmas, because then they could be justified, or at least rationalized, as acts of Christian charity. The transactions took place in the lobby of the old Manger Hotel, next to the Boston Garden. In the lobby, several of the councilors stationed bagmen who would sit in the hotel's overstuffed easy chairs, an open satchel beside them, into which the friends or relatives of convicted criminals would drop their cash-filled envelopes. In his day, Governor Jim Curley had called the council a "hock shop," but it was worse than that.

In 1961, the longest-serving member of the Governor's Council was from Billy's own district. Patrick "Sonny" McDonough was an old-time rogue who in many ways was the original Billy Bulger, both in personality and style.

Sonny, who was not related to Will McDonough, was fifty when Billy arrived at the State House in 1961. After a lifetime of watching the Curleys and the McCormacks, among so many others, Sonny had many theories about how to make a buck, and he wasn't shy about sharing them with his protégés, Billy among them.

For instance, Sonny detested cops, and suggested to his younger associates that they never use anyone with a badge as a bagman.

"I hate it when a cop gives me $300, because I never know if he's stolen $200 or $700," he would tell the younger pols in a reflective moment. "The problem with cops is, they think whatever they get is theirs."

Whitey, meanwhile, was doing hard time in the federal prison system. After his conviction in 1956, his first stop was at the Atlanta penitentiary, and it was there that he met Dr. Carl Pfeiffer, a professor at the Emory University medical school who was conducting experiments with a new drug—LSD.

It was 1957, long before Dr. Timothy Leary urged young people to "turn on, tune in, and drop out." Ken Kesey's electric Kool-Aid acid tests were still seven years in the future. Few had even heard of the drug when Dr. Pfeiffer began looking for volunteers at the local federal penitentiary.

"We were recruited by deception," Whitey began in the handwritten notes he left behind when he fled Boston in 1994. "We were encouraged to volunteer to be human guinea pigs in a noble humanitarian cause—searching for a cure for schizophrenia. We were told that they could induce all the symptoms of schizophrenia by a chemical LSD-25 . . .

"I was serving a twenty year sentence and was motivated by a desire for some kind of a reduction of sentence—3 days off my sentence for each month of participation—also I was a believer in the government to the degree they would never take advantage of us and also felt that I would be giving something back to society.

"Once a week we checked into the so-called Nuero [*sic*] Psychiatric Ward—a large room with bars + steel locked door in

[the] basement of the prison hospital . . . we were given the LSD in varying dosage—some times light some times massive that would plunge us into the depths of insanity and followed by periods of deep depression suicidal thought and nightmares and interrupted sleep."

Now Whitey was positioning himself as the victim of a mad scientist during a white, psychedelic version of the Tuskegee Project.

"Two men [who] went insane on the project were carried down the hall to a strip cell shipped to Springfield Mo and placed in the wing of the criminally insane."

Billy writes in his memoir that he and his father visited Whitey at least once in Atlanta and then again when Whitey was transferred to Lewisburg, Pennsylvania. He recalled Whitey's contempt for the correctional officers.

"You have to score very high in the stupidity test to be a guard in this place," Whitey told his brother.

But they were apparently smart enough to catch Whitey with what Billy described as "contraband of some sort," and in 1959, Whitey was shipped west to "the Rock."

In his early "acclimatizing" years, as Billy called them, he made few ripples at the State House. In his first term, he was the third youngest of the 240 members. By 1961, the Democrats' majority, expanding by a few seats each term, had risen to 153–87. On average, the Republican members were perhaps ten to fifteen years older than their Democratic counterparts. Those who weren't being picked off were dying off.

The legislature was also in transition from its tradition of part-time service—in many outlying communities, it had long been considered a sacrifice of sorts to serve a term or two in Boston. Now it was becoming a lucrative, full-time career, at least for those in the leadership, who controlled the flow of legislation to the floor. In 1961, though, no one would have thought to list their "profession" as legislator, as so many do now. The 1961–62 "bird book" of Massachusetts politics—the collection of photos and résumés of all the members of the legislature—includes as occupations of the House membership funeral director (6), firefighter (4), farmer (3), housewife (2), foreman (2), and one each of the following: factory worker, bowling alley manager, dentist, and barber.

In May 1961, Billy graduated from Boston College Law School, shortly after his wife, Mary, gave birth to their first child, a son, Billy Jr., on April 3. Between preparing for the bar exam and helping Mary with the baby, Billy wasn't much for the Beacon Hill nightlife. And for an ambitious young state rep, that was a problem, because the quickest way to rise in the House was to become a drinking buddy of the House speaker, John Forbes Thompson of Ludlow, known as "the Iron Duke." Only forty, he had been in the legislature since 1949, and legend had it that he'd never taken a drink until he arrived at the State House. He had been wounded in World War II, and many were willing to overlook his increasing dependence on alcohol because of the shrapnel that he still reportedly carried in his body. By 1961, though, the booze was his crutch, a way of life, a disease.

"He wasn't a bully," Billy wrote of the Iron Duke. "In fact, he was kind when he thought about it. But he rarely thought about much beyond his next drink. He was at best a spectator, in charge of nothing—least of all himself."

A backbencher, Billy saw himself going nowhere in such a dysfunctional legislature. He blamed his problems on the speaker, who spent his evenings carousing through the North End, promising jobs at the State House to waiters and bartenders. The next morning they would show up at the speaker's office asking when they could start work. Not remembering anything about the previous evening, the Iron Duke never turned any of them away, and the number of "court officers"—

door openers—continued to swell, leading future congressman Barney Frank to remark that the State House had to be the only building in the world with more door openers than doors.

Whitey's inmate number at Alcatraz was 1428. His initial psychological evaluation described him as "very self-centered in all he does and [he] has never developed any social responsibility."

Whitey's three years at Alcatraz would become another topic that in later years he would never tire of bringing up. He would discuss the Rock endlessly, with whoever would listen. There were no educational classes, no rehabilitation. Inmates saw two movies per month. It was not a happy time for Whitey.

"After I left Atlanta and arrived in Alcatraz," he wrote in his journal, "I realized I still had LSD problems—visual hallucinations and audio hallucinations—I never mentioned it to the officials or doctor—at that point I feared they may permanently commit me to a mental institution."

Whitey did his time on the Rock in its final days—only 148 more prisoners' names appear on the Alcatraz roster after his. His closest friend was a Native American from Oklahoma—Clarence Carnes, better known as "the Choctaw Kid." A couple of years older than Whitey, he'd been at Alcatraz since age eighteen, the youngest prisoner ever sent to the Rock, after his conviction on murder and kidnapping charges.

As Whitey arrived at Alcatraz in 1959, the Choctaw Kid, then thirty-two, had spent almost half his life on the Rock. In later years, Whitey told stories of a prison of unimaginable horrors, and thirty years later, at the Choctaw Kid's funeral, which he paid for, Whitey would say Carnes had saved his life.

Another of his Alcatraz pals was John Joseph O'Brien, a bank robber from Chicago with whom he had much in common. They were the same age, and both came from urban Irish political families—O'Brien's brother became a Cook County judge. But there was, however, one major difference between Whitey and O'Brien. To protect his family's good name, O'Brien quickly changed his name—he became known as "Barney Grogan." His fellow inmates called him "Dirty Shirt."

Whitey often talked about the racial tensions at Alcatraz. The blacks were segregated in Block B, and were not allowed in the shower room at the same time as the white prisoners. One day in the late 1970s, as Whitey chatted with some of his gangland associates in a restaurant in Boston, the talk turned to a state prison, MCI-Norfolk. One of Whitey's acquaintances at the table mentioned how "tough" he thought MCI-Norfolk was.

Whitey chuckled. "You think Norfolk's tough? I'll tell you what was tough. Alcatraz was tough."

Then he recounted a story about how one time a hulking black inmate had started making sexual advances to a smaller white con, sidling up behind him and telling him in graphic detail how he planned to rape him. Terrified, the white guy fashioned a scythe-type weapon in the prison shop, which he smuggled back to his cell. A couple of nights later, just before evening lockdown, the white con hid at the top of a stairwell that he knew the black inmate would soon climb.

As Whitey told it, when the black guy reached the top of the stairs, the white inmate stepped out of the shadows and swung his scythe at the black man's neck and took off his head. The inmates listened in their cells as the head bounced down the stairs one step at a time like a bowling ball.

Solitary at Alcatraz in the Treatment Unit—TU—was another of Whitey's favorite topics. He would tell the same stories time and again, until the eyes of his closest associates, Stevie Flemmi and Kevin Weeks, would begin to roll as he began another recounting of how the screws would strip you to your underwear and leave you in the unheated steel boxes. It wasn't called "the cooler" for nothing. In the winter the temperature often dipped under 50 degrees and everyone soon learned to sit in such a way as to minimize bodily contact with the steel.

Whitey Thompson, another former inmate of the Rock, described Alcatraz as "the land of forgotten men," and that was surely the way it seemed to Whitey. His father was dying, his brother had a growing family, and instead of being less than four hundred miles from Boston, as he'd been in Lewisburg, he was now more than three thousand miles away.

Billy passed the bar exam in the summer of 1961, and joined his old friend Tom Finnerty in a two-man firm at 41 Tremont Street in downtown Boston, just down Beacon Hill from the State House. Naturally much of his work involved cases at South Boston District Court, where Sonny McDonough controlled everything. In his memoirs, Billy paints a rosy, nostalgic glow on those days, with enough avuncular judges, nipping janitors, and inept burglars to populate a John Ford movie.

Nineteen sixty-two was shaping up as a big year in Massachusetts politics. In June, in response to the increasing public outcry about corruption in state government, the legislature reluctantly passed a bill establishing the Massachusetts Crime Commission, with subpoena power to conduct closed, grand-jury-like proceedings. The commission's chairman was an old Yankee Republican lawyer from the North Shore, whom Sonny McDonough immediately dubbed "a poor man's Cotton Mather."

The bigger story, though, was the impending election to fill JFK's old Senate seat. In most years, state Attorney General Eddie McCormack would have seemed a heavy favorite. But in 1962, the president's youngest brother, Ted, age twenty-nine, was running for the seat, with the blessing of the White House.

Billy, though, would side with Eddie McCormack. He

owed the McCormacks. It wasn't just the fact that Eddie's father, Knocko, had passed out the snow buttons to him when he was a kid, or that they were all from Southie. In the six years that Whitey had been in federal prison, Eddie's uncle, U.S. House Speaker John McCormack, had watched out for him. In his book, Billy described the speaker as the family's sole source of information about Whitey's life in prison. As first the House majority leader, and then speaker, McCormack's inquiries to the Bureau of Prisons were always answered promptly, and McCormack would relay the information back to an increasingly despondent James Bulger Sr., assuring the old man that his eldest son might someday change his ways, if only he could catch a break. McCormack was also close to J. Edgar Hoover, and when the FBI director spoke, Washington listened.

In short, the speaker had been there for the Bulgers, and now the Bulgers, or at least Billy, would be there for his nephew Eddie. The Kennedys understood, but that didn't mean they couldn't make a run at Billy. The approach would be made through Gerry Doherty of Charlestown, another young Boston state rep. Teddy wanted to sit down with him, Doherty told Billy, at Locke-Ober's, by far the most expensive restaurant in Boston.

They filed in for lunch, Ted and Billy and Doherty and a few others. Everyone else in the party took their cues from Teddy and ordered light. But Billy ordered the most famous and expensive item on the menu—Lobster Savannah, which cost $10, a fabulous sum for a meal in 1962.

All through lunch as the rest of the party implored Billy to jump the McCormacks' sinking ship, he kept shoveling it in. Finally, Gerry Doherty, the Kennedys' embarrassed emissary, asked Billy to put down the fork long enough to at least listen to their pitch. But Teddy shook his head.

"I don't know whether we should try to persuade him,"

Teddy said to Doherty. "I know we can't afford to keep feeding him."

Teddy Kennedy easily defeated Eddie McCormack in the primary, despite the attorney general's sneering comment to him in a televised debate that, "If your name were Edward Moore, your candidacy would be a joke." Suddenly, though, in October the focus shifted from state politics to international brinkmanship, as the Soviet Union placed missiles in Cuba, within easy striking distance of the U.S. mainland. President Kennedy demanded their immediate withdrawal, the Russians refused, and a naval blockade around the island began.

For several days, the world appeared to be on the verge of nuclear war. When the crisis ended, JFK's poll numbers soared, and not only did his brother Teddy win what had become the family's U.S. Senate seat, but Massachusetts narrowly elected JFK's Harvard '39 classmate, Endicott "Chub" Peabody, as governor. His first order of business was engineering the removal of the Iron Duke as speaker. Thompson had not been cooperative during the Cuban Missile Crisis when JFK had wanted a pro forma resolution of support from his home state's legislature. Among the rank-and-file reps, the years of frustration were finally boiling over, and several candidates emerged, one of whom was Michael Paul Feeney, a reclusive state rep from Hyde Park who had first been elected in 1938, and whose proudest accomplishment in politics was his two-digit license plate, 54.

Billy Bulger threw in his lot with Paul Feeney.

For some who followed Billy's career, it would be the first example of a problem that would haunt him through the decades—an inability to judge character or talent.

"Everybody knew what a pious fraud Feeney was," said a surviving legislative colleague. "But Billy was still right there with him."

Feeney's candidacy went nowhere, but Billy wouldn't budge. It was his year of lost causes—first Eddie McCormack, then Paul Feeney. On the eve of the vote, in January 1963, he received a phone call from the lame-duck attorney general, Eddie McCormack, asking him to come down the hall to his office right away. As soon as Billy arrived at Eddie's office, he received a call from Speaker McCormack, asking him to change his vote from Feeney to Thompson.

Billy was in a quandary. He felt he still owed the speaker, for Whitey, yet he also didn't want to ask Feeney to release him from his commitment to support him for speaker. McCormack told him not to worry, that Feeney would release everyone when he realized his cause was hopeless. He did, and the Iron Duke was reelected speaker, much to the irritation of JFK and his new, handpicked governor.

By then, Speaker McCormack had already delivered again for Whitey. He'd been transferred out of Alcatraz in 1962, a year before it was closed down. His last stop would be Leavenworth, where he had at least a couple of visitors from Boston. One was Will McDonough, now covering the Red Sox for the *Globe*. On a road trip with the team to Kansas City, McDonough rented a car and drove to Leavenworth, where he promised to take care of Whitey when he was released.

"I can get you a job," he said, and Whitey knew the kind of work Will had in mind—a patronage job somewhere. That might look good to his parole officer, but Whitey had his own plans, and they didn't involve punching a time clock.

Billy and Mary were now having one child per year. In 1964, old Jim Bulger died, but his widow, Jean, stayed on in the apartment on Logan Way. She was waiting for her oldest son, Jimmy, to come home to her. Which he did, finally. In March 1965, almost nine years since he'd pleaded guilty to bank robbery, Whitey Bulger was released from Leavenworth and returned to Boston.

In May 1965, the Massachusetts Crime Commission issued its final, blistering report on corruption in the state.

Part III dealt with the unchecked power of organized crime, and laid much of the blame for the state's endemic corruption on urban politicians who looked the other way.

"Until the electorates in these areas elect officials who will attack illegal gambling actively, or until there is law enforcement by a state agency, such local conditions will continue," the report concluded. "There is little indication that such electorates will change their voting habits in the foreseeable future."

The commission was prescient, if nothing else. Then the panel assessed just how the Mob was able to survive:

"— They exercise strong political power in some quarters;

"— They use bribery and physical violence without hesitation and with little fear of detection;

"— They command unlimited funds;

"— And they have a comprehensive spy system which enables them to exercise their power effectively."

The commission had laid out, in a few words, exactly how Whitey Bulger would rise to the pinnacle of organized crime in Boston over the next thirty years.

CHAPTER 3

As MISERABLE AS HIS TIME IN prison was, Whitey's enforced absence from Boston between 1956 and 1965 was the best career move he ever made, even better than hooking up with the FBI a few years later.

During the time he spent in Alcatraz and Leavenworth, the Boston underworld's internecine gang war eliminated large numbers of the hoodlums who would have become Whitey's competition in the decades ahead. Many were murdered, others imprisoned, while still more simply fled the area forever.

What became known as the Irish Gang War began on Labor Day weekend 1961. In Charlestown and neighboring Somerville, two predominantly Irish mobs coexisted relatively peacefully. The Somerville group, the Winter Hill Gang, was run by Buddy McLean, and the McLaughlins of Charlestown were headed up by Bernie McLaughlin, the oldest of the three brothers who gave the crew its name. As summer 1961 ended, members of both gangs were partying in Salisbury Beach, New Hampshire. The youngest of the McLaughlin brothers was drunk, as usual, and he made some unwelcome advances toward the girlfriend of a fringe member of the Somerville crew.

When Georgie McLaughlin refused to take no for an answer, he was severely beaten and dumped unconscious in front of the emergency room of a local hospital. A few days later his older brother Bernie demanded that the Winter Hill boss, Buddy McLean, turn over the guys who'd inflicted the beating on Georgie.

McLean refused. Georgie, he said, had had it coming. Bernie was not accustomed to getting no for an answer, and a few nights later the McLaughlins tried to wire a bomb to the car Buddy McLean's wife used to drive their children to school. Such a provocation could not go unchallenged. At noon the next day, on the McLaughlins' home turf of City Square, Charlestown, Buddy McLean shot Bernie McLaughlin in the back of the head in front of dozens of witnesses, none of whom offered to positively identify the shooter for the police.

The war was on, and before it was over, more than forty Boston hoodlums would be dead.

At the beginning of the Irish Gang War, the local Mafia watched, amused, as the Irish and their Italian allies who weren't in La Cosa Nostra slaughtered one another. Soon, however, the Italians realized their rackets were being adversely affected by the bloodshed and the resulting public attention. Individual Mafia members found themselves forced to choose sides, and they usually threw in with the gang whose members they'd been closest to during their last stretch in prison. It was a tangled situation, ripe for exploitation, and during Whitey's absence from the scene, a new force appeared on the local underworld scene—the Federal Bureau of Investigation. Over the next three decades, the FBI would realize its goal, practically destroying organized crime in Boston. But as it dismantled the competing criminal syndicates, the bureau's local office too would be devastated by the ethical compromises its agents had to make, compromises that quickly degenerated into outright corruption that included subornation of perjury, bribery, and even murder.

Until 1957, J. Edgar Hoover had denied even the existence of an American Mafia. But after Robert F. Kennedy was appointed attorney general by his brother, the pressure on Hoover to deliver Mafia scalps became overwhelming. Despite the Kennedy family's long-standing ties to organized crime, dating from the patriarch Joe's Prohibition bootlegging to the president's sharing of a girlfriend with Chicago mobster Sam "Momo" Giancana, Bobby despised the Mob and put the heat on the FBI to crack down. On March 14, 1961, Hoover issued a memo instructing the field offices to "infiltrate organized crime groups to the same degree that we have been able to penetrate the Communist Party and other subversive organizations."

In Boston, that task would fall mostly to H. Paul Rico, the Belmont native and Boston College grad who knew Whitey from the old days in Bay Village. Rico's partner was Dennis Condon, a Charlestown guy, conveniently enough. They had joined the bureau within a month of each other in 1951.

As the gang war dragged on, a couple of particularly deadly hitmen began to stand out among the crews of underworld killers stalking Boston. Their names were Joe Barboza and Vincent Flemmi (better known as "Jimmy the Bear"), and both of them became so feared that the city's newspaper photographers, a raffish lot themselves, often attached a note to the back of their arrest photos: "NO credit on photograph!"

Barboza was a Portuguese-American, from New Bedford, and he dreamed of being the first non-Italian to be inducted into the Mafia. But behind his back, Mafia boss Raymond Patriarca referred to him as "the nigger."

By 1964, Patriarca insisted that all of Barboza's hits be cleared through him. Discussions took place at his headquarters on Atwells Avenue on Federal Hill in Providence. In May 1965 the feds reported to Hoover on a conversation one of their informants had heard between Patriarca and his hitman Barboza, who wanted permission to whack an unidentified, but very hard-to-get, hoodlum whom Barboza had been tracking for months.

"He lives in a three-story house," Barboza told Patriarca. "So what I'm gonna do is, I'm gonna break into the basement and pour gasoline all around and torch the place, after which I either get him with the smoke inhalation or I pick him off when he's climbing out the window."

Barboza had worked out a plan for every contingency. He would bring three shooters with him, to watch each side of the house. They would cut the telephone lines to the houses, so that the victim couldn't call the fire department. And just in case one of the neighbors called, before setting the house on fire Barboza planned to phone in false alarms across the city to tie up every fire company.

Patriarca asked Barboza if anyone else lived in the house, and Barboza mentioned his victim's mother.

"You're gonna kill his mother too?" Patriarca asked.

"It ain't my fault she lives there."

Patriarca canceled the contract.

The other top gun in the city was Jimmy "the Bear" Flemmi. Unlike Barboza, he was a Boston native, from Roxbury, and he and his younger brother Stevie both worked with an older hood named Wimpy Bennett. A third Flemmi brother, Michael, would soon join the Boston Police Department.

In the mid-1960s, the Bear too was piling up bodies right and left. Once in 1964 he murdered an ex-con in an Uphams Corner bar and then chopped off his head. Flemmi left the headless torso in a South Boston housing project (the head was never found). In May 1964, FBI agent Condon filed a report on a conversation another one of his informants had had with Jimmy the Bear: "Flemmi told him all he wants to do now is kill people, and that it is better than hitting banks."

Finally, Gennaro "Gerry" Angiulo, who was running the Boston Mafia as Patriarca's underboss, held a sit-down with Jimmy the Bear inside an FBI-bugged barroom on Tremont Street. From now on, Angiulo told him, Patriarca—"the Man," as he was called—would have to approve each of his hits, personally, just as he did with Barboza.

"The Man says that you don't use common sense when it comes to killing people," Angiulo lectured. "Jimmy, you don't kill somebody just because you have an argument with him."

FBI agent Rico followed the bloodletting closely. Hoover's newfound obsession with the Mafia meant the agents had carte blanche to cut deals with anyone who could help them achieve their mission of destroying Italian organized crime.

For any criminal who could provide the FBI with information about the Mafia, no favor was too great. Buddy McLean, for example, became one of Rico's most valuable informants. In 1964, Ronnie Dermody, one of Whitey's old bank-robbing crew, was released from prison and fell in with the McLaughlins. Gunning for the Winter Hill Gang boss, one night Dermody wounded a civilian he had mistaken for Buddy. As he fled, Dermody was positively identified by Winter Hill hoodlums. In a panic, knowing that he was now marked for death, Dermody called Rico to arrange his surrender to police. When Dermody arrived at the agreed-upon spot, a few blocks from Rico's Belmont home, he was met not by FBI agents but by McLean, who shot him dead on the spot. It went into police files as another "unsolved" murder.

Rico couldn't recruit Mafia members themselves as informants, because they were the target, so he focused instead on cultivating sources who associated with the Mafia but who had not been inducted into La Cosa Nostra.

In March 1965, Rico wanted to flip Jimmy the Bear. Rico didn't care how many thugs Flemmi killed, as long as he could feed the FBI information on the Mafia. But even as Rico tried to recruit him, Flemmi was stalking his next victim, a small-time hood named Edward "Teddy" Deegan. It was the murder of this minor figure that would come to symbolize the corruption in the Boston FBI office.

At the time, though, it was just another hit in the ongoing war. After getting an okay from Providence, a plan to eliminate Deegan had been quickly hatched. One of Deegan's friends would tell him about a bank burglary in Chelsea, and he'd meet up with several guys from the Ebb Tide, a Mafia gin mill on Revere Beach. Flemmi's shooting party would include Joe Barboza. Once they got Deegan into the alley, they would open fire.

It seemed like a simple assignment. But the murder would quickly involve the FBI in a cover-up, followed by perjured testimony, and finally the railroading of four innocent men to prison for more than thirty years for a crime they did not commit. And thirty-five years later, the murder of Teddy Deegan would lead to a congressional investigation of corruption in the Boston office of the FBI. It was that probe that would cost Billy Bulger his job as the president of the University of Massachusetts, even though neither he nor Whitey had anything to do with the Deegan murder. Whitey, in fact, was still a few days from being released from Leavenworth when the FBI first got word that Deegan was going to be hit.

On March 10, 1965, Rico filed a report quoting an informant as saying that Jimmy Flemmi was going to murder Deegan and that "a dry run has already been made and that a close associate of Deegan's has agreed to set him up."

Two days later, despite their knowledge of the impending murder of Deegan, the Boston FBI office approved Jimmy the Bear as an informant, and assigned him to the agent who'd recruited him, H. Paul Rico. That evening, Teddy Deegan was shot to death by Jimmy Flemmi and Joe Barboza, among others, in an alley in Chelsea.

Within hours, J. Edgar Hoover had a memo from the Boston field office on his desk accurately identifying all the killers, the real killers, as opposed to the four innocent men who would be convicted of the crime on the false testimony of Barboza in 1968. For the FBI, it was more important to keep Flemmi, and later Barboza, on the street as informers than it was to prevent the framing of innocent men. In fact, the railroading of the four men served two purposes for the FBI—it would enable their informants to escape conviction for a murder they had committed, and it would also remove several Mafia soldiers or affiliates from the scene that the FBI had not been able to eliminate in a legal manner.

H. Paul Rico quickly became one of J. Edgar Hoover's pets. Perhaps once a year, he would fly to Washington and pick up an award for meritorious service, along with a small cash bonus, after which he would receive the ultimate honor for an FBI agent—having his picture taken with the director and Clyde Tolson, Hoover's top aide and reputed homosexual lover. The photos would be given prominent play in the Boston papers, especially the Hearst tabloid, the *Record American*.

Whitey was released from prison in March 1965, a few days after Teddy Deegan's murder. He moved back in with his mother in the projects, and quickly began dating a twenty-six-year-old single mother of four, Theresa Stanley, who would remain his most significant female companion until his final flight in 1994. The rest of the city's underworld might have been convulsed in a bloody gang war, but in Southie, nothing much had changed during Whitey's nine-year stint in prison. Organized crime still involved mostly truck hijackings, small-time gambling, and barroom shakedowns.

As Whitey readjusted to life on the outside, the Irish Gang War came to an end with the October 1965 murder of Winter Hill boss Buddy McLean, and then the 1966 slayings of the last two major McLaughlin gang associates, the brothers Connie and Steve Hughes.

Whitey, meanwhile, was providing muscle for Donnie Killeen, the fading top dog in Southie, who operated out of the Transit Café in the Lower End. Whitey's prospects for advancement in the underworld appeared uncertain enough that he decided to get "on the city"—he was hired as a "courthouse custodian" in September 1967. Records at the Boston Retirement Board indicate that although Whitey supposedly lived with his mother on Logan Way, he listed Billy's address—828 East Third Street—as his own. Will McDonough later bragged that he, not Billy, had gotten Whitey the job, because at the time Billy lacked "the clout" to obtain even a janitor's job for his brother.

His starting pay was $76 a week.

The job was, in essence, a no-show. Whitey appeared at the courthouse only on payday. Which left him plenty of time to worry about the threats posed to Killeen and himself both by "the kids" in Southie, and by two ambitious hoods from outside the Town who saw in the disarray across the bridge an opportunity to expand their own rackets.

The two outsiders were Frank Salemme and Stevie Flemmi, Jimmy the Bear's younger brother. Through his brother, Stevie had gotten to know FBI agent H. Paul Rico, and as Jimmy succumbed to the late 1960s lure of drugs, Rico sought out Stevie more and more often for reliable information. Unlike the Bear, who only cared about hits and parties, Stevie was a businessman, always out hustling, perhaps because he had two families to support, with at least six children by two women. At various points, he owned a real estate business, a garage, a variety store, and he even bought a funeral home in Roxbury, where he stored his fleet of vehicles. He too was a killer—in 1967, with some help from his friends, chief among them Salemme, he eliminated all three of the Bennett brothers, who had given him his start in organized crime.

By 1967, Flemmi was resisting overtures to become a made member of the Mafia, but he had no such qualms about being made by Rico as a paid FBI informant. He went into the files as "Top Echelon," which meant that his information was considered highly reliable. Stevie had his businesses, and the FBI, and Salemme had garages in Roxbury, and now they were just about ready to make their move in Southie.

But then Whitey got lucky. The feds had flipped a small-time hoodlum who was willing to testify against both Salemme and Flemmi. He would put them together on the murder of the last of the Bennett brothers, Billy, and he would also testify that he had seen them preparing the bomb that had blown up the car that belonged to Joe Barboza's lawyer.

By now, though, the FBI's rogue agents in Boston had no intention of allowing Stevie Flemmi to be taken off the board. He was simply too valuable, both as an informant and as a general go-to guy, always ready to perform a favor for his FBI pals. When Rico was gunning for the McLaughlins, Flemmi had provided him with a throwdown—an untraceable firearm that Rico could have planted on any of the Charlestown mobsters if he had ever gotten the opportunity to gun down any of them in cold blood while they were unarmed. With a throwdown on the body, Rico would have been able to plausibly claim he had acted in self-defense. After Georgie's older brother Edward "Punchy" McLaughlin was recorded in 1965 on an illegal FBI wiretap—a "gypsy wire"—describing Rico and Hoover as "fags," it was Flemmi (and Salemme) whom Rico sought out with the address where Punchy was hiding out in Canton. A few days later, they killed Punchy as he boarded a bus. Other favors were more mundane. When Rico smashed up his FBI motor pool car during business hours at the Suffolk Downs racetrack, it was repaired at Salemme's garage, free of charge.

So Rico owed them both. And in September 1969, Stevie and Salemme met with Rico at dawn on Revere Beach, and Rico delivered some bad news.

"There's going to be an indictment and you guys need to get out of town. Just get out of town and play it by ear."

Which meant that, with Rico's help, they could ride it out. So they went back to Salemme's garage on Massachusetts Avenue, picked up a Cadillac and some untraceable license plates from one of their people at the Registry of Motor Vehicles, and started driving. In Chicago they caught a plane to Los Angeles.

Both Stevie and Frankie had more pressing concerns now than muscling into Southie. Neither of them would be a problem for Whitey Bulger ever again.

The directive to the Boston FBI office to reach out to Whitey came directly from J. Edgar Hoover himself. On June 3, 1971, the director ordered the Boston special agent in charge to "promptly advise results of your contacts" with Whitey. With the Flemmis at least temporarily out of the picture, the FBI needed fresh eyes in the underworld. But Whitey was strictly a small-timer, with no contacts in the Mafia. It seems unlikely that Hoover would have singled him out for recruitment, unless perhaps he was doing another favor for the now retired McCormack and some of his most loyal constituents, namely the Bulgers.

Whitey certainly needed assistance from someone, because he found himself in a precarious position. He and the Killeens were embroiled in an open gang war with a faction that included Paulie McGonagle, Pat Nee, and Buddy Roache, whose brother was a young cop named Mickey Roache, and whose roommate was a pint-sized, hard-drinking street tough named

Jimmy Kelly, who would later become president of the Boston City Council.

Outnumbered and outgunned by the younger group, Killeen had recruited one of Flemmi's old associates, Billy O'Sullivan, a loanshark in the Combat Zone. Killeen had also hired a hitman to murder McGonagle, but the contract assassin ended up killing his twin brother by mistake, as well as a younger McGonagle brother, as he sat in a car. In February 1971, Buddy Roache demanded a sit-down with Whitey and O'Sullivan, during which he informed them he was going to "take out" Killeen.

"A violent argument ensued," Condon wrote later that year, and O'Sullivan ended up shooting Roache, paralyzing him. After that, the McGonagles were still more determined to even the score, and Whitey began taking extraordinary precautions. O'Sullivan didn't, and one Saturday night in March 1971, after returning from dinner with his wife, he was walking down Savin Hill Avenue when he was approached by several McGonagle hoods. He saw them coming and started running for a vacant lot across the street. He never made it. They shot him dead.

As soon as the memo from Hoover arrived, FBI agent Condon was assigned to reach out to Whitey. It was a task that once would have been handled by Whitey's old friend H. Paul Rico, but Rico had been transferred, at his own request, to the Miami office. After Condon and Whitey sat down in July 1971, Condon filed the first of hundreds of reports on Whitey's underworld observations that various Boston agents would write during the next twenty years.

That first report ran more than two single-spaced pages, and described the South Boston underworld landscape, or at least Whitey's version of it, at some length. But when Condon pitched him on becoming a regular FBI informant, Whitey initially rebuffed him. Condon wrote that he was too "preoccupied" with his own survival to work for the feds. Whitey said both he and Donnie Killeen had become "convinced that if they did not make a move, they would be eliminated."

Whitey had a plan, but it was one he couldn't share with the FBI or Killeen. He would reach out to the top non-Mafia gang in Boston—the Winter Hill Gang in Somerville. It was Buddy McLean's old crew, now run by Howie Winter, a career criminal who was six months older than Whitey. In later years, some journalists assumed that the gang took its name from its leader's surname, but it was just a coincidence. Ethnically, it was a mix of mostly Irish and Italians, and after the years of bloody conflict against the McLaughlins, "the Hill," as it was known, could hold its own against anyone, including the local Mafia. Whitey had to be careful, because Winter was tight with the McGonagles, and also because his assistance would come with a price tag attached. But Whitey had no choice if he wanted to survive.

Whitey journeyed to Chandler's, the new restaurant on Columbus Avenue in the South End that Howie Winter was now using as the Hill's headquarters in the city. There, Whitey told Howie Winter that there was no need for further bloodshed in South Boston. Once Killeen was gone, Whitey explained, the Southie gang war would be over. As part of the deal, it would naturally be Whitey's job to dispose of his boss.

May 13, 1972, was a Saturday, and it was the fourth birthday of Donnie Killeen's youngest son, Greg. The party was in the Killeens' new suburban home in Framingham, and Greg Killeen's big present from his father was a toy fire engine. Shortly after 9:00 p.m., with the sun safely down, Donnie went outside to his 1971 Chevrolet Nova, saying he was going to buy a newspaper.

As Donnie climbed into his car, the *Globe* reported, "Several men charged the car, rammed a submachine gun into the driver's side, and fired 16 bullets."

Killeen had seen them coming, and died reaching into the glove compartment for a .38-caliber pistol, which police later found on the front seat, under his body.

The next day, Donnie's sole surviving brother was walking hurriedly along the street in Southie when a car pulled up alongside him. Whitey rolled down the window and told him, "You're out. No more warnings."

On Monday, the last of the Killeens called an unprecedented press conference to announce that he was retiring from the rackets, although he didn't use that word. The Transit Café would soon be sold, and it eventually became Whitey's headquarters, Triple O's.

In case anyone was in doubt about the changing of the guard in Southie, the next day, at the funeral home, a large bouquet of flowers arrived for the Killeen family from a Brookline florist, collect.

The card read, "Au Revoir."

In the spring of 1972, the movie version of *The Godfather* was released. The surviving Winter Hill mobsters were amused to see that Alex Petricone, one of Buddy McLean's old pals, had a supporting role in the film, as the Jewish gangster from Las Vegas, Moe Green. Petricone had fled Somerville in 1962, moved to Hollywood, lost fifty pounds, and changed his name to Alex Rocco.

The same spring, a first novel about the Boston underworld was published to rave reviews. In *The Friends of Eddie Coyle*, former federal prosecutor George V. Higgins told the story of a minor hoodlum named Eddie Coyle who bore an uncanny resemblance to Billy O'Brien, one of Whitey's old bank-robbing associates who had been murdered in 1967. Like Eddie Coyle, O'Brien had just been arrested on federal charges, and the papers reported that O'Brien's associates, like the fictional Eddie Coyle's, were concerned that he might not stand up.

O'Brien's slaying was never solved, and neither was Eddie's. The fictional murderer was an ex-con named Dillon, who set up the failed truck hijacking for which Coyle was to be sent back to prison. Dillon owned a bar, and was a feared freelance assassin. The fictional Dillon was also an informant, both protecting and promoting his own interests by funneling information about his underworld competition to the police.

In other words, Dillon appeared to be a prototype of the gangster that Whitey would become, although novelist Higgins, just before his death, denied that he had based his Dillon character on the real-life Whitey.

"At that time," Higgins said, "Whitey hadn't yet become 'Whitey,' if you know what I mean."

That would soon change.

CHAPTER 4

JUST AS WHITEY BENEFITED from an event beyond his control—
the Irish Gang War—so too did both he and Billy benefit from
the ruinous attempt by the federal courts to integrate the Boston
public school system. During the 1970s, that experiment in social engineering transformed Southie from a predominantly law-
abiding working-class enclave into a festering backwater of
lethal class and ethnic tensions, overlaid with drug and welfare
dependency. Much of Southie's population that could afford to
fled to the suburbs, and those who remained behind came in
large measure to see themselves as victims, embracing both civil
and criminal disobedience against the larger society.

In many ways, it is hard to imagine the Bulgers becoming
what they became without busing. The more the community
was fractured, the more the brothers consolidated their power.

A few days after the Irish Gang War began with the murder of
the first of the McLaughlin brothers on October 30, 1961, a
forty-five-year-old housewife from South Boston named Louise
Day Hicks was elected to her first term on the Boston School
Committee. She seemed an unlikely crusader for Boston's white
ethnic neighborhoods. Traditionally, the School Committee was
about jobs—it paid nothing, but for many committee mem-

bers, the rewards were great, and they came in cash. Louise was a member of one of the F.I.F.'s—the First Irish Families of South Boston—that Billy had run against in his first campaign a year earlier. Her father was a lawyer, a part-time judge in the South Boston District Court, the owner of the "Irish" bank in Southie.

During Billy's first decade in politics, Louise would overshadow not only him but every other politician from South Boston, including U.S. House Speaker John McCormack. She would appear on the cover of *TIME* magazine. Within four years, she would become such a symbol of what would soon be known as "the Silent Majority" that Martin Luther King Jr. would journey to Boston to deliver a speech on the Common.

"Will you," he asked his supporters, "follow Louise Day Hicks or Martin Luther King?"

For Billy Bulger, the answer was obvious.

During her first term, Louise was just another job-hungry Southie pol. But then, in June 1963, a number of reform groups led by the Boston chapter of the National Association for the Advancement of Colored People charged that the Boston public schools had been deliberately segregated. They presented compelling evidence that the black schools tended to be older, and that the per capita spending on black students was lower than that spent on their white counterparts. At the time the report was issued, Governor George Wallace of Alabama was trying to block integration of the University of Alabama, and Medgar Evers had just been gunned down in Mississippi. From a public relations standpoint, the last thing President Kennedy needed was the Boston NAACP demanding an end to segregation in the public schools of his hometown. But Louise Day Hicks angrily rejected the NAACP's contentions, and almost overnight she became a fixture on the networks' evening newscasts, an overweight middle-aged housewife in frumpy clothes and funny hats denouncing "radical agitators" in a thick Boston accent.

At the White House, the Kennedys were not amused by this unexpected turn of events.

Both JFK's top aide, Kenny O'Donnell, and then his brother Attorney General Robert F. Kennedy called Louise. Neither got anywhere with her. Finally JFK placed a call himself, pleading with her to back off. By then, though, it was too late. Running for reelection to the School Committee in November 1963, she got 74 percent of the vote, twenty thousand more than incumbent mayor John Collins.

In both South Boston and the entire city, she had become almost a force of nature, Hurricane Louise.

Through the next two years, Louise Day Hicks and her supporters would duel with the civil rights groups over the segregation in the public schools, both in court and in the media. Outside Southie, though, the tide was running against the "neighborhood schools" that Louise professed to want to preserve. The national elections of 1964 produced a Democratic landslide, and in 1965 a new federal civil rights act would be passed. President Lyndon Baines Johnson would announce the beginning of the "War on Poverty."

The Massachusetts legislature followed suit, passing the Racial Imbalance Act, which decreed that a school was "imbalanced" if it was more than 50 percent black. Only three cities in the state had such schools: Boston, Springfield, and Cambridge, so it was an easy, feel-good vote for suburban legislators of both parties, whose constituents would never be affected, and that was what so infuriated white working-class Boston.

Billy seethed at the hypocrisy of the rich white suburbanites, who reminded him of the people Sonny McDonough dismissed as "the League of Women Vultures." But once more it was Billy's neighbor Louise Day Hicks who most candidly articulated the resentments of white ethnic Boston: "If the suburbs are honestly interested in solving the problems of the

Negro," she said, "why don't they build subsidized housing for them?"

As J. Anthony Lukas wrote in *Common Ground*, his study of court-ordered busing in Boston, "Louise had tapped a much broader sense of grievance, rooted less in race than in class: the feeling of many working-class whites that they had been abandoned by the very institutions—City Hall, the Democratic Party, the Catholic Church, the popular press—that until recently had been their patrons and allies."

Busing was still almost a decade away, but it was already clear that the next few years in Boston would be scarred by racial animosity and bitter class warfare. Incumbent mayor John Collins had no stomach for what lay ahead. In early 1967 he announced he would not seek a third term, and Louise quickly entered the race. At her announcement, the band played the old standard "Every little breeze seems to whisper Louise."

Her slogan: "You know where I stand."

There were a host of candidates, but the race quickly boiled down to Louise versus Kevin Hagen White, the secretary of state, the son and grandson of Boston politicians. White had been elected secretary of state in 1960, at the age of thirty-one. At the time he was so obscure that at a pre-election rally, JFK introduced him as "Calvin White."

By 1967, though, he had been elected statewide four times, and he became the consensus anybody-but-Louise candidate. The *Globe*, which was consolidating its own position as the newspaper of record for liberal Massachusetts, ended its ninety-year policy of no endorsements for political office to come out strongly for White, and he won easily, despite Louise's lopsided margins in the blue-collar, white working-class wards. White resigned as secretary of state, and the legislature selected House Speaker John F. X. Davoren as White's successor, which opened the way for Majority Leader Bob Quinn of Dorchester to become speaker.

For the first time, Billy had a friend—a neighbor, in fact—at the helm. But as his top deputy, Quinn picked David Bartley of Holyoke, who was two years younger than Billy. In terms of advancing in the leadership, Billy still appeared stuck on a treadmill to oblivion. And that meant he didn't have the political juice to deliver the number of patronage jobs to Southie that his constituents demanded.

In 1968, Billy even found himself on the short end of a legislative redistricting. For a time he looked like the odd man out in his three-person Southie district, so he appealed to Louise Day Hicks to campaign for him. On the stump, she quoted John Boyle O'Reilly, the Irish immigrant and poet for whom Billy's first public elementary school was named.

"'Loyalty,'" she said, quoting O'Reilly, "'is the holiest good in the human heart.' Billy Bulger has never forsaken his own."

Billy was reelected. It would be his last tough race.

Though his political future was secure, at least temporarily, Billy still wasn't making much money in his little two-man law firm with his fellow Southie native Tom Finnerty. Billy was always a little short of cash, especially with a new child continuing to arrive every other year. And it was during this period that he began to develop some bad financial habits that would later get him into some serious trouble, namely, investing with his law partner, Tom Finnerty.

In February 1968, Billy did his first land deal with Finnerty. With a group of five other wired Boston pols, he bought fourteen acres of land from the federal government in Winthrop on the old Fort Banks military base.

Beacon Winthrop won the land after an open bidding process, paying $201,818. Eventually, after a few more of the paper transfers of the sort that Whitey would someday perfect in his own real estate transactions, the land was sold off between 1970 and 1972 for $499,999—a 148 percent return.

It was all "strictly legit," as they would say at the State House. It was also Billy's first big score with Tom Finnerty. It would not be his last.

In March 1970 Speaker John McCormack finally announced he would not seek a twenty-third term, and for the first time since 1926, the South Boston Congressional seat was open.

It was Louise Day Hicks's for the taking.

But Senator Joe Moakley called Billy one night to give him the heads-up that, Louise or no Louise, he too would be running for Congress. And that meant that Billy could run for his open Senate seat, just as he'd run for Moakley's open House seat a decade earlier. This time, though, he would be the favorite. His only significant opponent would be an aide of McCormack's named Patrick Loftus.

Loftus never really threatened Billy, but the same could not be said of Whitey's attempts to intervene on his brother's behalf. In the summer of 1970, Billy heard from someone in Loftus's campaign that Whitey had been "sounding off" about taking care of Loftus. In 2003, under oath, Billy described to the congressional committee what happened next: "So I drove up the street, and I found him and I said, 'This is madness. Don't do this. . . .' I think probably he thought he was doing this for me and ultimately around this time I made it very clear to him. Please don't do it. He said, 'I assure you I will never be near any of us again.'"

Billy won easily, just as Louise Day Hicks defeated Moakley in the Democratic primary to win McCormack's seat. In January 1971, Billy was sworn into the state Senate. With forty members, compared to the 240 in the House, it was a much smaller pond, in which Billy would soon find himself a much larger fish than he had ever been before.

CHAPTER 5

By 1972 BOTH BULGERS had risen higher in their respective trades than anyone could have imagined twenty years earlier. But any further advancement seemed unlikely. Both Billy and Whitey found their paths to the top blocked. For Billy, the problem was the state senators ahead of him in the Democratic leadership—President Kevin Harrington and Majority Leader Joe DiCarlo.

Whitey was now the undisputed king of the rackets in Southie, and he rapidly began consolidating the protection racket. Even though he had still not been officially designated as an FBI informant, Condon remained in contact with him.

In September 1973 he filed this report on Whitey: "Informant advised that JAMES 'WHITEY' BULGER has been moving around the city pressuring bookmakers and shylocks for payments of money. BULGER was told that he had been coming on too strong and is going to curtail these activities in the future."

Whitey, obviously, had a different plan for the future. His goal was to curtail the activities of anyone in the underworld— or law enforcement—who could order him around. If any curtailing of activities was going to be ordered, Whitey wanted to be the one issuing the commands, not taking them.

But standing in Whitey's way was the Mafia. If he were ever to dominate organized crime in Boston, he would have to eliminate Gerry Angiulo and his brothers who hung out on Prince Street in the North End. But even before that, Whitey would have to somehow take over the non-Mafia mob that he now associated with—the Winter Hill Gang of Somerville.

The Hill operated out of a compound of buildings and a garage owned by Howie Winter on Marshall Street, on the corner of Broadway on Winter Hill in Somerville. Winter ran the gang along with Johnny Martorano, a former all-state football player from Milton whose father had run a gin mill in the Combat Zone, the city's red-light district after the demolition of old Scollay Square in 1961, a seedy stretch of strip joints, adult bookstores, and pornographic movie theaters along lower Washington Street. After graduating from high school, Johnny had turned down seven football scholarships and instead stayed in Boston, hanging out in the Zone and quickly moving into the rackets, as did his younger brother, Jimmy, a few years later.

Martorano had fallen under the sway of Stevie Flemmi, and by the age of twenty-five he was a professional hitman. Johnny rapidly became one of the city's most prolific killers, a reputation he solidified in January 1968, after a forty-seven-year-old black man made the mistake of beating up Flemmi in an after-hours joint. Martorano tracked his quarry to a car on Normandy Street in Roxbury, where the man was sitting with two people who turned out to be, not fellow criminals, but a nineteen-year-old girl and a seventeen-year-old boy. Johnny walked up alongside the car and calmly killed all three of them with his trademark .38-caliber Police Special revolver. From then on, in certain circles, Johnny Martorano would be known as "Sickle Cell Anemia." He was deadly to blacks.

The new, consolidated Winter Hill Gang soon began flexing its muscles. They wanted to control gambling north of the city, and that meant eliminating another crew of independent mobsters led by Indian Joe Notarangeli, who operated out of Mother's, a barroom under the elevated tracks of the Green Line at North Station.

The Notarangelis controlled a number of bookies in the Merrimack Valley, and they were stubborn. In March 1973, a bartender from Mother's was killed by machine gun fire at a stoplight in Brighton. He had no connections to organized crime. His fatal error: He drove a Mercedes-Benz that looked a lot like one owned by Indian Joe's brother Al.

Eleven days later, Whitey was in the front seat of an automobile with an Uzi machine gun as a Notarangeli hood named Al Plummer drove down Commercial Street in the North End. Whitey opened fire, practically decapitating Plummer and wounding another gangster in the car, an old associate of Stevie Flemmi's named Hugh "Sonny" Shields.

The third person in the car was a hoodlum named Frank Capizzi, who had been wounded twice earlier by Winter Hill hit squads, namely Whitey. After the third shooting, on Commercial Street, he and his family fled Boston, crisscrossing North America to escape. As he wrote to a judge in 2003, his children "had the job of cleaning festering wounds and picking out bits of lead from my back as they surfaced."

Four days later, on a Friday night, they caught up with Billy O'Brien, a thirty-two-year-old roofer and stevedore from South Boston (no relation to the Billy O'Brien who was murdered in 1967). O'Brien, who had served time for killing yet another hoodlum named O'Brien, in South Boston in 1964, was driving on Morrissey Boulevard. He had bought a cake at Linda Mae's before picking up his ten-year-old daughter, Marie, for the weekend. In the car with O'Brien was another rackets guy named Ralph DeMasi. As they headed north, another car pulled up alongside them and the passenger opened fire, again with a machine gun. O'Brien was hit seventeen times, and died instantly. DeMasi was wounded.

"I thought someone was taking target practice on the road," DeMasi said in a letter to a judge in 2004. "It was my good friend John Martorano."

The driver: Whitey Bulger.

Eleven days later, a different pair of Winter Hill killers flew down to Fort Lauderdale to murder an ex-boxer from the Notarangelis' hometown of Medford. When he opened the door to his apartment, the associate of Indian Joe was shot five times in the head.

By April 18, Indian Joe had abandoned Mother's. He retreated to his home turf, Medford Square, a bustling downtown area with heavy pedestrian traffic and narrow, clogged streets. About 3:45, he walked into the Pewter Pot coffee shop, used the pay phone, and then sat down and ordered a coffee.

He hadn't been there long when Johnny Martorano walked in, wearing construction clothes. Johnny shot Indian Joe twice, then walked out of the restaurant and jumped into a car driven by an older man with "stubby fingers," as one witness put it.

Ten months later, in February 1974, Johnny Martorano caught up with Indian Al, shot him in the head, and left his body in the trunk of a stolen car in Charlestown. Days later a couple of Charlestown teenagers took the car for a joy ride. The cops caught up with them in Somerville. In the trunk was the frozen corpse of Indian Al.

The Hill began calling in, one by one, the bookies who'd been laying off their action to the Notarangelis. One of the calls went out to Jackie McDermott, the top bookie in Lowell. McDermott was summoned, as he later told the story, to the Holiday Inn on the Somerville-Charlestown line and escorted to Room 13. Whitey was there, but Howie Winter did most of the talking, and McDermott did all of the agreeing. What choice did he have?

Finally, when all of the arrangements had been made,

McDermott was told he was free to leave. He nodded, but said he had just one question he'd like to ask.

"Why'd you hit Joe like that, in front of so many people? Right downtown there, in broad daylight?"

Whitey Bulger threw in his two cents' worth: "Because we wanted to show everyone how easy it is."

Whitey was in the gang, but he still wasn't of it. The other gangsters appreciated his impeccable Boston police and courthouse sources; even the Mafia would come to rely on Whitey to keep them informed. Gerry Angiulo would say to him, "Whitey, you can find out a little more than me . . ."

But he was still the odd man out in Boston organized crime, the one guy from Southie, the city's overwhelmingly Irish neighborhood. Somerville was at least as Italian as Irish; Howie Winter was married to an Italian woman. The Martoranos and Frank Salemme were half-Irish. Whitey, though, was what the others laughingly called FBI—full-blood Irish. It didn't disqualify him from membership in the gang, but it did set him apart from everyone else.

Now, though, the FBI was about to construct for Whitey his own little mini-crew, a gang within the gang. The two men who would become his closest associates—FBI agent John "Zip" Connolly and mobster Stevie Flemmi (from an Irish neighborhood, married to an Irish woman)—were about to return to Boston.

Flemmi had been on the lam since the fall of 1969. By early 1972, he was holed up in New York, but he wanted to return to Boston, and the FBI wanted him back. Flemmi was, after all, the best kind of organized crime informant—an Italian hood who was trusted by the Mafia, but who had no compunctions about informing on them. The problem was, he still faced a pair of outstanding warrants, for the Billy Bennett murder in 1967 and for the car-bombing of Barboza's lawyer, a semi-shady un-

derworld attorney named John Fitzgerald. The Bennett murder
was disposed of quickly, when two of the other defendants were
acquitted of the charges by a Suffolk County jury.

The Fitzgerald bombing, though, was more complicated. It
had occurred in Middlesex County, where it was more difficult
to broom a case than in Boston. And the lawyer was, at least in
the public mind, a civilian who had merely happened to be
in the wrong place at the wrong time. Fitzgerald had lost a leg
in the bombing, which made him an even more sympathetic
figure. In short, Middlesex County needed a scalp, and Condon
had one picked out—Stevie's old partner, Frank Salemme, who
was also hiding out in Manhattan.

If everything could be worked out properly, Salemme's capture would be good for everybody—except for Salemme, that
is. Rico and Condon wanted the credit for the pinch to go to
their new protégé in the bureau, Zip Connolly.

Zip was yet another native of the Old Colony Harbor projects. He'd graduated from Boston College in the same class
with Johnny Martorano's brother, Jimmy, then briefly, unhap-
pily attended law school. In 1968, Zip was at loose ends, and
he needed some advice. He ran into Paul Rico's partner, Dennis Condon, and Boston police detective Eddie Walsh, an old
friend of the Connolly family's. Both Condon and Walsh would
later brag that they had "recruited" Zip. Then Connolly
stopped by the State House to visit his old neighbor and now
state rep, Billy Bulger, to discuss career opportunities in law
enforcement.

On August 1, 1968, U.S. House Speaker John McCormack
wrote a personal note to his old friend J. Edgar Hoover on behalf of a constituent.

"Dear Edgar," the letter began. "It has come to my attention
that the son of a lifelong personal friend has applied to become
a special agent of the Federal Bureau of Investigation. . . ."

Zip was appointed to the FBI in October 1968. He began

his FBI career in Baltimore and then San Francisco before he was transferred back east to New York. But like Stevie, he still wanted to get back to Boston, to be closer to his ailing father. Condon and Rico were bumping up against the FBI's mandatory retirement age, but Connolly was just a kid, barely thirty. He could be their go-to guy in the Boston FBI office for the next twenty years, whatever their second careers turned out to be.

But first they had to get him back to Boston. Connolly was the guy who could take down Salemme. Every few days, Flemmi and Salemme would get together in Central Park. They'd sit on a park bench and swap secondhand gossip about what was going on back in Boston. One day, early in 1972, as soon as they sat down on a park bench, Stevie delivered some big news.

"I'm getting out of here," he told Salemme. "It's too hot down here."

His next stop would be Montreal, Flemmi explained to a stunned Salemme. And as Flemmi prepared to flee, Condon began establishing the paper trail to explain Connolly's impending capture of Salemme.

In 1998, under oath in federal court, Condon was asked about all the memos he sent to Connolly in the days before Salemme's arrest.

"I believe I sent him a couple of photographs [of Salemme] and said: See if you can spot—spark them up down there."

Once Stevie was safely out of New York, the plan to make Zip Connolly a hero could proceed. In 2003, Salemme told congressional investigators what happened almost immediately after Stevie fled.

"Shortly after that," Salemme said, "I was bumped into by John Connolly on 83rd Street and 3rd Avenue."

By the time Salemme was shipped back to Massachusetts to stand trial for the bombing, Stevie Flemmi was safely established in Montreal. He would say later that those were the best years of his life. On the witness stand, he later claimed, unconvincingly, that he didn't even want to return to Boston. He said H. Paul Rico made him come back. Working at a print shop, Stevie kept up with the Salemme trial in the Boston papers. The case went badly for Frank—he was convicted of bombing the car that belonged to John Fitzgerald and shipped off to state prison for sixteen years.

But the main witness against Salemme also testified that Stevie was not present at the bombing. Then he vanished, not to be seen again for twenty years. In May 1974 Rico called Stevie in Montreal and told him it was time to come home.

Once the charges against him were officially dismissed, Stevie was warmly welcomed back at the garage on Marshall Street. Stevie moved back in with his mistress, Marion Hussey, in Milton, and was soon sleeping with her fifteen-year-old daughter as well. He found another girlfriend, Debra Davis, at a Brookline gas station, and when her father objected, he drowned mysteriously. In short, it was business as usual for Stevie, and business as usual meant talking to the FBI.

But now there would be someone else in the mix—Whitey. Unlike Stevie, Whitey still hadn't been officially "opened" by the FBI as an informant. Later Zip invented a story about how he recruited Whitey as an informant as they sat in an FBI car on a moonlit night at Carson Beach in 1975.

But the reality was less cinematic, and more pragmatic. It was an arranged marriage between Whitey and Stevie, and the marriage broker was the Federal Bureau of Investigation. Once Zip was back in Boston, Billy told him to keep Whitey out of trouble. That would be Johnny Martorano's testimony, and Billy, under oath, didn't deny it.

As Flemmi testified in 1998: "[Whitey] didn't just approach me cold and say: 'Hey, here's what I'm doing,'" Flemmi said in 1998. "I mean, it didn't make sense. I would have been wondering what was going on here."

In court, Flemmi said that Whitey approached him one day in the garage in 1974 and told him he was talking to Connolly. Later, Whitey would tell Stevie that Connolly wanted to meet him, and that the introduction would be handled by Dennis Condon. They met in what Flemmi described as an "obscure" coffee shop in Newton. It was a cordial get-together. Flemmi asked how Paul Rico was, and Condon said he was fine. It was, Flemmi said, "like a transition."

By 1975, Whitey had officially joined Flemmi as a Top Echelon informant for the FBI. It was quite a feather in his cap, considering that he had spent almost his entire post-prison career in the South Boston rackets, and had practically no access to the information that the FBI was still most interested in gathering—about the Mafia. Stevie was much more tied into Prince Street and the Angiulos' satellite crews in East Boston and Revere. Stevie would talk to the Mafia, and pass on whatever he'd learned to Whitey.

And Whitey would pass it on to Zip, who would write it up, giving most, if not all, of the credit, to Whitey. The question that has always lingered is, why exactly did the FBI need Whitey if they had Stevie?

The answer was, they didn't need Whitey nearly as much as they needed his brother Billy. The retirement age for agents was fifty, and they always fretted about their post-FBI jobs. Their federal pensions weren't nearly as large as they would later become. It was easier for a retired agent to find a new job if he knew somebody, and if he hadn't made any enemies. And what was so wrong with helping out the brother of a rising legislator who might someday be in a position to put in a good word for a retiring, middle-aged agent?

Whitey was an informant, after all. He did meet, first with Condon, then Zip, and finally other agents as the years went by. And, according to FBI regulations, some informant had to be cited for every bit of information in each report—so why not Whitey? Stevie came up with enough information for two people, and if Whitey got credit for some of the tips, well, how exactly was that a problem? No money was changing hands, at least not yet. And if, down the road, some retired agent from the Boston office were to become Boston police commissioner or director of security for Boston Edison—well, so be it. It wouldn't be the first time either of those jobs had been given to a politically connected retired G-man.

As time went by, and Billy solidified his grip on state government, Zip would make a habit of inviting the new agents to a tour of the State House, where he would introduce them to the Senate president, "the most powerful man in the state," as one of the corrupted agents later described Billy.

Things were looking up for Whitey, but he still needed to eliminate some of his old rivals in the Town. Spike O'Toole, an old friend of the McLaughlin brothers, was the first to go. He was a regular at the Bulldog Tavern on Savin Hill Avenue, even though the bar's owner, an ex-prizefighter named Eddie Connors, was tight with Howie Winter. Connors tipped off Howie about Spike's pub crawls, and Winter told Connors to give him a call the next time Spike was tying one on at the Bulldog.

Sitting in a black car on a Saturday night in December 1973, Johnny Martorano waited for Spike to stagger out of the Bulldog, then machine-gunned him in front of the Avenue Laundry. Hit at least ten times, O'Toole stumbled out onto Dorchester Avenue, knocking over a mailbox as he toppled over. The black car then sped off, in the direction of South Boston.

O'Toole's murder put Paulie McGonagle at the top of what they all called the Hit Parade. Whitey handled that one himself, with help from a tough local barfly named Tommy King.

Whitey buried McGonagle on Tenean Beach—it was the first interment in one of the three death pits where five more of Whitey's victims would be interred over the next decade. Whitey drove McGonagle's car to Charlestown, pushed it off a pier, and then threw Paulie's wallet into the water. Whitey liked to make his victims "do the Houdini," as his acquaintances from New York City's Hell's Kitchen, the Westies, used to say. Everyone might have a pretty good idea what had happened, but they could never really be sure. And with any luck, McGonagle's remaining friends might decide he'd been done in by Charlestown hoods and take misguided revenge against the Townies, thereby thinning the herd of Whitey's rivals even further.

Next to go was Eddie Connors, the owner of the Bulldog Tavern, who'd fingered Spike O'Toole a year or so earlier. By 1975, Connors had been arrested in a botched robbery, which was bad enough, but he had also taken to bragging about his role in setting up O'Toole for Howie Winter. It was a dangerous sort of name-dropping, and Howie Winter coldly told Eddie to give him the number of a "safe" telephone where he could call Connors to discuss the matter. Once Howie got the number, he turned it over to Johnny Martorano, who from his sources at the telephone company discovered that it came back to a pay phone at a gas station on Morrissey Boulevard.

On June 12, 1975, Connors was to appear at the station at 9:00 p.m. to receive the call from Howie. One hundred yards away, 150 cops were enjoying a banquet. All would later report that they hadn't heard a thing. The only problem was a Metropolitan District Commission police traffic detail, almost directly across the boulevard from the phone booth. Whitey quickly found another phone booth and called in a false accident report to the MDC police. The traffic detail immediately left to answer the alarm, and moments later Connors pulled up in his Cadillac to await the call. When the phone rang and he stepped into the booth, Johnny Martorano, Whitey Bulger, and Stevie Flemmi pulled up next to the booth in a stolen car. Whitey and Stevie jumped out and riddled the telephone booth with bullets. Connors died at the scene.

It was Whitey's and Stevie's first hit together. It would not be their last.

All the murders were planned at Howie Winter's garage. The only legitimate business operating there was a body shop jointly owned by Stevie, Johnny Martorano's younger brother, Jimmy, and George Kaufman, Frank Salemme's old partner in the auto repair business on Massachusetts Avenue.

Kaufman always had an auto body shop or used car lot of some kind where the non-Mafia crews hung out; he was also a jack-of-all-trades for the Mob—a liaison to both the Jewish bookies they shook down and whatever gang members happened to be in prison at the time. He never made much money, though, because after a while, Kaufman's regular customers would realize who they were rubbing elbows with, and business would fall off and Kaufman would have to pack up and move again, and then Stevie and Whitey would show up once more and the same scene would play out all over again.

Inside the Marshall Street complex, the first office belonged to the guys who actually operated a garage. Further back in the building was the real inner sanctum of the crew—where Howie Winter and Johnny Martorano held court. No one who owed money ever wanted to be escorted into that part of the building. On the wall hung a poster of two vultures perched on a cactus overlooking a desert, with one vulture saying to the other: "Patience, hell. I want to kill somebody."

There were often females at the garage—wives, girlfriends, and neighborhood women who brought over food for the guys. Most of the crew enjoyed having them around, but not Whitey. He asked them inappropriate questions, and he glared at them, giving the women the you-don't-belong-here looks that any black teenager outside Southie High on H Street would have understood only too well.

Since so many underworld characters had their cars worked on by Kaufman, they would often stop by the office just to chat, with their keys in hand. If anyone of whatever status in organized crime ever twirled their key chains, Whitey would immediately demand that they stop.

"I can't stand that twirling," Whitey would say, in great agitation. "It reminds me of the screws at Alcatraz."

Still, Whitey had his strengths. He was handy with a machine gun, and he had those high-ranking police sources in Boston. One night, after everyone else had gone home, Stevie Flemmi and Jimmy Martorano were closing up the garage when a task force of cops raided the garage and began rifling through the desks. In Whitey's desk, one of the plainclothes cops discovered a list of undercover state cops, descriptions of their cars, and the untraceable license plates on the vehicles.

"Where'd he get this list?" one of them asked Stevie.

"That list?" Stevie said. "I thought everybody had one of those."

The cops left in a huff. No crimes had been committed.

Everyone kept their separate rackets—Whitey had the bars in Southie, Stevie had loansharking and prostitution in Roxbury—but they also had deals going together. At its height, the gang's most prominent members included Howie Winter and his bookkeeper, Sal Sperlinga, the Martorano brothers, and Whitey and Stevie. Also around were George Kaufman, and two other Irish guys from Somerville—Jimmy Sims and Joe McDonald, the oldest of the crew, born in 1917.

McDonald was typical of the gang. He was a skilled killer—he'd gotten a lot of experience during the Irish Gang War—but not nearly as effective at more routine criminal enterprises.

The Hill was quite proficient at killing rival mobsters to take over their rackets, but once they gained control, they had no idea how to run them. That was the lesson of Winter Hill's disastrous foray into gambling after wiping out Indian Joe's crew. In what should have been a fabulously profitable enterprise, Winter Hill lost its shirt.

One problem for the Winter Hill gangsters is that they enjoyed partaking in their own vices. Both Howie Winter and Johnny Martorano were themselves degenerate gamblers. Like their marks, they spent Sunday afternoons in the fall drinking beer and watching pro football on TV, often doubling up on the late West Coast games as they tried desperately to get even.

Whitey and Stevie learned from their mistakes.

"They didn't drink," said Salemme. "They didn't gamble."

As the years went by, Whitey and Stevie lost interest in running any kind of gambling operation. They would eventually only provide one service—protection. Bookies, drug dealers, truck hijackers—they all needed "protection," and Whitey and Stevie were only too happy to oblige them. "Protection" became one of their favorite words; they'd learned it from the FBI.

Meanwhile, Howie Winter and Johnny Martorano were going broke. Eventually they had to go to Gerry Angiulo to borrow money. To make the weekly payments, they began going into business with people they didn't know, and couldn't trust.

And that was where Fat Tony Ciulla came in. The son of an East Boston fish merchant, Fat Tony Ciulla was six foot three, weighed 350 pounds, and at age thirty-five had been fixing horse races for almost half his life, mostly at smaller East Coast tracks. He had also worked as a driver for Joe Barboza.

In 1973, Fat Tony began laying off bets on fixed races with a bookie connected to Winter Hill. Somehow, Howie Winter found out the races were fixed, and Fat Tony was summoned to a meeting at Chandler's. Fat Tony owed Howie $6,000, and six months after he paid it off, he started showing up at the garage.

Very soon Fat Tony was partners with Winter Hill. They supplied the cash and the mules to lay down bets across the country, and Fat Tony provided the doped-up horses and the bribed jockeys. Gerry Angiulo warned Howie Winter to steer clear of Fat Tony, but Howie and Johnny—and Stevie and Whitey and everyone else at the garage—didn't care.

The money was too good.

In November 1975, Whitey eliminated the final holdouts in the South Boston underworld. One of the guys he'd always liked least was Tommy King. Tommy wasn't terribly bright, but he was absolutely fearless. Tommy had tried to get with the new program in Southie, even assisting Whitey in the murder of Paulie McGonagle a year earlier. Now he was a potential witness against Whitey. Then he got the best of Whitey in a barroom brawl, and that rocketed him to the top of the Hit Parade.

Whitey began "lobbying," as Stevie later put it, for the elimination of Tommy King. As the top guy in the non-Mafia underworld, Howie Winter had to sign off on every hit, just as Raymond Patriarca did on Mafia assassinations. By 1975, Howie had enough headaches without having to worry about the Byzantine intricacies of the Southie underworld, so he finally gave Whitey the okay.

Once he had the green light, Whitey began lulling King into a fatal complacency. Like Don Corleone in *The Godfather*, Whitey was keeping his friends close and his enemies closer. After a while, Whitey told King he needed some help on a hit. Eddie Connors had a partner, and he was making noises about avenging his late pal. The guy that was to be hit, Whitey said, was named Suitcase Fidler.

So the boys would get together, and whack Suitcase. Everyone would show up at Carson Beach on the night of November 5, 1975. Stevie would pass out guns, and then they'd drive over to wherever Suitcase was and whack him.

It was a moonless night, and one by one they climbed into the car—Whitey and Tommy in the front seat, Stevie and Johnny Martorano in the back. Stevie had a paper bag with the .38s, and he handed them out. All were loaded except the one he gave to Tommy King.

Johnny Martorano leaned forward and shot King in the back of the head. They took his car keys, and then they buried him on the banks of the Neponset River on the Quincy-Dorchester line. For years afterward, whenever he drove past the spot, Whitey would tell whoever was with him: "Tip your hat to Tommy."

Once Tommy was gone, they went after his best friend, Buddy Leonard, one of Whitey's old neighbors in the projects. He had to go, for two reasons. First, he might try to settle the score for his old pal when Tommy turned up missing. Second, killing him would muddy the waters. Buddy was a heavy drinker, and Whitey knew he'd be drunk and therefore easy to take after closing, and he was. Just a few hours after killing Tommy King, they snatched Buddy Leonard outside a Southie bar and pushed him into a car—Tommy King's, of course—and then they shot him in the head. Whitey ditched the car in the projects and Stevie, who'd followed him in a second car, gave Whitey a lift home.

The next day, in the evening editions, police were described as "baffled" by the murder of Leonard in the automobile belonging to his best friend, who was now himself missing. But the cops suspected the two incidents might somehow be related.

Frank Capizzi had been on the run for years after being shot by Whitey on Commercial Street in the North End in the spring of 1973. Finally, though, he decided the heat had died down enough that he could return to Boston. But something had changed in the time Capizzi had been away. Whitey was now officially an FBI informant. He had friends in high places, and Frank Capizzi didn't.

When word got out that Capizzi was back in town, three cops showed up at his home in Winthrop for a pro forma interview—FBI agent Dennis Condon, Boston police detective Eddie Walsh, and the new kid in town, Zip Connolly.

In a letter he wrote to the federal court before Connolly's sentencing in 2003, Capizzi recalled his meeting with the cops.

"I looked directly into John Connolly's Machiavellian eyes and told [him], Mr. Connolly, James Bulger shot me three times!!! . . . Dennis Condon listened attentively, writing it all down."

Despite Capizzi's positive identification, Whitey was not arrested. Nor would he be, ever again. As a Top Echelon informant, Whitey was headed for the top of the rackets.

CHAPTER 6

SENATE PRESIDENT KEVIN Harrington and Billy Bulger, his number-three man, made an odd pair walking through the marble State House corridors—Harrington was six foot nine, almost a foot and a half taller than Billy. Billy was soon joking that he was spending so much time with Harrington that he had begun ducking whenever he went through a doorway.

But Harrington's closest ally was his majority leader, Joe DiCarlo of Revere. Billy had a four-year head start on him in the legislature, but DiCarlo had more than made up for lost time. A former teacher, he'd become a chairman in his first term in the House, in 1965, and three years later he knocked off a twelve-term Senate incumbent in the primary. Billy, of course, had never run against an incumbent, nor would he ever.

Another ambitious young senator, a former state rep and accountant from Oxford, was James Kelly (not the Jimmy Kelly who was a minor South Boston hoodlum who eventually became president of the Boston City Council). After winning the Senate presidency in 1971, Harrington had appointed Kelly chairman of Ways and Means. Kelly wrote the Senate's version of the state budget, and it wasn't long before Kelly was referred to in the press as "D-Ritz," for his table in the Ritz Café, where he held court. With Kelly it was pay to play, strictly cash 'n' carry, no reasonable offer refused. According to State House lore, he employed two bagmen.

A decade later, Billy would be blamed in the press for a trend begun by Jimmy "D-Ritz" Kelly that centralized even more budgetary power in the hands of the legislative leadership—the use of "outside sections" to surreptitiously enact legislation in the state budget. In the years to come, Billy would be suspected of using outside sections to settle scores with Whitey's foes. They would be filed anonymously, with no fingerprints, by the legislative leadership, and would become law without ever having been publicly filed, or heard in committee, or debated on the floor, passed by both branches, reconciled in conference committee and then signed into law. For instance, a major contributor to a legislative leader might need a parcel of state-owned land for a development that was opposed by the community in which the land was located. Under normal legislative rules, the affected municipality could block such a project. But by using an "outside section," the leadership could deliver the land, or any other favor, to anybody who hired the properly connected lobbyists, with no chance for any opponents of the measure, however odious it might be, to complain. Or a connected state worker recently convicted of a crime might need to add a few more years of government "service" to bolster his pension. A single vaguely worded paragraph, buried in hundreds of pages of innocuous boilerplate, would often get the job done.

Once the state Senate had been a proud deliberative body. Calvin Coolidge had served as its president. But by the early 1970s its membership had degenerated badly. Other politicians occasionally used to ask Harrington why he didn't appoint better people to committees. Harrington would throw the bird book, the illustrated legislative directory, at the questioner, and snarl: "You find somebody in there!"

Billy still devoted some time to his law practice. Representing constituents has always been considered part of the job, another service to be performed "on the arm"—for free. Still, despite the picture he later tried to paint in his memoir, Billy was far from destitute. By 1974, he had accumulated enough cash to buy a summer "cottage" in Mashpee on Cape Cod, the ultimate status symbol for an up-and-coming legislator. But he could have been making much more had not such a large part of his practice continued to be for short, if any, money. The cases Billy did handle often involved his political cronies. One such case he handled was for the father of the man who would succeed him as Senate president, Tom Birmingham.

Birmingham's father, Jackie, was a veterans' agent for the city of Boston. Jackie Birmingham and Billy Bulger were close, perhaps because of something they had in common—both their brothers were gangsters.

According to Billy's account in his book, his friend Jackie had approved unemployment benefits for one Suitcase Fidler, the Charlestown hood whose name Whitey would drop when he was successfully setting up Tommy King to be murdered.

Suitcase, according to Billy, was indeed a jobless veteran, but was in prison at the time.

Suitcase's family had needed the money, and now Jackie Birmingham was caught up in a corruption investigation by the Suffolk County district attorney's office. By his own admission, Billy intervened and "the result was that Jackie never appeared, never had to tell his story, never had to take his hit."

Billy hadn't been in the Senate for even a full year when the series of events that would deliver the Senate presidency to him began to unfold.

In 1971, the state auditor issued a scathing audit report of the ongoing construction of the new UMass Boston campus at Columbia Point in Dorchester. He was appalled by the cost overruns of a New York company that was overseeing the entire project—McKee-Berger-Mansueto. The Senate set up a committee to investigate, with DiCarlo as chairman.

MBM's executives knew they had a problem, and began trying to reach out to the legislators to see if something could be worked out. Eventually an MBM executive got to Republican Senator Ron MacKenzie of Burlington, who was tight with DiCarlo. The MBM executive mentioned something about . . . contributions. MacKenzie understood, and took the offer back to DiCarlo.

In November 1971 DiCarlo's Senate committee issued a report exonerating MBM, and two months later, according to court testimony, the MBM executive met Senator MacKenzie in the Point After lounge in the Back Bay and handed him $5,000 cash in $50 and $100 bills. MacKenzie returned to the State House and gave half the money to DiCarlo.

A month later, in the men's room of the Parker House bar, MacKenzie took another $7,000 in cash. The next meeting was again at the Point After, with a different MBM executive handling the delivery. MacKenzie stuffed the money into his coat and said he'd have to be very careful driving home.

"It would make quite a splash in the headlines," the Republican senator told the MBM executive, "if a senator was in a car with $10,000 on him."

The clock had begun ticking down on Joe DiCarlo.

In 1972, the House had amended its rules to change to a system of single districts, doing away with the old system of double- and triple-districts in the cities. The first tangible result was the election of several more black House members who for the first time formed a caucus and began lobbying for the creation of a new black state Senate district in Boston.

In hindsight, Billy was never in any real danger, but what the black legislators were proposing would mean serious changes in his own district, which contained most of what was then black Roxbury. The minority population of Billy's First Suffolk District amounted to about 30 percent overall, although the percentage of black voters was much smaller.

Among those white liberals pushing for a new black Senate district was a freshman state rep from Beacon Hill by the name of Barney Frank. Billy considered Frank's efforts to be a personal attack on himself, his career, and his neighborhood.

"What bothered Bulger," Frank said in an interview in 2004, "was the idea of the people who were involved in trying to change his district—liberals, blacks, a Republican governor from Dover. And busing was coming too."

In the end, a black Senate district was created, but it would be carved out of the two Jewish districts, one of which had been devastated by white flight in North Dorchester and Mattapan.

Frank now had a problem—he had crossed Billy. And Billy saw to it that any bill with Frank's name on it was torpedoed in the Senate. If any of his legislation was to have even the slightest chance of passage, Frank had to convince senators to put their names on his bills. Frank's name alone was enough to assure a bill's demise. That was how things worked in the Senate, even before Billy became president. If someone in leadership wanted something done, it was. To get along, as the saying goes, you had to go along. Anyone who refused to go along would quickly find himself persona non grata—another Barney Frank. Then, just to add insult to injury, Billy arranged for Barney's Beacon Hill district to be transferred into the South Boston Senate district, where Irish conservatives outnumbered Jewish liberals by at least a five-to-one margin. Barney couldn't "move up." He would forever remain a state rep, or so it seemed.

The decade-long struggle over the integration of the Boston public schools was finally coming to a head. For years the city, the School Committee, and the NAACP had been tangling in federal court, while on Beacon Hill the legislature proposed one unworkable solution after another.

Finally, the case had been taken over by Judge W. Arthur Garrity, a Kennedy liberal who lived in Wellesley. Fed up with the school committee's foot-dragging, in 1973 Garrity ordered busing to begin in the fall of 1974.

In the city, especially in South Boston, the white working-class population was outraged at the injustice of it all. They well understood that it was they and their children who would have to bear the brunt of a solution imposed by their more affluent neighbors, whose residence in the suburbs shielded them from the crime and racial polarization that increasingly plagued Boston. The suburbs would be insulated from the chaos that they were forcing by judicial fiat on blue-collar Bostonians who quite often worked, in one form or another, as their hired help—as cops, cabbies, teachers, and tradesmen.

At the time, Boston was the sixth largest metropolitan area in the country, but the city of Boston proper was no larger than the twentieth in the nation. In almost any other part of the country, many of Boston's affluent suburbs would have been part of the city—and any busing plan. If the suburbs had been included in Garrity's grand design, his neighbors—and Harvard classmates—would have surely brought their economic and social clout to the table to insist on a more equitable solution. But that was not the case, and as the years went by, even many white working-class Bostonians with the wherewithal to flee did. As white flight accelerated, those still stranded in the city saw their political clout dwindle even further, and outside Boston's declining white neighborhoods, there was no upside for any politician to come to the defense of the beleaguered Irish and Italians in the city. It would have offended the *Globe*. Particularly galling to Southie and Charlestown and East

Boston was the sanctimonious posturing of many of the residents of the town of Brookline, which was practically surrounded by Boston.

Brookline had once been predominantly Yankee, and was now heavily Jewish. Many of its residents had been part of the first waves of white flight out of Roxbury, North Dorchester, and then Mattapan. The symbol of Brookline's smug hypocrisy was former state representative Michael Stanley Dukakis. He had run for lieutenant governor with Kevin White in 1970 and lost, and now in 1974 was seeking the Democratic nomination for governor against Billy's old friend from Dorchester, Bob Quinn, the former House speaker who was now the attorney general. Quinn was the favorite, but with the Watergate scandal dominating national headlines, 1974 was not shaping up as a good year for conservatives or regulars from either party.

Dukakis was a strong supporter of Judge Garrity and the forced busing plan. For Billy, politics was always personal, and just as he could not quite let go of his grudge against Barney Frank, he never really forgave Dukakis for his stand in favor of forced busing in a city in which Dukakis did not live.

"I could never quite get over the pain of knowing that he harbored such contempt for me and my family that he would want my children shipped to inferior schools," Billy wrote in his book. "I wondered what the reaction of Dukakis and his wife, Kitty, would have been if told that their children were to be bused into a high-crime area."

For years Billy had talked about a judgeship, and as the 1974 election season heated up, the embattled Republican governor, Frank Sargent, decided to make a few friends for himself in a Democratic stronghold. Just before the Fourth of July 1974, shortly after the birth of Billy and Mary's final child, Brendan, the Republican governor nominated Billy for the open judgeship in the South Boston District Court. He would of course be confirmed by the Governor's Council; Sonny McDonough would see to that.

Billy was ecstatic at first, but he quickly began to get cold feet. He received a call from former U.S. House Speaker John McCormack telling him how disappointed he was that Billy was giving up politics. His resignation from the Senate would have meant a short, brutal primary fight—potential candidates would have included Louise Day Hicks, who had lost her seat in Congress to Joe Moakley in 1972. Others sure to run included the two state reps, Billy's friend Michael "Flats" Flaherty and Ray Flynn, a camera-loving former Providence College basketball player whom Billy already detested. For the Town as a whole, the timing of any primary couldn't have been worse—it would take place the same week that the court-ordered busing began.

There was another problem for Billy. The Governor's Council had just changed its rules, and now judicial nominees had to make at least limited financial disclosure. Billy didn't like that one bit. There was no need for his constituents to know how well he'd been doing; it would just give them something else to resent. As Dr. Samuel Johnson observed in 1775, "The Irish are a fair people; they never speak well of one another." Nothing had changed in two hundred years.

If Billy's neighbors in Southie found out about the "cottage" in Mashpee, or the real estate deals, many were likely to begin whispering that Billy was putting on airs, trying to rise above his station. He would be castigated for going, as they say, "high-hat."

The *Globe* soon reported that a Bulger "associate" believed that the new financial disclosure rules, in effect for only a month, should be "waived for a candidate like Bulger, who has been in the Legislature for 14 years."

There would be no waivers. And so Billy dithered. Few outside South Boston yet knew about Whitey's rise in his chosen

career. But as Billy considered the duties of a judge, he sometimes seemed to be thinking of his older brother, although he
would later tell Congress that he never heard any talk of "the
more terrible crimes."

In the *Sunday Globe* of July 14, 1974, he said he wanted to
"avoid even the appearance of impropriety. . . . I believe un-
popular clients need defense. I've always been stubborn about
that. They're entitled to representation. You're not defending a
murderer or a rapist. You're defending a human being, a person, who has been accused of rape or murder. And they have a
right to counsel.

"There are degrees of guilt. Every case is different. Every
person is different. I don't want to say anything now that seems
like a blanket statement."

Still, the reporter noted near the end of the lengthy profile
that some in Southie were "skeptical" that he would take the
judgeship. Eight days later, Billy hand-delivered a letter to
Sargent in the governor's Corner Office.

"I do not believe it appropriate for me to disengage myself
from legislative service at this time," he began. "You will understand, I hope, the difficulty and strain of reaching this decision, especially in the light of my initial reaction to accept
the appointment."

It was a blow, especially, to Representative Flynn. He was already running for Billy's Senate seat, and four candidates were
running for his seat in the House. Also surprised was the governor, a Republican struggling vainly to win reelection in the
wake of Watergate.

Six weeks later, court-ordered busing began in the city of
Boston.

Busing changed everything in South Boston, forever. A large
part of the Town's stabilizing influence—its middle class—
fled the chaos for the inner suburbs south of the city, while oth-

ers who could not yet afford to leave everything behind shipped their children out beyond the city limits to live with relatives on the more tranquil South Shore. Among those who remained in Southie, respect for the old traditions gave way quickly. Pathologies that had previously existed only on the fringes—drugs, family breakups, out-of-wedlock pregnancies—rapidly became the norm for ever-growing segments of Southie's population.

The disaster that unfolded over the next several years also dashed whatever faint hopes Billy might have had of someday running statewide. He became known as an anti-busing zealot, which pushed him further to the margins of the increasingly liberal and suburban Democratic Party in Massachusetts.

The court-ordered busing began on September 12, 1974, and it went smoothly throughout most of the city. But outside South Boston High School, in front of network TV camera crews, angry mobs gathered and chanted, "Niggers go home!" Six hours later, with the buses headed back to Roxbury on Day Boulevard—"that memorial to Louise Day Hicks' father," as J. Anthony Lukas noted—crowds gathered to throw rocks and beer bottles at the buses. Nine black students were injured by the projectiles and the broken glass.

Four days later, the city canceled an anti-busing protest march, and Southie teenagers attacked blacks at a subway station. The Boston Police Department had to break up brawl after brawl inside the schools. Attacks on solitary blacks in Southie led to retaliatory assaults on whites in Roxbury. Soon, Governor Sargent had to mobilize the National Guard.

The indignities for South Boston never seemed to end. The *Globe*, whose Yankee editor was from Lincoln, and whose editorials were written by a Cambridge Brahmin named Anne Cabot Wyman, would win a Pulitzer Prize for covering a phenomenon that did not adversely affect the lives of any of the paper's top editors, reporters, or, needless to say, its blue-blooded owners.

On October 7, someone fired gunshots from Morrissey Boulevard at the presses of the *Globe*. Mayor White stationed police sharpshooters on the roof of the building. Billy was in the thick of things in Southie, appearing informally before Judge Garrity in court, often haranguing crowds on the street. One radio reporter, Dick Levitan, later recalled Billy singling him out during one particularly vitriolic speech, pointing at him and saying that the crisis was all the fault of "Zionists like Dick Levitan." Billy denied he'd ever said such a thing.

Like most of his constituents, Billy was obsessed with busing, the utter unfairness of it. To describe the situation, he often resorted to the word "Orwellian." The swells, the outsiders who foisted school integration on Southie—the *Globe*, Ted Kennedy, the judge from Wellesley, the lawyers from Brookline—they were a "manicured mob." As the furor over busing wore on, relations between the police and the community deteriorated to the point of open hostility. The brunt of the tough law enforcement in Southie fell to a special Boston Police unit, the Tactical Patrol Force, the TPF.

The police commissioner was Robert diGrazia, one of those credentialed out-of-staters that Kevin White relied upon so heavily during his first two terms as mayor. Billy couldn't stand diGrazia. One day in 1974, when the police had arrested some demonstrators outside Southie High, Billy yelled at the cops, calling them "Gestapo"—an epithet he tossed around carelessly in those days.

DiGrazia threw it right back at Billy.

"If you had any guts," he said, "you'd tell those people to get their kids into school."

Bulger stared at the outsider, the blow-in, the drifter ordering him and his people around.

"The community," he told diGrazia, "has a message for you, Commissioner. Go fuck yourself!"

With the situation near anarchy, Louise Day Hicks was still in the forefront of the anti-busing forces, but she was . . . Louise, yesterday's news. Billy's leading rival in Southie politics was now Ray Flynn, a state rep who was everything Billy was not—a heavy drinker, a graduate of Southie High, a nonlawyer, an ex-athlete.

Billy loathed him, and not just because he was a maverick in the legislature, or because, like Billy, he wanted to run for mayor in 1975. He also distrusted Flynn's tentative olive branches to the communities beyond the bridge, and to the media. To Billy, Ray Flynn was simultaneously a lightweight and a traitor.

He was also a media hog. Billy had gotten along well enough with the boozy State House press corps of the 1960s. He played hearts with them on occasion, and would make sure they had copies of speeches he planned to deliver in the afternoon, so they could get their stories into the evening editions. But now the era of the legmen, mostly high school dropouts, phoning in stories to rewrite men back in the city room for the "replate" editions, was passing. The trade of newspapering was becoming the profession of journalism. And Billy didn't much care for the new breed of Ivy Leaguers that *Globe* editor Tom Winship was hiring.

In the winter of 1975, Billy was still uncertain about his future in the Senate. There were occasional stories in the newspapers about a federal "probe" of payoffs to unnamed state legislators by McKee-Berger-Mansueto executives, but as the months dragged on, the investigation seemed to be going nowhere.

The two agents doing much of the legwork were Dennis Condon and Bob Sheehan. Both were nearing retirement, which meant they had entered the go-along, get-along phase of their careers. Condon was even known to be a friend of the majority leader, occasionally hanging out in the DiCarlo family's furniture store on Hanover Street.

If DiCarlo survived, Billy was all done in the Senate. There wasn't room for two forty-one-year-olds from Suffolk County in the two top spots.

The 1975 mayoral race would be between Kevin White and state Senator Joe Timilty, a former city councilor and ex-marine whose uncle, Diamond Jim, had been Curley's police commissioner. Timilty was a street guy, a high school dropout who lived in Mattapan. He had a driver named Tom Menino, who in 1993 would become mayor himself. With busing overshadowing everything else, 1975 became a brutal fight. Billy continued with his anti-busing harangues, both on the floor of the Senate and on the streets of Southie.

On November 3, 1975, White narrowly won a third term for mayor over Timilty. White—beset by busing and the early signs of the corruption that would dog his later years at City Hall—decisively lost the white vote in the city. Only the black wards stuck by him, and for years Timilty's supporters claimed that fraud had been rampant at the polls. As for White, he later claimed that "the Mob" was behind Timilty.

Kevin White had always tried to keep himself at arm's length from the darker, more paranoid, self-pitying side of the "shanty Irish," as the residents of hardscrabble neighborhoods like Southie and Charlestown were often called by those who'd made it out. Kevin White was originally from West Roxbury, Ward 20, a neighborhood of single-family homes and shady, tree-lined streets. Kevin had gone to Williams College rather than Boston College. He seldom drank—his father, a career Boston politician, was an alcoholic—and Kevin didn't even belong to the Knights of Columbus. As an adult, he lived on Beacon Hill. But as assimilated as the mayor was, he was still able to grasp instinctively how both Bulger brothers were simultaneously tightening their respective grips on South Boston.

In 1978, White sat for an end-of-year television interview with Christopher Lydon of Channel 2's *Ten O'Clock News*. After the formal interview ended, as the cameraman began recording a few setup shots for later use as cutaways, White began talking about the media's reluctance to take on the connection between the two brothers—Whitey and Billy.

"You don't want to touch the tough ones," he said, apparently thinking he was speaking off the record. "The point is, if my brother threatened to kill you, or you thought he would kill you, you would be nothing but nice to me. You just wouldn't want to get too close to investigating the mayor."

Then the mayor recounted an incident during busing, when he played tennis one night at an athletic club in South Boston, and came out at 11:00 p.m. by himself, or so he told Lydon.

"I was never more scared in my life. I almost slept in the club, 'cause I figured if they pump me out—which, why not? Whitey would be crazy enough to do it even then. . . . And if they shoot me, they win all the marbles. They draw [Gerry] O'Leary as mayor. So why not shoot the son of a bitch?"

Whitey didn't, but that summed up his emerging philosophy rather succinctly.

CHAPTER 7

THEY WERE PARTNERS NOW—Whitey and Stevie and the FBI. And from the very beginning, it was a one-sided deal. Each side would do "favors" for the other, but the FBI's were a lot more valuable than the cash and gifts that Whitey and Stevie would pass on to their agents.

"Me and Whitey gave them shit," Stevie said later, "and got back gold in return."

The FBI would tip them to informants and make sure they were cut out of indictments. They would scare off potential witnesses, so that Whitey and Stevie could continue their two-man crime wave. In return, Stevie would claim in 2005 that he and Whitey bribed a half-dozen agents, thoroughly corrupting the Boston office and destroying the FBI's reputation in New England for more than a generation.

In the mid-1970s, as the deal began to take shape, the FBI bailed Whitey and Stevie out of one jam after another, and in return, their two Top Echelon organized crime informants gave up Johnny Martorano's younger brother, Jimmy.

Jimmy Martorano had to go because the FBI needed a scalp, quickly, to show Washington how well its new informants were producing. The G-men would naturally have preferred some higher-profile Mafia types, but at that moment Stevie could offer nothing from Prince Street other than gossip—mostly lists of guests at Mafia weddings and the dates of restaurant openings on Hanover Street.

But then Whitey saw an opportunity to do a favor for the FBI. Jimmy Martorano was owed $2,000 by a bar owner in Revere. One of Martorano's drinking buddies at the garage was an ex-con named Brian Halloran, who would later figure in what were perhaps Whitey's most spectacular pair of murders. In October 1974 Jimmy asked Halloran to collect the debt for him, and Halloran, drunk as always, pulled a gun on the bar owner and then stole $445 out of his cash register. The terrified victim went running to the FBI and was placed under the protection of a new agent named John Morris.

Jimmy Martorano and Halloran were arrested and charged with loansharking. But Jimmy thought he had a solid defense—he was going to claim that he had actually loaned the money to somebody else, who had then given the $2,000 to the bar owner. If this person were willing to testify that the $2,000 was actually his, then Jimmy and Brian Halloran could argue that they were simply doing a favor for the first guy in getting his money back from the bar owner. It might still be robbery, or assault, but those were relatively minor state crimes, and even if they were convicted, it wouldn't mean heavy prison time, especially not from a judge in Suffolk County.

One morning, at the garage, Martorano announced he was going downtown to talk to his lawyer about his impending trial. Whitey and Stevie asked if they could tag along, and Jimmy, suspecting nothing, agreed. The two new FBI informants got to listen in as Martorano and his lawyer confidently discussed their plan to have their secret witness testify.

The next morning, FBI agent Zip Connolly and the new guy in the office, John Morris, suddenly appeared at the new witness's home and asked him if he had received a $2,000 "loan" from Martorano. Frightened by the agents' brusque questions, the potential witness suddenly concocted a new story about the money—he told the agents he had in fact taken the $2,000 from his wife, who had been saving to buy some furniture. He mentioned nothing about borrowing any money from Martorano.

As soon as he heard about the FBI agents' visit, Jimmy knew he was gone. If the man were now called as a defense witness, and told the original, exculpatory story under oath, Morris and Connolly would then be sworn as witnesses to impeach his testimony. In short, their star witness could no longer testify for Martorano and Halloran. In June 1976, Martorano was convicted on the loansharking charges. (Halloran, already in state prison on gun charges, was acquitted.) Now, on the big Winter Hill scores, there was one fewer guy to split the pot with. And Whitey's guy in the FBI had a notch on his belt.

Much later, after he had confessed to being an informant, one of Stevie Flemmi's co-defendants asked him why he and Whitey had ratted out their alleged friend Jimmy Martorano for something as seemingly inconsequential as allowing Zip to score a few brownie points with his bosses in Washington. Stevie shrugged.

"Somebody had to go," Flemmi said, "and Jimmy did good time."

One down, many to go.

Despite their proficiency in destroying their competition, the Winter Hill Gang was ripe for the picking. They were deeply in debt and they were getting sloppy. With their bookmaking business still in the red, most of their cash was coming from Fat Tony Ciulla's fixed horse races. But Ciulla, like Howie Winter and Johnny Martorano, was a compulsive gambler. He too was always short of cash, and when he and one of his underlings tried to supplement their race-fixing earnings with a robbery, they botched it, and ended up exchanging gunfire with the intended victim.

The problem for Ciulla was that they had added a third gun for the heist, a guy named James Sousa, and now Fat Tony fretted that the hired hand was a weak link who could be flipped. Ciulla went to the garage and asked for help, and Johnny Martorano got the contract. He lured Ciulla's accomplice to an apartment on Winter Hill and murdered him. Sousa's body was never found.

The fact that the Somerville guys were now killing people for Fat Tony should have told them something was seriously wrong. But they needed money.

Now that they had a secret to share, Whitey and Stevie were soon spending more and more time in each other's company. They often drove together to the garage from Boston, and eventually they decided to go into business together. As Howie and Johnny became more and more reckless, their Boston associates fretted about the future of their joint ventures. So with George Kaufman, Whitey and Stevie set up a company to install vending machines throughout the city. Their salesmen basically had one pitch—mentioning the names of Bulger and Flemmi.

They had barely set up the operation before Kaufman convinced a bar to switch to the Bulger-Flemmi machines. That meant that the machines owned by Melotone, the established vending machine company in Boston, had to go. When the Melotone owners found out what had happened, they immediately went to the FBI. There was talk of wiretaps and bugs, but before any court orders could be obtained, Zip Connolly decided to pay a visit to Melotone's corporate offices. Zip informed the owners that if they decided to cooperate, they should be prepared to join the Witness Protection Program and leave Boston.

As Flemmi explained on the witness stand in 1998, "It probably was a threat. I don't know. I wasn't there. All I know is what the results were."

The results were, Melotone's owners lost interest in prosecuting Whitey and Stevie. The criminal investigation was ended, and Whitey and Stevie pulled their machines out of the disputed bar, assuring that there would be no more complaints, or probes. No harm, no foul. Melotone moved its machines back in, and shortly thereafter, Whitey and Stevie folded their company. There would be easier ways to make money.

Stevie's flow of usable information, as opposed to gossip, was little more than a trickle, but the FBI's protection never flagged. Zip Connolly's next save came in early 1976. An ex-con and businessman named Francis Green owed $175,000 to a finance company with ties to Winter Hill. Accompanied by Johnny Martorano, Stevie and Whitey drove to the Back Side restaurant in Dedham to put the squeeze on Green. The deal was, they would receive a cut of whatever money they could wring out of him.

As they walked into the restaurant, Martorano spotted one of his old grade-school classmates—Bill Delahunt, the new district attorney of Norfolk County. As Whitey and Stevie found a table, Martorano walked over to say hello to the prosecutor. After a few pleasantries, they traded verbal jabs, and finally Delahunt told Johnny to stay in Boston and out of Norfolk County.

By then Green had joined the Bulger party, and Martorano walked over and sat down with them. From across the restaurant, Delahunt was now staring at the gangsters, but that didn't deter Whitey.

"If I don't get my money," he said to Green, "I will kill you. I will cut your ears off. I will stuff them in your mouth, and then I will gouge your eyes out."

Green went first to the Norfolk County district attorney, but the office punted to the FBI. And there the case died. It was becoming a pattern. Dennis Condon wrote the report, describing Green in the first sentence as "a convicted swindler." He pointedly mentioned that Whitey was trying to collect for a woman, "a friend of theirs." He wrote nothing about the threats.

Condon, however, would soon retire, taking a job in the administration of Governor Michael Dukakis. Another of Condon's contemporaries, Bob Sheehan, would take his federal pension and become the state comptroller. The old guard was changing at the Boston office of the FBI. H. Paul Rico had retired from the bureau's Miami office in 1975 after twenty-four years on the job. He soon had a new job—director of security for World Jai Alai, a gaming company based in Florida. Rico would soon be back in the middle of everything in Boston, but for now, he was relaxing in the Florida sunshine.

Meanwhile, Connolly was putting together a new FBI crew. Other than Zip, the most important agent for the future would be John Morris, who'd helped out on the Jimmy Martorano case. Morris and Dennis Condon both lived in Lexington and would commute into the city together. Soon Morris was one of the boys, and eventually Zip decided it was time to introduce him to Whitey.

In federal court, Morris later recalled Connolly's instructions as to how he should handle Whitey: "Be sure to treat him with respect."

When Morris finally met Whitey, he was surprised to see that Stevie Flemmi had also shown up. According to FBI regulations, informants weren't supposed to be interviewed together; they weren't even supposed to know who else was giving information to the bureau. But no one on either side seemed terribly concerned about the bureau's rules.

"I wasn't sure if they knew they were informants," Morris said, in all seriousness.

Whitey still had provided no information of any consequence to Zip. He'd turned over the license plate numbers of a few troublesome Southie hotheads he wanted taken off the board, and he'd also passed on some negative, self-serving gossip about several political figures, including District Attorney Delahunt and at least one of Mayor Kevin White's political operatives in Southie. Zip dutifully wrote up the "tips," although he couldn't have been satisfied with the quality of the information.

But as Whitey discovered, there were other ways to keep an FBI agent happy. In June 1976, the same month Jimmy Martorano was convicted, Whitey presented his first gift to Zip Connolly. It was a stolen diamond ring. Zip gave it to his first wife, as she would testify during his racketeering trial in 2002.

Meanwhile, the flow of "gold" out of the FBI office to South Boston continued unabated. Whitey next learned that a bookie named Richie Castucci had become an informant for the FBI. Castucci ran the Ebb Tide, the old Mafia hangout on Revere Beach where the Teddy Deegan hit had been planned back in 1965. Castucci was tight with Winter Hill—he'd introduced Flemmi and Johnny Martorano to a major New York bookmaker when they were organizing Fat Tony's race-fixing scheme. But then Castucci started feeding information to the FBI, and he passed on some information about two fugitive Winter Hill gangsters—Joe McDonald and Jimmy Sims. He knew they were hiding out in New York's Greenwich Village, and he told the feds.

The penalty for such treachery was death. The Hill decided Richie Castucci had to go, but before they killed him, they planned to make a lot of money off him.

All through the fall of 1976, everyone in the gang bet football games heavily with Castucci. Even Whitey and Stevie, the nongamblers, took the plunge, because they had no intention of ever paying off Castucci, except with a bullet. For about half the season, the Hill remained ahead, and Castucci dutifully paid them off each Monday. But as the season wore on, the boys went into the red. They kept doubling up on their bets, but they couldn't get even, and by Christmas, they knew it was time for Castucci to go.

He was told he could pick up his money in Somerville at the garage. When he got there, as Johnny Martorano later confessed, he handed Castucci a bagful of cash and told him to go to an apartment with two guys and count it. The two guys were Whitey and Stevie. Castucci was sitting in the apartment kitchen sorting the bills, with his back to the front door, when Johnny Martorano walked in and shot him in the head. Whitey and Stevie cleaned up the blood and wrapped the body in a blanket. Then they put Castucci's body in the trunk of his car and drove it back to Revere, where they abandoned the vehicle in the parking lot of an apartment building.

To protect Whitey and Stevie, Connolly immediately began filing reports suggesting that Castucci was deeply in debt to both the Hill and the Mafia, and that Castucci settled with Winter Hill first. That was a fatal breach of organized crime protocol, Connolly wrote, because the Mafia always insisted on being paid off first. But the murder of an FBI informant required more than the usual duplicity. The day after Castucci's body was found, the feds convened a multi-agency meeting to figure out who had murdered their informant. Representing the FBI was Zip Connolly. He suggested that the hit bore all the hallmarks of a Mafia assassination.

"Winter Hill doesn't kill like that," he said.

The legend of Whitey Bulger continued to grow, at least in the FBI reports filed by Zip Connolly. Soon Zip was claiming that Whitey had saved the life of an undercover FBI agent named Nick Gianturco.

Gianturco had been working undercover out of a warehouse in Hyde Park as "Nick Giarro." The sting, which was called "Operation Lobster," involved Gianturco setting himself up in operation as a fence, buying stolen goods from truck hijackers, mainly from Charlestown.

At one point, an associate of Stevie Flemmi's asked if "Giarro" had any protection, because the associate was planning to rob him and didn't want any repercussions.

Stevie phoned Whitey, who called Zip, who immediately got in touch with Gianturco and asked him if he had any meetings planned. Gianturco told him that he did, that night, but he'd already decided to blow the crew off because, wisely enough, he didn't trust them.

As the years went by, Connolly and Morris increasingly exaggerated the importance of the tip. Morris eventually cited it as one of the two occasions on which Whitey's information had prevented the murder of an FBI agent. During his testimony in 1998, Morris was asked to name the second agent.

"I cannot recall," he said.

Whitey and Stevie had tried vending machines, and now Howie Winter and his associate Sal Sperlinga decided to put pinball machines into all the bars and veterans clubs in Somerville. First they got the Somerville aldermen to repeal the city ordinances outlawing the machines. But once pinball was legal, other, more legitimate businessmen quickly moved in, undercutting the Hill's high gangster prices. In no uncertain terms, Howie Winter informed his would-be competitors that it was the Hill that had brought pinball back to Somerville, and that it was the Hill that would now enjoy the fruits of its monopoly. But instead of knuckling under, some of the other companies went straight to the Middlesex County district attorney, and soon the lantern-jawed first assistant district attorney, John Forbes Kerry, was announcing the arrests of Winter and Sperlinga.

The pinball arrests in late 1977 were a major break for Whitey and Stevie. Howie was the undisputed boss, and Sperlinga one of his top money men. With both of them off the street, Johnny Martorano was the last remaining at-large Winter Hill hoodlum who outranked them, so to speak.

The pinball machines, though, were just the beginning of Howie Winter's troubles. One of Fat Tony Ciulla's crooked jockeys had been arrested in New Jersey, and he flipped. Once the Garden State jockey implicated Ciulla, Fat Tony cut a deal for himself with prosecutors, and then he sold his story to *Sports Illustrated*, which put it on the cover of its November 6, 1978, issue. In the piece, Ciulla didn't mention the names of anyone from Boston, but in New Jersey, a judge ordered Fat Tony to reveal the names of the gangsters who were involved in fixing races with him in Massachusetts.

"Your Honor," he complained, "I don't know if I am allowed to say these names here in open court."

The judge didn't care about federal grand juries. "You are here now," he said.

Fat Tony took a deep breath and began speaking.

"Fellows that were partners of mine," he began. "One's name is Howie Winter. One name is John Martorano. M-A-R-T-O-R-A-N-O. Whitey Bulger. Stephen Flemmi."

It was the first time Whitey's name had been mentioned in a federal courtroom since 1956.

By January 1979, Whitey was in deep trouble. During Fat Tony's run, he and Stevie had been in charge of finding bookies willing to take action on the fixed races. Like everyone else, they'd made a lot of money over the years, but now Fat Tony had put them squarely in the middle of the conspiracy, along with everyone else in the gang. With Howie Winter and Sal Sperlinga already in state prison on the pinball machine case, it looked like the end of the line for Winter Hill.

But then Zip Connolly went to bat for Whitey. He had to—he was already on Whitey's payroll, often leaving his government paychecks uncashed in his desk at the JFK Building in Government Center for months at a time. Zip's new sidekick, John Morris, would also soon be accepting Whitey's cash. Now the two feds would really have to earn their keep, by deep-sixing a much higher-profile case than that of shakedown victim Francis X. Green or the botched takeover of the vending machine racket. The FBI agents went to Jeremiah O'Sullivan, the head of the federal organized crime strike force. They made a simple pitch: The FBI was preparing to bug Gerry Angiulo's Mafia headquarters, the Dog House, at 98 Prince Street, and they needed both Bulger and Flemmi as sources. It was an easy sell, and the race-fixing indictment was quickly rewritten to include both Whitey and Stevie only as unindicted co-conspirators.

Everyone else in the gang was indicted for fixing horse races, and those who weren't convicted, fled. Using information from their new friends in law enforcement, Whitey and Stevie got word to Johnny Martorano ahead of the indictments, and he vanished. But before leaving, Johnny turned over some valuable names to Stevie Flemmi, one of them a state trooper who had funneled inside information about various investigations to Martorano over the years.

Martorano also passed on the names of his contacts at the telephone company, who had provided numbers for, among other things, the Eddie Connors telephone booth hit in 1975. Martorano still had his loansharking money out on the street, but during the seventeen years he was on the lam in Florida, Whitey and Stevie would send him about a million dollars in cash. In return, Martorano would come in handy as a hitman in the years to come.

Once they dodged the race-fixing indictment, it was back to work, shoveling underworld shit to the FBI in return for federal gold. Now that Richie Castucci had been murdered for

being a rat, the FBI needed someone else to help them keep
tabs on fugitive gangster Joe McDonald. This was a perfect
chore for Whitey, and he took up where Castucci had left off
when he was murdered for providing the sort of information
that Whitey would now willingly pass on to the feds.

Three times in the summer of 1979 Connolly filed reports
on what Whitey told him about McDonald's activities, whereabouts, and drinking habits. Based on Whitey's information,
the FBI made no arrests, and no one was hit for tipping off the
feds. The Boston office of the FBI wasn't really interested in arrests, only in deluding its superiors in Washington that it was
keeping tabs on organized crime. And Whitey wasn't truly
concerned about rats, only about making money off them. He
just wanted to rip them off, the way he had Castucci, before
murdering them on the grounds that they were informants.

On October 16, 1979, Jimmy the Bear Flemmi died of an apparent drug overdose at the state prison in Norfolk. In 1975,
while serving an eleven-to-eighteen-year sentence for assault
with intent to commit murder, he'd received one of the state's
first weekend furloughs from prison. Like an early Willie Horton, Jimmy had immediately fled, and was not apprehended
until three years later, in Maryland. He was forty-seven when he
died.

Meanwhile, Stevie's mother had been mugged again in Mattapan, by a mob of fifty blacks, and a photo of her sitting outside her car, on the pavement, dazed and bloody, had appeared
on the regional Associated Press wire. Stevie was fed up.

He needed to relocate his parents to a "nice" neighborhood—an all-white neighborhood. He asked Whitey if he
knew of anything available in Southie, and Whitey told him
that the house at 832 East Third Street, next door to his
brother Billy's at 828, happened to be for sale.

It would be a good place for the Flemmis, Whitey told Stevie. And it would be a convenient place for everyone to meet—Whitey, Stevie, their FBI agents, and even, on occasion, Billy. The house included an enclosed sun porch, which, if weather-proofed, would be usable year-round. The sun porch would be perfect for storing things—machine guns, silencers, even the bodies of young women.

As always, Whitey was thinking ahead.

CHAPTER 8

IN SEPTEMBER 1976, Majority Whip Billy Bulger got the break he'd been waiting for. Senate Majority Leader Joe DiCarlo was finally indicted for extortion, after years of fitful investigations by the FBI. Within fifteen months, the scandal would destroy the careers of the only two men who stood between Billy and the Senate presidency.

DiCarlo was charged with taking payoffs from McKee-Berger-Mansueto, the New York consulting firm that had managed the construction of the new University of Massachusetts campus at Columbia Point in Dorchester. Just a year earlier, U.S. House Speaker Tip O'Neill had assured DiCarlo that he was in the clear. But the turning point in the long probe came when the Boston FBI office abruptly moved two of its older agents—Condon and Sheehan—off the case. Two young go-getters named Connolly and Morris were temporarily transferred from the organized crime unit and sent to Lubbock, Texas, to reinterview two former MBM underlings.

As his lawyer, DiCarlo hired a lobbyist, Walter Hurley. Hurley worked for Tom Joyce, a Beacon Hill power broker who was a close friend of Billy Bulger's. Every morning, the defense team would meet in Joyce's office across Beacon Street from the State House—the defendants, their lawyers and aides, along with Joyce, Harrington, and one other person: Billy Bulger.

On January 23, 1977, after a four-week trial, DiCarlo and his bagman—Republican senator Ron MacKenzie of Burlington—were convicted on all eight counts. On February 28, Billy was appointed majority leader, but the MBM scandal turned out to be the gift that just kept on giving. In late 1977, DiCarlo and MacKenzie's new lawyers filed an appeal for a new trial, charging that their previous lawyers had mishandled the case by not introducing as evidence important details implicating other prominent politicians in the scandal, among them Senate President Kevin Harrington.

According to documents included in DiCarlo's desperate appeal, his onetime mentor Harrington had received a $2,000 corporate check in 1970 from MBM. Harrington, who was struggling to mount a campaign for governor against Dukakis, offered the feeble defense that he had "no memory" of receiving the check, which he had not deposited, but cashed, in a bank in his hometown of Salem.

Kevin Harrington was never charged with any crime, but he was finished, both as a candidate for governor and as Senate president. It was just a matter of time now until Billy inherited the gavel.

As for the defense lawyers for the two convicted senators, both would be appointed to state judgeships by Michael Dukakis. Joe DiCarlo has remained silent about his downfall, and its aftermath, for more than twenty-five years, but his friends never fail to mention the judgeships for the defense lawyers. Or that DiCarlo's lawyer, Walter Hurley, was eventually forced to retire from the bench with a special sweetheart pension deal approved by the Governor's Council. Hurley's ouster came after he was implicated in a low-grade scandal involving preferential treatment for some lawyers at the Boston Municipal Court. Among those connected lawyers was a former state senator, George "Gigi" Kennealley, who also had a job at the State House as counsel to the Senate. Among Kennealley's employees: Jean Bulger Holland, Billy's oldest sister.

In August 1978, after the year's budgetary work was completed, Harrington announced he was quitting, and Billy, his number-two man, was quickly confirmed as his successor by the Democratic caucus. Normally, Billy would have appointed his own majority leader, but his support was shaky, especially among the suburan liberals, who remembered with distaste his endless anti-busing harangues. So, in an unprecedented move, Harrington dropped down, from president to majority leader. That way, the dissidents could not coalesce behind someone who might threaten Billy in January 1979.

Billy then selected one of the Senate liberals, Chester Atkins of Concord, as his Ways and Means chairman. Not only was Chester a liberal, he was a Yankee. It was a sop both to the liberals in the Senate and to the Yankees at the *Globe*.

Meanwhile DiCarlo's appeal went nowhere. The only thing accomplished by DiCarlo's public revelations about Harrington's $2,000 check was the demolition of the career of his old friend. The only two people who had stood in Billy's way had turned on each other, both had been destroyed, and only Billy was left to fill the vacuum of power.

Tom Finnerty, Billy's original law partner, had been elected district attorney of Plymouth County in 1974, but now he was having a tough time making ends meet on a prosecutor's salary. He knew he could make more money in private practice. Still, county prosecutors had wide discretion over how criminal cases were handled and they also controlled large numbers of patronage jobs. District attorney was not a job any political organization would relinquish easily, especially not one in which Billy Bulger had a say.

But there was an obvious solution, so obvious that it would be used again and again by Billy's cronies through the years. As the filing deadline for candidates in the district attorney's race approached in the spring of 1978, Finnerty gathered the signatures on his nomination papers. But his top aide, William O'Malley, was quietly informed that his boss would not seek reelection, and that he should start getting his own signatures.

On the final day to file, with only a few hours before the deadline, Finnerty called reporters into his office and announced he wouldn't be running. O'Malley then filed the nomination signatures he'd surreptitiously gathered, and ran unopposed in the Democratic primary.

Now Billy Bulger's allies would continue to control the district attorney's office in Plymouth County, and all its jobs, and Tom Finnerty, Billy's old partner, could return to the private practice of law.

Edward J. King was the longest of long shots to upset Governor Michael Dukakis in the 1978 Democratic primary. The former chief of the Massachusetts Port Authority, King was fifty-two and a member of the postwar generation at Boston College that included, among others, H. Paul Rico and state treasurer Bob Crane. King had a thick Boston accent and was a daily communicant at Mass—Michael Dukakis, needless to say, couldn't stand him, and had in fact fired King from his beloved Massport post in 1975, almost as soon as he became governor.

On the stump, King was stiff, wooden. But it didn't matter. Dukakis had made too many enemies. He had raised taxes, he was arrogant, he was against the death penalty, and he hadn't rewarded his supporters with the sorts of patronage jobs many had been expecting when they backed him as an underdog candidate in 1974. On primary night 1978, liberal Massachusetts was stunned as King took 50 percent of the Democratic vote to

Dukakis's 43. At the victory celebration at Anthony's Pier 4 in South Boston, King's street manager, a former state legislator from Hyde Park, put it succinctly: "We put all the hate groups into a pot and let them boil."

King crushed a liberal Yankee Republican legislator in the final election. He was sworn in as governor in January 1979, the same month Billy was elected to his first full term as Senate president.

Philosophically, Ed King and Billy were simpatico, but there was a wariness to their relationship. King was an Irishman from East Boston, and it was the old story with Billy: He could get along better with Republicans—and even liberal Democrats—than he could with his own kind. His own kind held him to higher standards than the Republicans and liberals.

Once King was sworn in, one of Billy's first chores was to set up his younger brother in a job that didn't involve any heavy lifting. Jackie was the runt of the litter, average in every respect, with a pair of brothers who were not, to say the least, average. Jackie worked at the MBTA, the Massachusetts Bay Transportation Authority, once known as the MTA but now most commonly referred to simply as "the T." He supplemented his income by working part-time at a fish store in Roslindale Square. But he wanted more, and soon Jackie had a job at the Boston Juvenile Court, just a block or so away from the State House. Next Jackie wanted a promotion to clerk. It would mean extra money, and behind that, a larger pension. There was only one problem for Jackie: the Juvenile Court already had a clerk. But that logjam was eliminated when Governor King appointed the clerk to a judgeship and then filled the vacancy with Jackie Bulger, Boston English High School Class of 1956.

On the day of Jackie's pro forma confirmation hearing before the Governor's Council, Billy walked across the hall and presented himself to the Governor's Council.

"Never have I seen a person so qualified," Billy said, "a person so deserving, a person so capable in every material respect, a person so clearly without peer as the candidate in whose behalf I speak today: probably the most brilliant choice ever to come before this council—my brother!"

The vote to confirm was 8–0.

Whitey and Billy's mother, Jean, died in January 1980. All the children gathered for the wake—all, that is, except Whitey. He had to wait until after visiting hours to join his siblings mourning in the parlor of the funeral home. Neither Billy nor Whitey wanted an errant snapshot of the brothers together appearing in the paper.

Soon after Jean's burial, Sonny McDonough suddenly checked himself into the hospital. Billy's beloved mentor was dying of cancer. As he reached what Billy always called "the checkout counter," he requested that Billy take care of his son, Patrick Jr. He hadn't even graduated high school, but so what? Like Jackie Bulger, he too wanted to be a clerk, and he had his eye on the Boston Housing Court, which was presided over by Judge E. George Daher.

There was only one hitch: Eighteen other candidates had applied for the clerk's job, all of them attorneys, and one in particular stood out: a black lawyer named Robert Lewis. Lewis got the clerk's job, and then, according to newspaper accounts, he was supposed to appoint Patrick as his assistant. If the Jackie Bulger scenario could be repeated, and why shouldn't it have been, then soon Lewis would be a judge, and Patrick would have the clerkship Billy had promised his old man.

Lewis got the job, but then declined to appoint young McDonough. And Judge Daher backed him up. There would be trouble, and it wasn't long in coming.

As Daher later recalled, one court administrator pointed a finger at him and said, "What the Senate president gives, he can take away."

On a courthouse elevator, a judge was even blunter with Daher: "Don't fuck with Billy Bulger on this one, okay?"

But he did, and it wasn't okay. The next budget contained an "outside section" that folded the Boston Housing Court, which had been independent, into the Boston Municipal Court. That meant that Daher was no longer a presiding judge—his pay was automatically cut $2,500—and his support staff was eliminated.

Governor King vetoed the reorganization, but the pay cut stood. The judges had learned the lesson from one of their own: Don't fuck with Billy Bulger.

And there was one other lesson everyone learned: Billy could hold a grudge.

A few years later, at the St. Patrick's Day breakfast, one of Billy's allies joked that Judge Daher had been reduced to "holding court in a Winnebago," and that he desperately needed an increase in his budget. Billy smiled and leaned in close to the microphone.

"He'll have to wait," Billy said, "until I hear from Sonny."

In 1980, the voters of Massachusetts overwhelmingly approved a referendum question that capped increases in local property taxes at 2½ percent a year, unless the voters, rather than elected officials, approved an override. Because of the mandated percentage, the new law became known as Proposition 2½, and it changed politics in Massachusetts profoundly, by making the cities and towns more reliant than ever on financial aid from the commonwealth. Suddenly, state government was playing a larger role than ever in the daily lives of the population.

Then the city of Boston was dealt another financial body

blow. For years, it had been assessing commercial property at a higher rate than residential. Finally, however, the commercial interests had gone to court, and prevailed. The city owed millions in rebates, and, because of Prop 2½, had no way to raise the money it needed to pay off the court judgment.

In 1981, the fiscal crisis in Boston gave Billy the opportunity to bail out the city and simultaneously concentrate still more power in his hands. The plan was developed not by Billy, but by the staff of his Ways and Means chairman, Chester Atkins. No one called Chester a liberal anymore. Bob Crane, the state treasurer, used to say, "When the boys from the suburbs go home, the boys from Boston go to work." Chester, the Yankee from Concord, was now one of the boys from Boston.

Since Billy had become president, in fact, Chester had been the Bulger team's MVP. He had a keen eye for talent, and he soon brought on a young man named Mark Ferber. He was Jewish, which meant he didn't have much in common with Billy, but he was smart, and Billy did appreciate that, at least in his aides who did not represent a potential threat to his power. It was Ferber who came up with the idea of how the city could pay off its court-ordered settlement to the commercial-property owners.

The city would sell some of its prime real estate to the state, for cash. The Hynes Convention Center on Boylston Street in the Back Bay was the obvious choice—the city needed a new hall, and couldn't afford to build one. But the state government could issue bonds to pay for the new hall, and the resulting debt could be paid off with revenue from the city's most successful cash generator, the parking garage under the Boston Common.

To build and then oversee the new convention center on Boylston Street, the state would set up the Massachusetts Convention Center Authority (MCCA). Under the informal agreement worked out with Mayor White and Governor King,

Billy's appointees would dominate the MCCA board, and with that power came control of the jobs.

The MCCA would provide jobs for friends of both Billy and Whitey. The fact that it was an "authority" made its financial records, not to mention its payroll, less accessible to the press. And the money, through the garage and later a hotel-motel occupancy tax, would flow endlessly.

The enabling legislation flew through the General Court, and Governor King signed it into law. Except for one member appointed by the House speaker, everyone on the board was a friend of Billy's. The chairman of the MCCA board was state Treasurer Bob Crane, Billy's old House colleague, a fellow BC grad, and another Irishman from Boston. Mayor White had an appointee too—he selected Bob Crane's son-in-law. Tom Finnerty, Billy's old law partner, was also appointed.

The actual day-to-day management of the MCCA would be handled by longtime Bulger aide Franny Joyce. The MCCA board bestowed on him what was at the time one of the sweetest deals ever for a state employee—a $75,000 annual salary, with lifetime security. Of course, the board had to post the open position for a director. At the board's first meeting ever, Chairman Crane announced with a straight face that only one person had applied for the lifetime $75,000-a-year job.

Francis Xavier Joyce of South Boston.

"It was a nationwide search," Crane said to the State House reporters, as the other members of the board nodded.

The MCCA board met in Crane's second-floor State House office, one floor down from Billy's plush Senate chambers. Whenever the board considered anything that related to Billy, Crane would roll his eyes toward the ceiling and say, "This is for the little man upstairs."

The MCCA became exactly the kind of money-pit its critics had predicted it would be. The final bill for the new Hynes Convention Center, including interest on the bonds, was $450 million—approximately $200 million overbudget. The potential for luring major conventions to a city with a cold climate like Boston's turned out to have been greatly overestimated, and soon the Hynes was advertising its availability for wedding receptions and bar mitzvahs—competing with local union halls and private function rooms.

The annual MCCA deficit was supposed to be covered by a new tax on hotel rooms in the city, and by the revenues from the Boston Common garage, which had always been such a reliable cash cow for the city. But under the new MCCA management, maintenance work on the Boston Common garage was neglected, and eventually it had to be closed for massive repairs that cost more millions and plunged the authority even deeper into the red.

But the MCCA did provide jobs for the friends of the Bulgers.

One of Joyce's first hires was Nancy Stanley, the daughter of Whitey's girlfriend Theresa Stanley. Another early hire was Lisa Martorano, the eighteen-year-old daughter of Johnny, who was already on the lam. She soon stole $21,000 in MCCA funds; her uncle, Jimmy, who was out of prison by that time, had to reimburse the agency. The payments were renegotiated between Jimmy and an MCCA executive named Bob Sheehan, yet another former Boston FBI agent. Despite spending hundreds of thousands of dollars every year on outside legal assistance, the MCCA also employed an in-house legal counsel. He was Harold Clancy, the former editor of the old *Record American* and a longtime friend of Billy's.

State Senator Alan Sisitsky of Springfield was proving to be a real headache for Billy. They'd served in the House together, and never gotten along. Now in his early forties and unmarried, Sisitsky appeared to be losing his mind. He would wander the State House halls, unshaven and disheveled after sleeping in his office, carrying a barbell, grabbing passersby by their lapels and haranguing them.

His hatred of Billy became an obsession. Somehow, it seemed, he resented that someone like Bulger—a Boston bigot, as Sisitsky used to call him—could rise so far. Sisitsky began charging his fellow senators, mainly Billy and Chester Atkins, with corruption. He was also writing letters to the attorney general, demanding investigations into how various bills had been passed. Sisitsky had taken a job as a law school teacher—in Tacoma, Washington. He spent much of the week in airports. As one who had "never been on the cutting edge of fashion," as Billy dryly observed in his book, Sisitsky now looked like a homeless person. He was fixated on the high-handed way in which Billy had punished Judge Daher by having his pay cut. One night, from O'Hare Airport, he phoned into a radio talk show in Boston and announced: "Senator Bulger will be arrested tomorrow at noon."

The host was astounded. He inquired as to the charges.

"Federal agents will be waiting for him when he arrives at his office," Sisitsky said.

As Billy recounted in his book, one day Sisitsky told the Senate, "The Senate president's brother, Whitey Bulger, is listening. He hears everything we say."

More than fifteen years later, several FBI agents, as well as Stevie Flemmi, would testify that they suspected the same thing, and no one would accuse any of them of insanity or paranoia. But Sisitsky had worn out his welcome, not just with Billy, but with the entire Senate membership. Sisitsky was drawing too much attention to a body that had come to prefer scheduling its most important votes in the evenings, often after midnight.

Finally, one day, as Sisitsky sat slouched in the Senate chambers, insulting one senator after another, Billy had had enough. Hearing no objections from anyone, Billy ordered his removal from the Senate. As the court officers, many of them from

Southie, converged on Sisitsky, he yelled one final insult toward his nemesis on the rostrum.

"Being thrown out of this Senate," he screamed, "is like being thrown out of a brothel."

The budgetary constraints imposed by Proposition 2½ gave Billy an opportunity to run the Senate with an iron hand. The mantra was that everyone had to tighten their belts, but the reality was that some belts wouldn't be tightened as much as others.

In South Boston, Mayor White was threatening to close the L Street Bathhouse, where kids like Billy (not to mention gangsters like Frank Salemme) had hung out in the summer ever since Curley was mayor. To shutter such a Southie tradition was unthinkable to Billy. Suddenly, a state agency assumed control of L Street from the city, and the agency received a $280,000 appropriation for the next fiscal year to keep the venerable Southie institution open.

The power was starting to go to Billy's head. As Senate president, everything had to go through him. One way or another, everyone who had ever crossed him would have to come to him, sooner or later, hat in hand, for one favor or another.

It was always payback time for somebody. The next one to feel the heat would be Barney Frank, who as a freshman state rep had tangled with Billy over the proposed state Senate redistricting in the early 1970s. Now Frank was a freshman congressman. And after the 1980 census, Massachusetts was scheduled to lose one of its twelve House seats.

None of the incumbents wanted to retire, so that meant someone would have to be redistricted out of office. Under the congressional redistricting plan approved by the legislature, Barney was gerrymandered into the district of Margaret "Peg" Heckler, an entrenched seven-term Republican incumbent from Wellesley. Initially, the plan was to cut most of Brookline and Newton—Barney's liberal, Jewish base—out of the new district. But U.S. House Speaker Tip O'Neill of Cambridge had insisted that Barney at least have a fighting shot at survival. Besides, Tip didn't particularly want Brookline and Newton added to his overwhelmingly Irish-Italian district.

As it turned out, 1982 was not a good year for Republicans. Barney ousted Heckler, who was then appointed ambassador to Ireland by President Reagan.

Even Billy couldn't win them all.

CHAPTER 9

IT WAS THE BEGINNING OF 1980, and what was left of the Winter Hill Gang needed new headquarters. After the race-fixing trial, everyone from Somerville was either in prison or a fugitive, so from Whitey's perspective, it made sense to move the operations into the city. The "gang" was now reduced to two people—Whitey and Stevie—and they were both from Boston. So it was an easy call for Whitey and Stevie to base themselves at George Kaufman's new garage in the West End of Boston. The West End was a much quicker commute from South Boston than Winter Hill.

Whitey, of course, had his own hangouts in South Boston, including Donnie Killeen's old Transit Café in the Lower End. As a felon, Whitey couldn't personally own a liquor license, but Kevin O'Neil could, and Whitey set him up as the West Broadway bar's straw owner. O'Neil was a hulking thug who had been arrested back in 1968, along with two other future Whitey Bulger associates, for murdering a black man in a street brawl. The charges were dropped after O'Neil hired Billy Bulger as his lawyer.

Triple O's—the name referred to O'Neil and his two brothers, the other owners of record—was all right as a place for Whitey to meet local hoods, but few outsiders cared to come into Southie. Plus, there was practically no parking, pedestrian traffic was heavy, and the bar was so close to the Broadway MBTA station that the cops could have easily kept a close eye on the underworld comings and goings had they so desired.

The West End, on the other hand, was neutral turf, a semi-deserted urban no-man's-land where few strangers ventured, except on nights when there was a game at the nearby Boston Garden. It was an old ethnic melting-pot neighborhood that had been "redeveloped" in the early 1950s into high-rise apartment towers and bleak state office buildings within walking distance of the Garden and North Station. Kaufman called his garage Lancaster Foreign Motors, and in the morning, before the gangsters arrived, it actually was a functioning garage. But around noon, Whitey and Stevie would arrive and the place would become a den for them and other underworld figures.

Ironically, it was the FBI that first discovered that Whitey had relocated to the garage. In January 1980, Whitey decided to kill the twenty-four-year-old son of Stevie Hughes, the McLaughlin hitman who had been murdered by Stevie Flemmi and Frank Salemme in 1966. Steve Hughes Jr. had just gotten out of prison, and he was talking about avenging his father's death by killing Stevie and Whitey.

But he was murdered first, in a Charlestown housing project, shot five times with a high-powered rifle from the roof of a building across the street. It was just another routine gangland murder, but on February 4, an FBI informant report included this information about how the Hughes job was arranged: "George Kaufman received a telephone call to get the [getaway] car outside of a garage on Lancaster St., Boston, Mass., just before the hit."

Even though it was less than a five-minute walk from the FBI offices, no agent bothered to check out the garage where notorious hoodlums were stashing hit cars. The report was filed away and forgotten.

It wasn't until April that the State Police found out about the garage, when a Statie driving by noticed George Kaufman standing on the sidewalk out front. The cop parked nearby and, reconnoitering the area, spotted Whitey and Stevie. The Staties returned a few times and saw a parade of familiar and unfamiliar faces making their way inside. Obviously, they were on to something, but street surveillance wouldn't get them much. The streets themselves were too narrow, parking too difficult, and unless you were either gay or a wino, you stuck out like a sore thumb—which was just the way the boys inside liked it.

An undercover state cop rented a room above the gay bar across the street from the garage, and they began monitoring the comings and goings at Lancaster Foreign Motors. They quickly noticed one new face—Nicky Femia, a former associate of Joe Barboza's, who had finally been murdered by the Mafia in San Francisco in 1976.

Whitey had realized the need for additional muscle, which explained Femia's presence. He was one of the leading suspects in the Blackfriars Massacre of 1978, when gunmen had burst into a downtown bar after hours, stolen a large amount of cocaine, and murdered five men—including a former TV reporter for Channel 7—in cold blood. When Femia began hanging around the garage, Whitey wanted it established in the FBI files that his new associate had nothing to do with the Blackfriars murders, although he probably did. Whitey didn't need any heat from some ambitious cop making a run at him just because of his association with a higher-profile killer like Femia. Soon a brief notice appeared in one of Zip Connolly's FBI reports clearing Femia of any involvement in Blackfriars. (Later, after Whitey and Femia had parted ways, Zip put yet another report into Whitey's file, suggesting that Femia had indeed been one of the triggermen in the Blackfriars killings. Femia eventually would be shot to death in a botched robbery in East Boston in 1983.)

Femia, who was both overweight and a cocaine addict, was not a good fit with Whitey. As he aged, Whitey was becoming more obsessed with physical fitness. He wore tight jeans and T-shirts, and grew increasingly disgusted with Femia's gut. One time, when Femia returned from the nearby McDonald's on Causeway Street with a bag of Big Macs and fries and began spreading out his fast food feast on the hood of Whitey's black Chevrolet, Whitey went crazy, screaming and pelting him with French fries.

Femia wasn't the only one to bear the brunt of Whitey's new rants about clean living. George Kaufman's son, Peter, sometimes worked odd jobs at the garage. At the time, Peter Kaufman smoked, and sometimes when he left he'd neglect to take his smokes with him. On his return, he'd shake a Marlboro out of the pack and notice that Whitey had taken a pen and written across the cigarette: DON'T SMOKE.

Soon the state cops surveilling the garage began seeing new faces showing up, sometimes with briefcases or small paper bags. One of Whitey's new visitors, they would later discover, was one of the largest marijuana importers in New England.

Whitey had been shaking down local bar owners for protection ever since he'd taken control of the rackets in Southie in the early 1970s. But now he began expanding his collections of "rent" to include local drug dealers. A payoff here and there, and they could use the beaches of Southie, Dorchester, and Quincy to off-load their product, and then store it in the grimy warehouses of the Lower End. Whitey didn't need a lot of muscle to retain control of this racket; all he had to do was guarantee that the dealers wouldn't have any interference from the police. That was an easy promise for Whitey to keep.

Some of the money was still being funneled to the beleaguered associates of Whitey and Stevie. Johnny Martorano was delivered money in Florida. And every Friday night, at his Marconi Club in Roxbury, Stevie would meet Frank Salemme's brother, Jackie, and hand him $200 for Frank, who was still in state prison for the 1967 bombing of the car belonging to Joe Barboza's lawyer. That was little enough money for Stevie to pay, considering how much Salemme knew, and how tightly he was keeping his mouth shut.

But money was all they would provide to their old colleagues. When Sal Sperlinga, out on work release, was murdered by a junkie, from prison Howie Winter demanded that the killer be whacked. In mid-January 1980, according to an FBI report, Howie reached out to the Angiulos for assistance in avenging his partner's murder. The Angiulos were surprised by the request, and asked Howie's envoy why he was coming to them rather than to his own crew, Whitey and Stevie.

"Because," the messenger said, "them two guys don't give a fuck."

Neither did the Mafia. The junkie was not hit.

In the summer of 1980, after several months of surveillance, the Staties finally got a court order to install bugs in the garage. But there were problems. One of the devices was planted in a couch, and every time one of the gangsters, particularly the 250-pound Femia, collapsed onto the sofa, it sounded like an earthquake. But the most crucial bug—the one in the garage office—worked perfectly. The conversations were clear, the voices distinct. The Staties figured it was only a matter of time before Whitey and Stevie incriminated themselves.

But then the Staties began to notice a not-so-subtle change in the tone of the conversations. Suddenly Whitey began to go on, sometimes at great length, about what a wonderful job the State Police were doing, particularly with their speed traps along the Mass. Turnpike. When criminals arrived to discuss business, Whitey would direct them out of the bugged office, and into his car, or out onto the street.

The bug had been blown. It has never been proven con-
clusively who tipped them. But however it happened, the
compromising of the bug precipitated a spate of interagency
finger-pointing and name-calling that didn't subside for
more than two decades. As for Whitey, he stopped coming to
the garage. He began conducting much of his business from
a bank of pay phones at the Howard Johnson's on the South-
east Expressway. The angry Staties soon picked up the trail
of Whitey's black Chevrolet and followed it to Hojo's. Every
afternoon, they would watch Femia arrive in the Howard
Johnson's parking lot. Once he determined that the phones
were safe, Whitey and Stevie would arrive. One day, the
troopers saw Femia, with a small handgun tucked into his
belt, standing behind Whitey and Stevie as they greeted a
man later identified as the Mafia's top drug importer in New
England.

The State Police got a wiretap order on the bank of phones,
but in what was becoming an all-too-familiar scenario, as soon
as the phones were bugged, Whitey never appeared at Hojo's
again.

Less than ten years earlier Whitey had been a hunted man in
Southie, and he was still sensitive to any threats, perceived or
otherwise, on his home turf. One of the top bookmakers in
Southie was Louie Litif, who was one of Zip Connolly's hand-
ball partners at the Boston Athletic Club. Earlier than most, he
realized that drugs, not gambling, were where the money
would be made in the future. One of the local drug dealers was
named James Matera, and he somehow crossed Litif.

Litif ordered Matera to a sit-down at the bar he hung out in,
Hap's Lounge. The place was deserted, except for the bartender,
Kenneth "Bobby" Conrad. Then Litif appeared and ordered
Matera into the basement.

"Hey Bobby," Matera yelled over his shoulder toward the

bar, as he walked down the stairs. "If I'm not back in fifteen minutes, come looking for me, 'cause I'm probably dead."

He was. Litif killed him. And soon thereafter, Bobby Conrad vanished. When Conrad's daughter went to the FBI for help in finding her father, the case was turned over to Zip Connolly. Zip's goal, as with every crime committed in Southie, was to make the case go away. Litif worked for Whitey, and if the heat suddenly came down on Litif, he might be tempted to try to cut a deal, by turning on Whitey.

So Litif would have to go. He hadn't been authorized to kill anyone, but he had, and the penalty for that was death. Whitey's theory was, if you let your people start doing freelance hits, clipping guys might get to be a habit, and that meant anarchy. Look what happened to Donnie Killeen.

But first they had to deal with Conrad's daughter. As she later recalled, when she went to the FBI looking for answers about her father's fate, Zip told her bluntly what had happened.

"Honey," he said, "your father's dead. They knifed him. But don't worry. They got him drunk first."

How did he know, she recalled herself asking him in a 2001 newspaper account.

"I saw it," he said.

Zip told her that if she went to the Boston police, it might jeopardize some very important underworld informants. The daughter's problem was that her family badly needed the money from her father's life insurance policy, but couldn't collect without a death certificate. Zip straightened everything out with a single letter to the insurance company on FBI stationery. Two decades later, the Conrads were able to produce a letter from the carrier stating that the case had been resolved thanks to the efforts of "agent Connolly."

Whitey next summoned Litif to Triple O's. Brian Halloran, Jimmy Martorano's friend and co-defendant, had just gotten out of prison and was hanging around, so Whitey sent him to meet Litif. They drove back to Triple O's in Litif's car, and Halloran dropped him off at the front door. Litif went upstairs, to Whitey's makeshift office, where Whitey murdered him.

After Whitey and Halloran wrapped the body in a blanket, they dragged it downstairs and put it in the trunk of Litif's car. The next question was, where to drop off the body? Whitey always liked a body to make a statement, either by disappearing completely, or ending up somewhere as a message. This time, the message would go to Larry Baione. Like Stevie, Whitey had never particularly liked the blustery, hard-drinking Mafia crew chief. Litif had spent a little too much time in the North End for Whitey's liking. Whitey considered it somehow disloyal. And even more recently, Whitey had been watching as a young South End hoodlum named Bobby Sullivan built up a thriving drug business. Sullivan operated out of the Baione family's tavern on Shawmut Avenue, and had come up under Baione's tutelage. But because his name was Sullivan, Whitey felt he should be the one providing "protection." But that was not to be—not yet anyway.

So Whitey instructed Halloran to park Litif's car on Shawmut Avenue in front of Larry Baione's laundromat. It was just a reminder, both to Baione, not to even think about messing with Southie, and to Sullivan and his crew, that the Mafia wasn't the only game in town. Halloran parked Litif's car, wiped down the steering wheel and doors for fingerprints, and then walked back to South Boston, where he assumed his natural pose, on a bar stool at Triple O's. Litif's body was discovered the next day; neither newspaper mentioned the significance of where it had been found.

A week or so later, Paul Corsetti, a Vietnam veteran and second-generation police reporter for the *Herald American*, the Hearst-owned daily, was sniffing around the Litif murder, and

Whitey's obvious involvement in it. After several days of reporting the story, Corsetti got a call at the paper telling him that if he wanted more information on the Litif hit, he should show up at 6:00 p.m. at P. J. Clarke's, a popular watering hole in Quincy Market. The caller dropped just enough tantalizing tidbits to pique Corsetti's interest.

That evening, Corsetti was sitting by himself at the bar when an average-sized, middle-aged man pulled up the stool next to him.

"You're Paul Corsetti, aren't you?" he said.

Corsetti nodded, and the garrulous fellow made more small talk, until finally Corsetti said, "I'd like to talk to you, but I'm waiting for somebody."

The man's smile disappeared. "You're waiting for me, motherfucker," he said. "I'm Jimmy Bulger and I kill people."

He then pulled a piece of paper out of his pocket and began reading to Corsetti—first Corsetti's address, in Medford, and then the make, model, and license number of his car, and then his wife's car. Finally, he mentioned Corsetti's preschool daughter, and where she was dropped off for day care every morning, and at what time. Then Whitey walked away.

The next morning, Corsetti arrived in the city room with a .38-caliber revolver on his hip. He had reason to be worried. Whitey was bad enough, but at that point Nick Femia was still on the gang payroll, and he had likely already murdered at least one reporter, at the Blackfriars in 1978.

Corsetti arranged a meeting at police headquarters. The cops too were concerned; one of them told Corsetti that they "had" Bulger for "at least 50 murders," none of which they could prove, of course. They suggested that Corsetti might have better luck if he reached out to Mob sources with more influence on Whitey. So he immediately sought out Larry Baione, who had himself been thinking about Whitey since the discovery of Litif's body outside his laundromat. Baione greeted the reporter warmly at his "clubhouse" on North Margin Street in the North End. Then he asked Corsetti what he could do for him. Corsetti only got as far as the words "Whitey Bulger" when Baione interrupted.

"Anything else I can take care of," he said. "But Whitey—he's fucking crazy. I can't do nothing with him."

Eventually, Corsetti got word that Whitey, for some unknown reason, had been concerned that the newspaper was working on a story about his brother Billy. Through intermediaries, Corsetti made it clear to Whitey that he was interested only in Louie Litif, not Billy Bulger. Soon, anonymous tips began flooding in, and Corsetti was able to cobble together a passable, if incomplete, story on a subject that promptly vanished from the public prints. Paul Corsetti's confrontation with Whitey would be long remembered, at least in the city's newsrooms, and it would be five years before the Boston media mentioned Whitey again in anything more than passing.

The State Police were still incensed that their bugging operation at the garage had been blown. The issue of who informed Whitey has never been definitively resolved, and Stevie did have at least one reliable source in the State Police who later went to prison. But given his other services to the gang over the years, Zip Connolly still seems the most likely suspect. The State Police brass certainly thought so. To vent their anger, they had insisted on meetings with their FBI counterparts, which quickly degenerated into loud, angry exchanges of accusations. The top feds in the Boston office knew that the State Police were likely correct in their suspicions, and they wondered if this particular pair of wiseguys was worth all these headaches. Zip Connolly, who had by now become a confidant, neighbor, and employee of Whitey's, was frantic that his boss and Stevie were about to be terminated as informants. So he went into overdrive. He filed a report about the charitable deeds Whitey had performed, including rescuing a young white woman from the clutches of a black pimp. Then, on October 15, he and Morris met with Whitey and, according to their report, advised Whitey that it was now "common knowledge" that he was an informant and his life was in jeopardy.

Whitey shrugged off the warning, saying anyone capable of killing him wouldn't believe he was an informant. He was more worried, he said, about the Mafia figuring out how weak his gang was.

"Informant reiterated," Zip wrote, "that in his opinion, if he is ever murdered, it will be as a result of gangland warfare rather than him being identified as an informant."

In other words, Whitey believed that if he ever got hit, it would be over money, not a matter of principle. As far as he was concerned, the old saw was correct. There was no honor among thieves.

In a follow-up report on October 30, Connolly wrote that Whitey told him that "State Police hierarchy speculate that SA Connolly possibly tipped off Whitey Bulger [to the garage bug] through his brother, Senate President William Bulger."

It was incendiary stuff for Zip to put down on paper—an accusation against himself, and Billy. But he had to portray Whitey as a mere pawn in a political dispute, a victim of petty, paranoid State House politics. Out on the street, though, Whitey remained as cocky as ever. On October 19 another FBI informant quoted him as bragging that "Stevie Flemmi and I are not worried about nothing." Two days later, Billy Bulger's name was mentioned by another informant, who told the FBI that Whitey had "gone to his brother . . . to obtain aid in the release" of a convict.

By November 1980, Connolly's bosses had come to the conclusion that Whitey and Stevie were far more trouble than they were worth. They would be terminated as informants, at the worst possible time imaginable, just as the FBI was about to place a bug in the Mafia's Boston headquarters in the North End. Once the Angiulos were removed, "my Irish," as Connolly called the Bulgers, could take over organized crime in Boston. The crew formerly known as the Winter Hill Gang might be but a shadow of its former self, but the Mafia likewise wasn't what it had once been. Over the years, Angiulo had eliminated any Italians who might pose a threat to him, much as Whitey and Stevie had in their own spheres of influence.

Now Angiulo too was having to cope with a severe shortage of talent. A few months later, he would be recorded on an FBI bug, bemoaning his mob's dire situation, specifically, the dearth of "intelligent tough guys."

In addition to Whitey's ambitions to take over the Boston underworld, the other reason it was imperative for him to remain as an informant was that once the bugs were installed, the feds were sure to hear discussions about the crimes of both Whitey and Stevie. And that would likely lead to their indictments, unless, of course, they were still federal informants, in which case Zip could protect them, just as he had in the race-fixing case.

To get a court order to bug Prince Street, the FBI needed affidavits from informants as to the nature and scope of the criminal enterprise being conducted at "the Dog House." If Flemmi and Bulger stopped by the Dog House, Connolly could list them as sources of information in the FBI's official application for a bug—a Title III. If they were included in the Title III, it would be almost impossible for the feds to cut them loose later, if only because it would give the Angiulos grounds for an appeal.

The problem with Zip's plan was that neither Whitey nor Stevie was keen on the idea of dropping in on their Mafia counterparts. Neither totally trusted the Angiulos, for good reason. But they both knew it had to be done, to protect their status as informants. And so, on November 20, 1980, Whitey and

Stevie dropped in at 98 Prince Street. During a mundane discussion with three of the Angiulo brothers, they learned from Donato "Danny" Angiulo they had "concern that revenue was down." Then a young mobster walked in and they all talked about collecting a $65,000 blackjack debt owed to Larry Baione. Then Whitey and Stevie left.

And this, Connolly wrote in a memo to his superiors, was the sort of incredible inside Mob stuff they'd lose forever if they dumped Whitey and Stevie because of the controversy over the blown bug on Lancaster Street.

But the visit to the Dog House didn't close the deal. It still appeared that the top feds were leaning toward terminating Whitey as an informant. So on November 25, Connolly and Morris decided that the only way to save their guy was to have him sit down with Lawrence Sarhatt, the new FBI boss in Boston. That day Whitey spent four hours with the Boston SAC in a hotel at Logan Airport. Whitey laid it on thick, probably as thick as he ever laid it on.

His love for the FBI, he said, stemmed from his early relationship with H. Paul Rico. He did not mention the gay bars of Bay Village.

"SA RICO," Sarhatt wrote, "was such a gentleman and was so helpful that he, Informant, changed his mind about his hate for all law enforcement. Additionally, he has a close feeling towards SA JOHN CONNOLLY because they both grew up in the same neighborhood in Boston and had the mutual childhood problems, as well as his deep hatred for La Cosa Nostra."

Whitey vehemently denied that the FBI had tipped him to the bug in the Lancaster Street garage. The tip came from a state trooper, he said. Asked by Sarhatt to name the state cop, Whitey refused "because this source is not doing it for monetary benefit but as a favor to him because of his close association with him."

On another subject, "Informant also related that he is not in the drug business and personally hates anyone who does [sell drugs]," Sarhatt wrote. "Therefore, he and any of his associates do not deal in drugs."

It was nonsense, and Sarhatt knew it, writing in his post-meeting memo that he was "not certain" if Whitey was "telling the full story of his involvement."

Whitey had one final point to make to Sarhatt before the meeting broke up. On the subject of Lieutenant Colonel John O'Donovan, the much-decorated state trooper most adamant in his assertions that the FBI was in bed with Winter Hill, Whitey said he had sat through several meetings with the legendary O'D, and had been shocked by O'D's disdain for the FBI.

"He [O'Donovan] made very disparaging and derogatory statements about the professionalism of FBI personnel," Sarhatt wrote of Whitey's recollection of his meeting with O'Donovan. "He [Whitey] took great umbrage inasmuch as his association with the FBI has been nothing but the most professional in every respect."

How exactly a criminal can have a "professional" relationship with a cop was not explained. And how could Whitey, a gangster, ask the FBI to take his word over that of their brother law enforcement officer?

O'Donovan had been a thorn in all their sides for far too long. He had arrested Jimmy the Bear three times, in addition to both Martoranos, and now he had tried to hang Whitey and Stevie out to dry. Myles Connor, another career hoodlum, had once shot O'D and still survived. Nobody, it seemed, could rid them of that pain-in-the-ass honest cop once and for all.

After spending four hours with Whitey, Sarhatt wanted to terminate him as an informant. Unlike so many other FBI agents, he had not been charmed by Whitey's banter about Alcatraz and his Cagneyesque childhood. But the final call had to be made by the prosecutor running the federal organized crime strike force, Jeremiah O'Sullivan. It was O'Sullivan who would be handling any prosecutions that arose out of the bugs that would soon be installed in the Dog House.

Four years earlier, Connolly had convinced O'Sullivan's office to rewrite the Winter Hill race-fixing indictment to make Whitey and Stevie, who had been in the middle of the conspiracy, merely "unindicted co-conspirators."

Now Connolly was once again able to convince O'Sullivan's office that there was, as the prosecutors noted in a report, "sufficient justification for continuing him [as an informant] regardless of his current activities to be able to eventually prosecute LCN [La Cosa Nostra] members."

With another assist from O'Sullivan, Connolly had recorded one more "save" for Whitey. In return Whitey was taking care of him with cash, free appliances, and below-market-value deals on condominiums in Southie, but Zip would have been a bargain at twice the price. Whitey was still getting gold in return for shit.

CHAPTER 10

As 1980 DREW TO A CLOSE, Whitey knew that if he were to survive, either he and Stevie or the FBI was going to have to eliminate the Angiulos and their crew at the Dog House on Prince Street. With the flashier Somerville guys now scattered, the Mafia was constantly head-counting, trying to figure out just what remained of the old Winter Hill Gang. Again and again they arrived at the same number: two. Whitey and Stevie. Others might come and go—George Kaufman, Nick Femia, various younger Southie thugs—but in the end it all came down to Whitey and Stevie.

They enjoyed being the only game on their side of town. They didn't have to split up the money with anybody else. But now it was making them a target of opportunity.

John Morris called Whitey around Christmas that year and said he had to talk to both him and Stevie right away. He suggested the sprawling Lechmere's parking lot in East Cambridge. Whitey called Stevie, and after meeting in Southie they drove over to East Cambridge and climbed into Morris's FBI car. Morris had a tape recorder with him. He wanted them to listen to something the FBI had just picked up off a wire—a fifteen-minute conversation between Angiulo's top enforcer,

Larry Baione, the Mafia hoodlum reporter Paul Corsetti had sought out, and Baione's driver.

"Graphic detail," Flemmi recalled of the conversation in 1997. "They said that they were looking for the right opportunity to eliminate Jim Bulger and myself . . . John Martorano [and] Joe McDonald, they were both on the lam at the time. Howie Winter was in prison. There was just myself and Jim Bulger, and they figured . . . we would be vulnerable. They wanted to make sure that we were completely eliminated and disappeared."

Whitey and Stevie understood. That was their modus operandi as well—unless they were trying to deliver a message, as with Louis Litif or Indian Joe, they too preferred their enemies to vanish enigmatically. Better to pick up the newspaper and see an old mug shot of their victim over a caption that said, "Missing from usual haunts" or "Foul play suspected," than a series of gory front-page photographs of machine-gunned cars and bullet-riddled bodies on the side of the Revere Beach Parkway.

Two months earlier, another FBI agent had filed a 209 report that confirmed much the same information, but also included one additional fact: that the Mafia figured that if they could kill Whitey and Stevie, the "remaining Winter Hill people [Martorano and McDonald] would be fugitives; the Mafia would have the FBI and the police as allies against the fugitives."

The Mafia was plotting to do to Winter Hill what Winter Hill, or at least Whitey, was plotting to do to them. They planned to use cops as their enforcers.

As thin as Winter Hill's ranks were, the Italians weren't in much better shape. Their top hitman, Joe Russo, was on the lam after murdering Joe Barboza in San Francisco. His half-brother in East Boston was such a half-wit that Gerry Angiulo had forbidden him, on pain of death, to ever enter the city proper.

Even by Mob standards, Gerry Angiulo was an unlikable sort. He was an egomaniac—his boat was named the *Gennaro*. He had a habit of referring to cops as "Irish pieces of shit," and he was even more obsessed than most mobsters with money. When he heard that one of his loansharking victims had died, he began screaming, "He can't be dead! He owes me $13,000!"

The FBI had been after him since the early 1960s, when they planted an illegal bug in a bar he owned on Tremont Street. In 1976, FBI agent Bob Sheehan, shortly before he retired to the state payroll, had approached Sonny Shields, the hoodlum Whitey had shot and wounded in 1973. Sheehan offered Shields the keys to the Angiulos' Prince Street headquarters, and a machine gun, and pleaded with him to wipe out the Angiulo brothers.

Shields politely turned him down.

The Angiulos seemed ready to be taken. Although they preferred, for safety's sake, to stay out of the North End, Whitey and Stevie were familiar enough with the security at 98 Prince Street to be able to advise the feds on possible weaknesses that could be exploited. This information was better than Whitey's usual "shit," perhaps because if the feds could put it to good use, they would no longer have to worry about the Mafia: "The brothers communicate by walkie-talkie. GERRY ANGIULO is known as 'Silver Fox'; DANNY ANGIULO is known as 'Laughing Fox' or 'Smiling Fox'; and NICK ANGIULO is known as 'Harry Fox.'"

Whitey, who was fascinated by the newer forms of technology, even advised the feds what equipment they would need to monitor the Mafia—a "Bearcat 210 Automatic Scanner . . . Source [Whitey] will attempt to ascertain the frequency number for the C.B. units."

Instead, the feds planted bugs, and not just at the Dog

House. In January 1981, they also installed one at 51 North Margin Street, near Regina's Pizza, where Larry Baione maintained both a clubhouse and a high-stakes poker game. Unlike the bugs they'd planted at Patriarca's headquarters in Providence back in the 1960s, these were court-authorized, which meant everything would be admissible as evidence in court.

The Prince Street bug captured all of Gerry's megalomaniacal boasts. He lorded it over everyone, even his son, Jason, whom he derisively called "the college boy."

Jason had been given an entry-level Mob job, running Las Vegas nights for local charities. One night, when Gerry found out that his son had been trying to cut expenses by using old decks of cards, he exploded and ordered him to change decks every few hands.

"That's a fuckin' order," he said, "'cause you're a fuckin' idiot."

Another time he ordered one of his soldiers to murder a loanshark victim who was thought to be a target of the grand jury.

"Strangle him!" Angiulo said. "And get rid of him. Hit him in the fucking head. . . . You stomp him. Bing! . . . Just hit him in the fuckin' head and stab him, okay. You understand American?"

When the mobster didn't answer Angiulo's questions about his preparations quickly enough, Gerry exploded.

"You ain't got a hot car. You ain't got nothing. You think I need tough guys? I need intelligent tough guys."

The audiotapes the FBI recorded from January until April 1981 were better than anyone could have hoped for. Late one evening, for example, Gerry Angiulo and Baione were discussing the Racketeer Influenced and Corrupt Organizations (RICO) statute, and Gerry argued that it didn't apply to them because it only covered the infiltration of legitimate business.

"I wouldn't be in a legitimate business for all the fuckin' money in the world to begin with," Angiulo said.

"That's right," chimed in Baione.

"Our argument is, we're illegitimate business." At this point, Baione and Angiulo become a kind of alternating chorus.

Baione: "We're a shylock."

Angiulo. "We're a shylock."

Baione: "Yeah."

Angiulo: "We're a fucking bookmaker."

Baione: "Bookmaker."

Angiulo: "We're selling marijuana."

Baione: "We're not infiltrating."

Angiulo: "We're, we're, we're illegal here, illegal there, arsonists? We're every fucking thing."

Baione: "Pimps!"

Angiulo: "So what?"

Baione: "Prostitutes."

Almost as soon as the FBI agents began recording the Angiulos' screeds, it was clear that they were finished. But now Whitey and Stevie had a new concern. Their informant status might protect them from indictment, but once prosecutor O'Sullivan and his crew began playing the tapes, it would be almost impossible for them to remain in the underworld shadows where they had flourished for so long.

The fact was, Whitey and Stevie were never far from the thoughts of Gerry and Larry. One night, Angiulo and Baione even discussed the way the Hill had split up its territories after the race-fixing convictions had decimated the gang two years earlier.

"Whitey's got the whole of Southie," he says. "Stevie is [*sic*] got the whole of the South End. Johnny's got niggers. . . . Howie knows this."

Billy's St. Patrick's Day breakfasts were mandatory stops for Massachusetts politicians. This one, in 1992, includes, left to right, then-Governor William Weld, future State House Speaker Tom Finneran, then-Speaker Charles Flaherty, Billy, former state Treasurer Bob Crane, former Speaker Tommy McGee, and former state representative (and future judge) Michael Flaherty (no relation to Charles) of South Boston, all singing their hearts out.

Billy Bulger on parade, wielding a ceremonial shillelagh on St. Patrick's Day.

Senator and Mrs. John F. Kerry at Billy's last St. Patrick's Day breakfast in 1996.

Billy and Ted Kennedy.

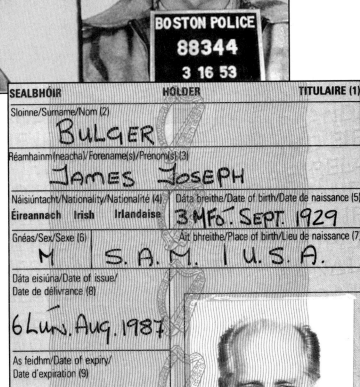

Whitey Bulger at different stages in his career: top, in a 1953 mug shot, and bottom, his Irish passport, issued in 1987.

BOSTON POLICE
88344
3 16 53

SEALBHÓIR	HOLDER	TITULAIRE (1)

Sloinne/Surname/Nom (2)

BULGER

Réamhainm (neacha)/Forename(s)/Prénom(s) (3)

JAMES JOSEPH

Náisiúntacht/Nationality/Nationalité (4)
Éireannach   Irish   Irlandaise

Dáta breithe/Date of birth/Date de naissance (5)

3 MFó. SEPT. 1929

Gnéas/Sex/Sexe (6)

M

Áit bhreithe/Place of birth/Lieu de naissance (7)

S. A. M.   I U.S. A.

Dáta eisiúna/Date of issue/
Date de délivrance (8)

6 LúN. AUG. 1987

As feidhm/Date of expiry/
Date d'expiration (9)

6 LúN. AUG. 1997

Údarás/Authority/Autorité (10)

Ard-Consalacht na h-Éireann
Consul General of Ireland
Boston

Síniú an tsealbhóra/Signature of holder/Signature du titulaire (11)

Whitey poses for an undated gag photo in Provincetown, on Cape Cod.

Stevie Flemmi and Whitey in an undated surveillance photo.

Gennaro (Gerry) Angiulo, Mafia underboss of Boston until 1983, top, in a 1947 mug shot, and bottom, much later, in a defiant pose.

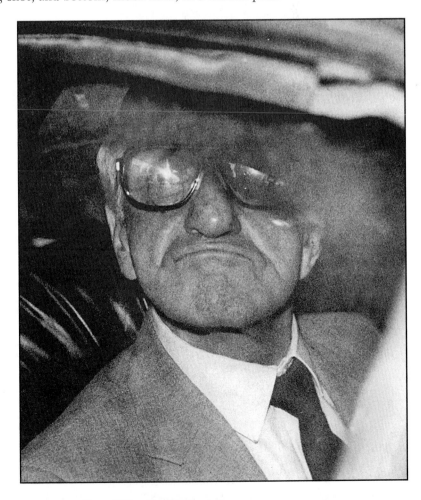

Frank Salemme, onetime head of the Boston Mafia, and a former cohort of Stevie Flemmi's.

Bottom, body of Billy Bennett, the third Bennett brother murdered in 1967 as the Boston underworld was consolidated into two groups—the Mafia and the Winter Hill Gang.

Hitman-turned-informant Joe Barboza on his way to testify in the 1968 murder trial that eventually led to congressional hearings into corruption in the Boston FBI office more than thirty years later.

FBI agents John "Zip" Connolly (left) and Nick Gianturco escort Francesco "Frankie the Cat" Angiulo after his arrest in 1983. The arrests of the Angiulo brothers (Danny can be seen behind Frankie) essentially left Boston's criminal world in the hands of Whitey and Stevie.

Stevie Flemmi in custody after his return from Montreal, 1974.

Vinny "the Animal" Ferrara was Whitey's last Mafia rival.

Kevin "Two Weeks" Weeks.

Larry Baione in particular was obsessed with them. When he was sober, as he was when he was recorded on the tape Morris played for Whitey, he plotted to kill them. When he was drunk—which he was most nights—he would sometimes grow sentimental about Whitey and Stevie. To him they were "kids," who, he inexplicably, and incorrectly, claimed, "are not big money guys."

More importantly, Baione knew they would have no qualms about murdering anyone in the Mafia who got in their way. One night a small-time hustler named Jerry Metricia was called to North Margin Street. According to Baione, he was "stealin' with" one of Baione's crew, a politically wired made man named John Cincotti, whose state senator, Mike LoPresti, had been feverishly lobbying the Boston police to issue the felon Cincotti a permit to carry a gun. What concerned Baione was that Metricia, during the race-fixing days, had been given $50,000 cash by Whitey and Stevie to bet in Las Vegas on a fixed horse race. Instead, he'd blown the dough at a casino, and had never settled up with the Hill.

Baione was now concerned about the fact that his unarmed man Cincotti was spending so much time with a guy who he knew was now marked for death.

"I know," said another of Baione's mobsters, "if Stevie or Whitey sees him—"

"They're going to hit him," said Baione.

And if Cincotti was there with him, he'd go too. That was the way Whitey and Stevie operated. Baione didn't care what happened to Metricia, but he didn't want to lose Cincotti in a senseless crossfire that would also ignite a gang war. So Metricia was brought in, and Baione got right to the point. He might be plotting to kill Whitey and Stevie every day, but with this small-timer Metricia, Baione wanted to maintain the polite fiction that organized crime protocol concerning unpaid debts mattered above all else.

"If you fuck someone that's friendly with us . . ." Baione began. "So you just understand me, do you know that the Hill is us? Maybe you didn't know that, did you?"

"No," said Metricia, softly. "I didn't."

"Did you know Howie and Stevie, they're us? We're the fuckin' Hill with Howie . . . You know that they're with us. You didn't know that?"

Metricia said he didn't know that.

"You make sure," Baione said, "you make a score, I'm going to see Whitey and Stevie get the money, and Howie. You understand? After all, you fucked them. These are nice people. These are the kind of fuckin' people that straighten a thing out. They're with us. We're together. And we cannot tolerate them getting fucked."

Whitey and Stevie got filled in on what was happening, of course. One night in early 1981, as both Morris and Flemmi would later testify, the FBI agent called and told them to meet him in a room at the Colonnade Hotel. When Whitey and Stevie arrived, with several bottles of wine, Morris was waiting for them with a tape recorder and a fresh audiotape he wanted them to hear, in which Gerry Angiulo badmouthed both of them in particularly profane terms.

They all laughed, and Morris started guzzling the gangsters' wine. Two bottles later, he was too drunk to drive, and Whitey relieved him of the keys to his government car. Whitey drove the FBI vehicle out to Morris's Lexington home, with Morris snoring softly in the front seat beside him. Stevie followed in Whitey's car, and after getting Morris inside his own house, they drove back to Southie. From then on, Whitey always called Morris "Vino." And they decided to keep the unedited tape that Morris had left behind in the hotel room. It might come in handy some day, if Vino ever got out of line.

Most of Whitey's information about the tapes, though, came

from his old reliable, Zip Connolly. He had to pull the occasional shift in the FBI's van in Charlestown, monitoring the conversations that the bugs were recording. Angiulo was always complaining about the fact that Whitey and Stevie were still on the hook to him for the money Howie Winter and Johnny Martorano had borrowed from back in the mid-1970s when their football card racket collapsed. With vig, the debt was up to $245,000, and yet Gerry hadn't been able to set up a sit-down with Whitey and Stevie to arrange for the $5,000-a-week payments he'd been assured would be forthcoming.

"Jesus Christ all fuckin' mighty, why haven't these guys been in touch with me? I don't understand it. Fuck me maybe, they don't like me. They got a right not to like me. It's not a problem . . . But they been jerkin' me around."

Whitey, of course, had no more intention of repaying Angiulo in 1981 than he had had of repaying Richie Castucci in 1976, and for the same reason—Gerry Angiulo wasn't going to be around much longer.

The bugs were pulled out of both 98 Prince Street and 51 North Margin Street on April 17, 1981, and it would take more than a year to transcribe the tapes. Gerry Angiulo was arrested on September 13, 1983, at his favorite restaurant, Francesco's, and would never return to the street. But Zip Connolly was already so concerned about the continuous references to Whitey that he felt compelled to slip a report into the file that claimed "source [Whitey] is not a 'hit man' for Gerry Angiulo as has been contended."

He neglected to mention that Angiulo had been recorded as quoting Whitey and Stevie saying, "We kill people for that guy," that guy being Gerry Angiulo. But quibbling over such details didn't matter as much now. With their Mafia rivals on their way out, Whitey and Stevie could begin to flex their muscles elsewhere. The feds had the situation in the North End well in hand.

CHAPTER 11

IN 1982 MICHAEL DUKAKIS won "the rematch" against Governor Edward J. King. John Forbes Kerry, the decorated Vietnam War hero who had prosecuted Howie Winter in the Somerville pinball case, won the Democratic nomination for lieutenant governor, and the Dukakis-Kerry ticket romped to an easy victory over a weak Republican in November.

The liberals were back in charge of the Massachusetts Democratic Party. But Dukakis had changed during his four years in exile, or so his supporters claimed. He now understood that he couldn't snub the legislature's urban street pols like Billy Bulger. The Duke, as Dukakis was called, would give them what they wanted, and in exchange for their beloved patronage jobs and judgeships and low-numbered license plates and the appointment of sheriffs who would eventually end up in their own jails, they would give the Duke his new programs and higher taxes.

It didn't matter much to Billy who won the governorship. Whoever the governor was, he was going to have to play ball with Billy, and abide by his rules.

Billy controlled the Senate absolutely. Over in the House, Speaker Tommy McGee had to deal with an occasionally feisty Republican minority, as well as a band of Democratic dissidents, both liberal and conservative, who would soon oust him from the speakership. Billy, though, brooked no dissidence. Whatever he said, went.

As he settled into his middle years as Senate president, Billy grew accustomed to an ever more lavish lifestyle. He was starting to enjoy foreign junkets, at taxpayer expense. In 1982, he journeyed to China, and there was an outcry in the papers. But as the trips became more and more frequent, the negative stories became less frequent. In June 1984, he was off to Israel, and in September 1985 he journeyed to Ireland with nary a mention in the press.

For years afterward, as he traveled abroad more often, Billy worked his trips into his St. Patrick's Day routines.

"If Dukakis goes, it's a trade mission," he would say. "If I go, it's a junket."

Kevin White had been mayor almost sixteen years. Since his near-defeat in 1975 he was a changed man. Busing had ended his national ambitions. Now he just wanted to survive, and so he used the city payroll to build a political machine of neighborhood people, from wards he felt no particular need to visit, except in election years.

The White machine soon became a magnet for criminals and grifters. At least two of his twenty-two ward bosses were ex-cons. In the amoral atmosphere of Kevin White's fourth term, other White operatives drifted into criminality—stealing grant money or faking disability pensions. Even the city's low-numbered license plates began disappearing.

It was a situation made to order for an ambitious prosecutor, and his name was William Floyd Weld. After his appointment as U.S. attorney in 1981, Weld immediately focused his attentions on bringing down Kevin White and his City Hall machine.

He quickly won convictions against White's two top operatives in Southie, then indicted the mayor's chief fund-raiser and his budget director. At the State House, Billy watched in fascination as the feds decimated both White's organization and his reputation. Billy began to wonder if he could parlay White's failing fortunes into something more—the mayoralty itself. Billy had never really gotten over his disappointment at not being able to run in 1975, and now it appeared he might have another shot. After all, he could serve as both Senate president and mayor; there was no law against it, and Ray Flynn, among others, had been both a state rep and a city councilor simultaneously.

In October 1982 Billy floated the first of his trial balloons, to a reporter at the *Globe*. Billy, of course, was officially noncommittal, saying, "There are all the obvious reasons not to run, family and so on."

The reporter wrote that Billy's mention of his family was an "apparent reference to his nine children." Whitey's name did not appear in the story.

On May 26, 1983, a battered Kevin White announced that he would not seek a fifth term as mayor. Billy moved quickly—suddenly, he was speaking to reporters again. White's favorability ratings had plummeted into the single digits, but he still had a citywide organization he could turn over. A week after his decision to pull out of the race, White and his wife gathered with Billy and state Treasurer Bob Crane and their wives for a lengthy, Friday night dinner at Anthony's Pier 4. The very public message: Mayor White would support Billy.

Billy was so ecstatic that he commissioned a poll. Stories appeared that the business community was "urging" him to run.

In Billy's own mind, at least, he seemed the perfect candidate. Was the electorate concerned about the city's lack of revenues? That would no longer be a problem, because Billy would remain president of the Senate, assuring a steady flow of state revenues to the neighborhoods.

Billy would be the next Josiah Quincy 3rd, who had been elected mayor of Boston while serving as Senate president in 1844. He was already calling most of the shots; now he would have the title to go along with the power. Surely the voters would understand the power Billy could wield . . . for their benefit, of course. Through his control of the state budget, he could funnel enough money to balance the city's books, while keeping the property tax rates low. The most powerful man at the State House would also be running City Hall. What could be better?

Then he got the poll results. Even the city's voters, it seemed, had grown to distrust Billy. He was running in fifth place, with a mere 8 percent of the vote. The poll jolted Billy with a cold dose of political reality. At age forty-nine, he was not only unelectable statewide, which he had long known, but he probably couldn't even win an at-large seat on the Boston City Council. Billy immediately issued a statement announcing his decision not to run for mayor. Family considerations were cited.

Billy had little impact on the 1983 mayor's race. He endorsed no one—it would have been the kiss of death for anyone he embraced. In the end, Ray Flynn was the last white candidate standing, up against Mel King, a dashiki-clad black state rep from the South End. Flynn won easily, and Billy Bulger fumed. Southie had finally elected a mayor, and it wasn't him.

Flynn became mayor in 1984, Billy gave him one opportunity to prove that he was a team player—for the Bulger team, naturally. Billy would forgive Ray for becoming mayor—on one condition. Zip Connolly would have to be appointed police commissioner of Boston.

Flynn refused Billy's request. Instead he chose Francis "Mickey" Roache, another Southie guy, a career Boston cop and the brother of Buddy Roache, the hood that Whitey's gangland pal, Billy O'Sullivan, had shot and crippled in 1971 as Whitey looked on.

Mickey Roache's brother-in-law, Mickey Dwyer, had also been involved in the same gang war. Dwyer had somehow run afoul of the Killeens, and one night outside the old Transit Café, one of the Killeen brothers had run outside, jumped Dwyer, and bitten his nose off. A passerby had found the nose on the sidewalk, and Donnie Killeen had wrapped it in a bar napkin with a few ice cubes and then sent the nose off to the emergency room at Boston City Hospital in a taxi.

In early 1984, U.S. senator Paul Tsongas was diagnosed with cancer, and he soon announced that he would not run for a second term. Another political free-for-all was shaping up, and one of the candidates for the Senate seat was the incumbent congressman from the Merrimack Valley, James Shannon. His decision to run opened up the Fifth Congressional District seat, and Billy's loyal Ways and Means chairman, Chester Atkins, prevailed, even though his opponent continuously assailed him as "Billy Bulger's butler."

What saved Chester in the end was the fact that his opponent was also a state senator, which meant that he too could be tarred with the Bulger brush. But Chester was an exception. Billy's ties continued to doom most politicians who were close to him.

The same day that Atkins won the Democratic nomination for Congress, Billy's majority leader, "Ditto" Dan Foley, was defeated by a reform candidate in his Worcester district. As he left the Senate chambers the next day, reporters crowded around Billy for a comment about the demise of Ditto Dan.

"He was a fine fellow," Billy said. "He laughed at my jokes."

Whatever Billy wanted, Billy got. When he decided he needed a three-digit license plate, he was given 979. Then it turned out that 979 had been improperly confiscated by the Registry of Motor Vehicles, and Billy had to return it. In its place, the Registry gave him an even lower tag for his white Oldsmobile—226. The new plate was issued, a spokesman for the Registry said, "to ease the pain."

On the Massachusetts Convention Center Authority board, there was one dissident—Nick Rizzo, the appointee of the House speaker. He would later go to prison for embezzling money from the 1992 presidential campaign of Paul Tsongas, but in the early 1980s, Rizzo wasn't yet considered dirty. He was the press's main source of information about what was going on inside the MCCA. Rizzo just wasn't with the program.

Mike Dukakis didn't want any trouble. In July 1983, when Rizzo's term expired, he was not reappointed to the board. A year later, Tom Finnerty's term expired. He was a team player. Dukakis reappointed him.

Life was getting better and better for Billy. As the unquestioned boss of Beacon Hill, his lecture fees rose to $3,000 a speech. He bragged about not owning a television set, and buffed his intellectual credentials by quoting John Adams and Aristotle when he came out against a bill that would have allowed reporters to shield their sources. He joined the Union Club on Park Street, where the old Southie city councilor John E. Kerrigan had once been a busboy. In Southie it began to be whispered that Billy was putting on airs, but the Union Club was a nice place to entertain his new friends like Robert Novak, the nationally syndicated columnist. And as long as Billy didn't rock the boat for their guy Dukakis, the *Globe* might leave him alone.

CHAPTER 12

JAI ALAI IS NOT A SPORT EVER likely to be featured on ESPN. It's a handball-like game, played primarily by men from the Iberian Peninsula who have long curved wicker baskets strapped to their hands.

Like dog racing, it exists, despite what its fans may say, for one reason only: gambling. Played in arenas called frontons, the sport has always been plagued by scandals. Opponents of legalized betting on professional major league sports sometimes cite jai alai as an example of what happens when gambling on human beings is legalized—sooner or later, the contests inevitably begin to be fixed. Still, despite the Winter Hill Gang's disastrous foray into horse racing, by 1980 Whitey and Stevie couldn't resist another shot at a gambling enterprise. But this time, in line with their emerging new philosophy, they would merely provide protection.

The company they would protect, World Jai Alai, dated back to the 1920s, and had always been owned and controlled by Bostonians. It was World Jai Alai's founders who had actually paid for the legislative campaign to legalize the sport in Florida. By 1980, the company owned frontons in Tampa and Miami, in addition to one it had recently purchased in Hartford, Connecticut.

It was through Hartford that Whitey became involved in a string of at least four and possibly as many as six murders, two of which remain officially on the books as unsolved, too gruesome for anyone ever to have taken responsibility for.

Whitey was brought into the organization by a Boston businessman, John Callahan, an overweight, Yale-educated certified public accountant for Arthur Andersen who liked hanging around wiseguys. He had, as a Boston police detective later put it to the *Miami Herald*, "a bad case of gangsteritis." For a while, he even shared an apartment in Boston with Jimmy Martorano above the Rusty Scupper, a popular 1970s-era waterfront singles bar. In the mid-1970s, the descendants of the original owners of World Jai Alai hired Callahan to run their very profitable, privately held corporation. He would only control the company for two years, but that was more than enough time to allow its thorough infiltration by organized crime.

Soon after Callahan's hiring, H. Paul Rico retired from the FBI's Miami office, where he had worked since 1970. Callahan, at the suggestion of his Winter Hill drinking buddies, had a job waiting for Rico, as vice president of security for World Jai Alai. Rico was the perfect man for Florida, that sunny place for shady people, as Graham Greene would say. He knew the players on both sides of the law, and he knew how to keep them happy, especially those on the FBI side. He quickly hired the wife of one of his former Miami colleagues as his secretary, and was soon squiring her FBI agent husband and at least one other Miami agent on all-expenses-paid trips to the Bahamas.

After World Jai Alai took control of the fronton in Hartford, Callahan began fretting that with the fronton's proximity to New York, one or more of the city's five Mafia families would try to muscle in. But Rico had just the pair to handle any problems—his old friends Whitey and Stevie.

In those days before cocaine became the focus of Whitey's criminal empire, World Jai Alai was his steadiest, greatest source of income: $10,000 a week, skimmed from World Jai Alai's parking revenues in Connecticut and delivered every week to South Boston. In return, he and Stevie protected the Hartford fronton from Mafia shakedowns and infiltration.

Everything at World Jai Alai was running smoothly until the late 1970s, when the descendants of the original owners decided to cash out. The State Police in Connecticut had always been wary of Callahan's ties to organized crime back in Boston, and shortly after he brought in Whitey and Stevie, Callahan was spotted at the Playboy Club in Park Square in the company of several known mobsters. Connecticut authorities pulled his license to run a pari-mutuel, that is, a pooled betting operation. Without a license, Callahan was unable to manage the fronton, and in 1977, he was out as president.

Soon afterward, the owners of World Jai Alai sold out to a fifty-five-year-old Massachusetts native named Roger Wheeler. Wheeler, who now lived in Tulsa, Oklahoma, had heard all the stories about jai alai and organized crime, but he figured he could handle it. He'd made a fortune in electronics and cashed out some of his profits, and now he wanted a good return on his investment. What really made up his mind to buy World Jai Alai was the impeccable reputation of his vice president for security, H. Paul Rico.

If there were any problems with the Mob, Wheeler decided, H. Paul Rico would know how to deal with them. Plus, he was hiring other newly retired FBI agents from the Miami office to work at World Jai Alai. Some of them, like Rico, had even known J. Edgar Hoover.

For $50 million, World Jai Alai looked like a steal. With annual profits of $6 million, Wheeler could quickly pay off his loans. But he should have recognized some warning signs. The First National Bank of Boston, where Callahan was well known from his days as a bank consultant, gave him good terms on the loan, except on one point. The bank insisted that Wheeler hire an associate of Callahan's as his president.

In addition, much of Callahan's old crew remained in place at World Jai Alai and so the skimming deal with Winter Hill remained in effect, if off the books. Wheeler suspected there was a problem, but Callahan had been a skilled enough accountant to paper it over. The new owner proceeded cautiously, auditing the books, trying to figure out just how much money was being skimmed, and how serious the theft problem was.

Peggy Westcoat was a cashier at the Miami fronton. She knew all the players in all the World Jai Alai frontons. So Wheeler approached her first. Did she know what was going on in Hartford? Callahan still had his own sources inside the company, and once he learned about Wheeler's investigation, he made sure to tell Whitey, who began an investigation of his own. He had to find out what Westcoat had told Wheeler, and how much he now knew about the Connecticut skim.

She lived with her boyfriend in a single-family home in southwest Dade. In December 1980, two men broke into her house and hanged her boyfriend near the front door. Then the killers dragged Westcoat into the kitchen, looped a rope around her neck, and pushed her up against the sink. One man turned on the garbage disposal, and began feeding the rope into the grinder. Then they turned off the disposal, and, with the rope still wrapped tightly around her neck, they questioned her about the new management. When she'd told them everything they wanted to know, they turned the garbage disposal back on.

When the cops found the two bodies the next day, they chalked it up as another Miami drug deal gone bad.

In December 1980, Wheeler's phone rang in Tulsa and one of his Florida managers told him the news. Peggy Westcoat had been murdered in Florida, but World Jai Alai's most immediate problem was Connecticut. Two months later, Wheeler put the Hartford fronton on the block. There were too many mobsters, and Wheeler felt that by selling the Hartford fronton, he would break World Jai Alai's long-standing ties with both the Mafia and Callahan's gangster crew in Boston.

But selling Hartford was not an acceptable solution to Whitey, Stevie, H. Paul Rico, or John Callahan, who still dreamed of regaining formal control of World Jai Alai. No one could afford any serious investigations of the skimming—it would mean the end of the $10,000 a week for the Hill, and exposure of both Callahan's role in setting up the skim and Rico's acquiescence in the scheme.

There was only one way to avoid exposure. They would have to murder Wheeler.

It was at this point that Whitey made an uncharacteristic tactical error. For the Wheeler hit, Callahan wanted to use Brian Halloran, the Winter Hill hanger-on whose ham-handed attempt in 1974 to collect a loansharking debt for Jimmy Martorano had landed Johnny's brother in prison (after an assist from Whitey and Stevie to the FBI). Halloran's own rap sheet was dotted with similar screw-ups; once he and Jimmy had been arrested in possession of several unregistered firearms after he crashed their vehicle into a telephone pole while trying to outrace a police car.

He was, in short, a notorious fuck-up, and the idea of using him on an out-of-state contract assassination was simply unthinkable, except that Callahan made the suggestion. Callahan was not only an "earner," he had also helped out Johnny Martorano when he went on the lam, lending him both his car and his apartment in Florida until he got on his feet. Callahan was the mule for the cash that Whitey and Stevie were sending south to Johnny.

In January 1981, a month after Peggy Westcoat's murder,

Callahan invited Halloran up to his waterfront apartment in Boston. Halloran arrived to find Whitey glaring at him.

Whitey didn't like Halloran for any number of reasons. He was a drunk, he snorted coke, his brother was a state cop, he was a link to the old crew—he was tight with Howie Winter and Joe McDonald. Whitey called him "Ballonhead." But his biggest problem was that he had driven Louie Litif to Triple O's a year earlier. He was a potential witness against Whitey in a murder case.

Callahan laid out the deal to Halloran, who listened, and then asked if there was any alternative. Whitey didn't like questions like that. They told Halloran they would get back to him later.

A few weeks later, Callahan called Halloran and told him to stop by the apartment again. Callahan was there by himself. He handed Halloran a bag, and when Halloran looked inside, he found $20,000 in cash, two hundred $100 bills.

"We shouldn't have involved you to begin with," Callahan said.

Halloran bought himself a new car, parked it at Logan Airport, and then flew off to Fort Lauderdale, where he went on a bender.

Stevie Flemmi also headed for Florida. But Stevie's destination was Miami, to meet his old FBI contact, H. Paul Rico. Rico's task was to set up his boss, just as he'd set up Ronnie Dermody and Punchy McLaughlin more than fifteen years earlier. It would be an easy hit—Wheeler was a square, a creature of habit, who often played golf at the Southern Hills Country Club, an exclusive club that had hosted the U.S. Open.

This time, Whitey and Stevie called in a pro—Johnny Martorano, the fugitive they had taken to calling "the cook." Flemmi got the details from Rico in Miami and passed them on to Martorano, who was living in Boca Raton with a teenage girl. Johnny called in Joe McDonald, another Winter Hill fugitive. They flew to Tulsa and scouted out the city and the getaway routes from the golf course. Via bus, Whitey shipped down several untraceable .38-caliber Police Specials.

On the afternoon of May 27, 1981, after finishing his weekly round of golf, Roger Wheeler walked out into the parking lot of his country club and climbed into his Cadillac. Johnny Martorano, wearing a fake beard and sunglasses, was waiting for him. With Joe McDonald behind the wheel of a rented Pontiac, Martorano hopped out of the car, hurried across the parking lot, and shot Wheeler through the window right between the eyes, killing him instantly. Seconds later, the Pontiac was gone. Witnesses later recalled hearing tires squeal.

The cover-up began almost immediately. The Tulsa Police Department got cooperation from the local office of the FBI, but was stonewalled by the bureaus in Boston and Miami. Relying heavily on information from H. Paul Rico, the FBI went into its blame-the-victim mode.

"Roger M. Wheeler was a self-made millionaire several times over," read an FBI memo sent to its field offices, "with a very aggressive, abrasive personality who usually made money at the expense of others. He had a strong dislike of paying taxes. He was best known as a trader rather than as a business operator and would sell anything he owed for the right profit . . . He was often involved in lawsuits, many [of] which he initiated."

As for any eyewitnesses to the murder at the golf club coming forward, the FBI office in Tulsa was not optimistic.

"[They] are black, uncooperative and do not want to become involved in rich 'white man' affairs."

Brian Halloran was next. He knew too much. In the fall of 1981, someone fired an errant shot at him outside his Quincy apartment. A few weeks later, drunk and stoned as always, Halloran found himself in a Chinatown restaurant after last call, sitting in a booth with Frank Salemme's younger brother, Jackie, and across the table from a drug dealer named George Pappas.

When Pappas got up to take a phone call, Halloran rose from his side of the table, pulled out a gun, and shot him in the head, killing him instantly. Then, as a dozen witnesses watched, and Jackie Salemme cowered under the table, Halloran ran from the restaurant, leaving behind his car keys and his trademark scally cap.

It was the work of a junkie, which is what Brian Halloran had become. But it was a lucky break for Whitey, because Halloran, in killing Pappas, had put the Mafia in a very awkward position. Jackie Salemme was one of their guys, and if Halloran went on trial, Salemme might end up on the witness stand. That alone was reason enough for the Mafia to want Halloran dead. So now Whitey could point the finger at the Mafia when he did what he had to do.

Halloran stayed on the run for a month, then turned himself in to the Boston police and made bail. By then, Whitey had already begun dictating Halloran's obituary, in Zip Connolly's FBI files. On October 2, 1981, Connolly filed the first of many reports on who was going to kill Halloran.

"Source advised that the Mafia want Brian Halloran 'hit in the head' to shut him up as a potential witness."

Halloran knew that without protection, he was a dead man. He also knew he was fresh out of friends in the Boston underworld. He started talking to the FBI.

In the fall of 1981, Whitey had other concerns beyond World Jai Alai. One was a girlfriend of Stevie's named Debbie Davis. She was now twenty-six, a beautiful blonde, and Stevie had been with her, off and on, almost since he had returned to Boston in 1974 after his years as a fugitive in Montreal.

By age twenty-six, she was fed up with her life as a moll in Stevie's harem. As Frank Salemme later described Flemmi, "He was a womanizer. That was his MO all along, his money and his women, not necessarily in that order." Debbie had watched Stevie eyeing her dark-haired thirteen-year-old sister, Michelle, whom he took to calling "Ava Gardner." Looking for a change, Debbie had started dating a Mexican on the side, a dangerous proposition, considering that one young man who had flirted with her had already ended up dead, shot in the back of the head in the Blue Hills Reservation. There was no way she could break up with Stevie, simply because she knew too much.

She would have to go.

One morning in September 1981, with Stevie's parents gone for the day, Stevie brought Debbie Davis back to the Flemmis' house in South Boston. Whitey was waiting for her. He jumped Davis and strangled her, as Stevie watched. Then they stripped her body, cut off her fingers and toes to prevent identification, and wrapped her corpse in a plastic sheet. After dark, they drove down to the same marshes by the Neponset River where they'd buried Tommy King back in 1975.

When he decided to go to the FBI, Halloran had known enough to steer clear of Connolly and Morris and the rest of the organized crime squad. He'd instead approached an agent he knew who was assigned to the labor racketeering squad. In the weeks that followed, Halloran was shifted from safe house to safe house, three in all.

The decision to formally protect him as a federal witness was up to Jeremiah O'Sullivan, the head of the organized crime strike force, who was by then preparing the indictments of the Angiulos. Preoccupied with the Mafia, O'Sullivan probably dismissed Halloran as a drunk and a druggie, a minor hood with a first-degree murder charge hanging over his head who wanted to roll over in return for uncorroborated testimony.

Others, though, including the agents who'd brought him in, thought Halloran could be a valuable tool against Winter Hill. With the law enforcement debate over Halloran continuing, Whitey dictated another FBI report, this one to Morris, on April 23, saying "that the 'outfit' continues to be interested in having Brian Halloran killed. Source advised that the 'outfit' consider Halloran to be a weak person and are concerned that he may make a deal with the DA's office to give up Salemme."

This was the classic Whitey swerve: attribute his own motives to someone else. When he hit Halloran, there'd already be a paper trail leading back to the Mafia.

In the end, O'Sullivan cut Halloran loose, refusing to okay his entrance into the Witness Protection Program. The new number-two FBI agent in the Boston office, Robert Fitzpatrick, was so stunned by the decision that he approached Bill Weld, the U.S. attorney. In court in 1997, Weld recalled the FBI agent's premonition.

"You know," Fitzpatrick said, "people always say there's a danger for this snitch or that snitch. I'm telling you, this guy—I would not want to be standing next to this guy."

Whitey had opened up an appliance store at F Street and West Broadway, out of which his top money-launderer Kevin O'Neil could deal hijacked stoves and refrigerators. On the afternoon of May 11, 1982, Whitey was hanging around the store, along with one of the younger gang members—Kevin Weeks, twenty-five years old, a project rat who had gotten his start as a bouncer at Triple O's. Weeks now had a job at the MBTA, and he supplemented his income doing the store's "bull work"—delivering the appliances.

That afternoon, an older hood from Charlestown stopped by

and mentioned casually that he had just seen Brian Halloran drinking at the Pier, a bar on Northern Avenue. Whitey suddenly snapped to attention and immediately pulled Weeks aside.

"Meet me down the club," Whitey said, referring to the City Point Athletic Association, on O Street between Second and Third. When Weeks arrived, Whitey was pacing the floor. Whitey had Weeks drive him to Theresa Stanley's house and then told him to go back to the club and wait for him.

Fifteen minutes later, Whitey pulled up in what Weeks described as "the blue Chevy," a hit car with a souped-up engine. With the push of a button, the vehicle would emit a billowing cloud of blue exhaust. Another button opened a specially built tank, allowing Whitey to dump gallons of oil onto the street, causing any pursuing vehicle to spin out.

Whitey had donned a light brown wig and a floppy mustache. He looked a lot like Jimmy Flynn, another member of the Winter Hill Gang with whom Halloran had been feuding. It was a perfect disguise.

Whitey told Weeks to drive down to Jimmy's Harborside, a well-known restaurant on Northern Avenue across the street from the Pier, where Halloran was still pounding them down, and wait for him. A few minutes later, Whitey arrived in the blue Chevy. In the back seat was another man, wearing what Weeks later described as a ski mask. No one else recalled anyone in a ski mask, but it meant Weeks could claim he couldn't identify the man Whitey had recruited as a backup shooter.

"He handed me a police scanner and a walkie-talkie," Weeks later testified. When Halloran left the bar, Weeks was to radio a brief message to Whitey: "The balloon is in the air."

A few minutes later, Halloran exited the Pier with a casual friend, Michael Donahue, who had offered him a ride home. As Halloran waited for Donahue to bring his small blue car around to the bar's front door, Weeks gave the signal.

"The balloon is in the air," Weeks said. With a roar of the

engine and a squeal of tires, Whitey pulled alongside the blue car.

"Brian," he yelled, and Halloran, bleary from an afternoon of drinking, looked up just as Whitey opened fire with a full automatic carbine. Donahue's car lurched forward, then began drifting across Northern Avenue until it finally crashed into a building. Whitey circled around, trapping the car, and continued firing his carbine into it as Weeks sped away.

When the police arrived, Donahue was dead, but Halloran was hanging on, drifting in and out of consciousness. The cops asked who had shot him.

"Jimmy Flynn," he said, and then died.

Whitey's luck held throughout the evening. He got the hit car back into one of the gang's garages in the Lower End, and Weeks retrieved the guns from the vehicle and sawed them up before tossing the pieces into the ocean in Quincy.

A couple of hours later, some friendly feds, including Zip and John "Vino" Morris, showed up at Whitey's apartment. They didn't want answers, they wanted beer. And Whitey was only too happy to serve them as much as they wanted. As usual, Vino was soon drunk, and once he was, he casually mentioned to Whitey that they had gotten the license plate number of the hit car. As soon as they left, Whitey called Weeks and told him to leave the hit car in the garage where it was. It, and the garage, were untraceable.

"Thank God for Beck's beer," Whitey said. "Thank God for Beck's."

As the murder investigation unfolded, Zip quickly laid down a trail of false leads back to people who had either crossed Whitey, or might represent some threat in the future. On the day after the Halloran-Donahue murders, Whitey tried the same ploy he'd first used eight years earlier, after murdering

Paulie McGonagle. He blamed Charlestown, advising Zip that "the wiseguys in Charlestown supposedly heard that Brian Halloran and his brother, who is a MA State Trooper, had met with Colonel O'Donovan of the MA State Police and that Halloran was going to cooperate with the law."

The next day Whitey advanced a new theory: the killers were Flynn and a guy named Weasel Manville, from the old Mullens gang, who used to run the O Street Club for them.

On May 21, Whitey fingered a guy from Charlestown as Flynn's wheelman and then, for good measure, invented a "backup van" with three more other Townie thugs. And Whitey put the State Police and Lieutenant Colonel O'Donovan back in the mix, because, he said, Halloran was cooperating with them, this time not on drugs, but on bank robberies, which would have put him in the crosshairs of the Charlestown crews.

Finally, on July 7, with the heat starting to die down, Whitey, through his amanuensis Zip Connolly, took one more run at the State Police, saying that Halloran was dead because the Staties "let the cat out of the bag." This time it was the FBI using the Whitey swerve, blaming someone else for what they had done.

Now there was only one person left to kill.

In June 1982 Johnny Martorano was summoned to a meeting with Whitey and Stevie in a hotel near La Guardia Airport in New York. The topic of the meeting was John Callahan. He had to go. His name was all over the papers, linked to Halloran. They'd been seen drinking together too many nights, by too many cops and reporters, at the Rusty Scupper. Everyone, including the press, knew that Callahan had run World Jai Alai, and after Halloran was hit, Callahan's name was mentioned in several of the sidebars about Halloran's criminal career. It was only a matter of time until the feds would have to pick up Callahan for questioning. And when push came to shove, Callahan was a civilian, not a wiseguy, and civilians flipped, always.

Whitey patiently pointed all this out to Johnny Martorano, and told him that they had no choice but to kill Callahan. Johnny Martorano shook his head and refused to accept the contract. Callahan had done the right thing by him, more than once. And Callahan was perhaps his imprisoned brother Jimmy's best friend.

"Well," said Whitey, "so then tell me something. Is he going to do ten years? Is he going to do twenty years?"

Johnny Martorano, not the smartest guy in the world, thought about it for a moment.

"No, he's not," Martorano said. "He's gotta go."

As in Tulsa a year earlier, the guns would be shipped down via bus. Callahan would be picked up at the airport in Fort Lauderdale by Johnny Martorano and Joe McDonald and from there it would be up to them how to handle it, although Whitey did have a couple of suggestions.

Even before the hit, Whitey had Connolly begin sending law enforcement off in the wrong direction. On July 7, Zip reported that Callahan had stopped going to Florida so often because of "a Cuban group who he was impressed with as being very bad."

Whitey added that "lately Callahan's relationship with this group has cooled and Callahan is supposed to be avoiding them."

On July 31, Callahan flew to Fort Lauderdale and was met by Martorano and McDonald, who drove off with him in a van. A day later, a garage attendant at the Miami International Airport noticed blood dripping out of the trunk of a silver Fleetwood Cadillac. When the police opened the trunk, they found Callahan's supine corpse, two bullet holes in his head, a dime on his chest. It was a Hollywood touch—a message, supposedly, for snitches.

The only personal effect missing from Callahan's body was a distinctive ring, and as soon as the body was found, Miami-Dade police received an anonymous phone tip about a strange ring that had been dropped in a small trash receptacle on Eighth Street—the heart of Miami's Little Havana district. The cops—Miami-Dade, FBI, even the Tulsa police still investigating the Wheeler hit—all scrambled to follow up on the Little Havana clue.

"We spent weeks chasing our tails on that ring," Tulsa police detective Mike Huff said later. "We thought it was Cubans for sure."

Whitey's only criticism of the hit was that he thought Martorano and McDonald should have disposed of Callahan's corpse before dropping the ring off on Calle Ocho for the cops to find. A missing body would have added even more mystery to the case.

Zip Connolly had come through, big time. And so had his supervisor, John Morris. Without their aid, Halloran might have survived to become a witness. The hit car might have been found. Whitey decided to do something nice for Morris.

At the time Morris was sleeping with one of the secretaries at the office. Her name was Debbie Noseworthy. About a month after Halloran's murder, Morris flew to Glencoe, Georgia, for drug training. He had told Debbie how much he wanted to take her with him, how they could have set up a little love nest at his motel on the FBI's tab, and how no one ever would have been the wiser. But the airfare—Morris said he just couldn't swing it. His wife would know for sure.

The next morning, Debbie was sitting at her desk, watching Zip Connolly talk on the phone. She could tell by his mannerisms that he was talking to Morris in Georgia. When he hung up, he walked over to her desk and handed her an envelope.

"John wanted you to have this," Zip said.

She opened it, and out tumbled ten $100 bills.

"Where did John get this?" she said. He was always complaining about being short.

"He's been saving it," he said. "It was in his desk and he wanted me to give it to you, and it's for you to go down to visit him in Glencoe."

It was the first payoff Morris took from Whitey. It would not be the last.

Joe McDonald had just turned sixty-five, and he was tired of being on the lam. So he decided to return to Boston, by train. He informed only his closest associates in the gang.

On the afternoon of August 16, 1982, as the Amtrak train pulled into Penn Station in New York, the FBI was waiting. They burst into McDonald's compartment and arrested him. He was still on the FBI's Most Wanted List for robbing a coin dealer back in 1973.

Less than seven years earlier, Richie Castucci had been murdered by Johnny Martorano for daring to speak to the FBI about Joe McDonald's whereabouts. As Whitey saw it, though, his betrayal of McDonald to Zip wasn't the same thing at all. It wasn't personal. It was strictly business. McDonald's usefulness to Whitey was at an end, and Whitey knew McDonald would never roll over on him. He was a Winter Hill guy, and everyone knew Winter Hill hoods never ratted out anybody.

Callahan might be dead, but there was one more score to make off him. At the time of his murder, he had been a partner with several other local businessmen in the development of an office building on High Street. Flemmi brought one of Callahan's partners to a bar in Southie, where Whitey pointed a machine gun at the businessman's crotch and told him that Callahan had died owing the gangsters "a lot of money."

Callahan's partner was also told that he shouldn't even think about going to the FBI, because Whitey would find out. Within weeks of Callahan's murder, Whitey and Flemmi collected $500,000 from the High Street partners and a Swiss bank account controlled by Callahan's associates.

Meanwhile, back in Southie, the crisis seemed to have passed. The $10,000-a-week skim was over, but all the potential witnesses were dead. Sometimes, though, Whitey wondered if it was really over. He used to tell Kevin Weeks about how difficult it was to get away with murdering anyone with serious clout.

"His words were, Roger Wheeler's family was a zillionaire and politically connected and it will go on forever."

As usual, in the years to come, Whitey would be proven correct.

CHAPTER 13

FOR A SOUTHIE GUY, Steven "Stippo" Rakes had a head for numbers, and he didn't mind working. From an early age he was buying and selling real estate. For a while he owned a sub shop, after which he bought a liquor store. By 1983, Stippo had sold his interest in the package store, and had his eye on a new location, on Old Colony Avenue, at the rotary, right between the two public housing projects.

Keeping his plans for the site to himself, Stippo took a $500-a-month lease on the property with an option to buy. Next, he took his wife, Julie, to an auction at City Hall, and she won a bid for a liquor license that had once belonged to a package store on Essex Street in the city's adult entertainment district, the Combat Zone.

The priest at the nearby church was opposed to the transfer, but Stippo knew a city councilor. The license transfer was approved by the Licensing Board on a 3–0 vote.

There were eleven liquor stores in Southie, and none of them had any parking. Just the fact that Stippo had nine parking spaces in front of his store would give him a huge advantage over his competition. Ditto, his location on the rotary, between the two housing projects. He would name it Stippo's Rotary

Discount. Soon Stippo was in for about $80,000—he installed signs, an alarm system, and new plate glass windows with steel rolltop grates, a wise precaution, considering the neighborhood. He didn't know it at the time, but every night that summer, after he went home, Whitey and the boys had been checking out his progress.

Stippo's Rotary Discount finally opened just before Christmas 1983. In the first four days, Stippo's did $25,000 worth of business. Every other liquor store in Southie was down, some as much as 20 percent, during what was normally one of the busiest weeks of the year. And so the calls started—death threats. The first one came when Julie was behind the counter.

"Listen," the caller said, "we like you. But we're gonna blow the place up." Click.

Julie immediately called Stippo, who was home at their second-floor apartment on East Fourth Street, baby-sitting their two daughters, two-year-old Nicole and one-year-old Meredith. She told him what had happened.

He was speechless in disbelief. "I thought this shit only happened in movies," he said later.

It was about seven o'clock on the fifth day the store was open. Stippo was baby-sitting again, and Julie was down at the store. The doorbell rang and Stippo reflexively buzzed his visitors in. Moments later, he heard a rapping on the door. Stippo opened it and saw in the hallway his old South Boston High classmate Kevin Weeks and, beside him, a fifty-something guy, about five foot nine, in a leather three-quarters-length coat. No introductions were necessary. Whitey's reputation preceded him. And like everyone else in Southie, Stippo knew that Weeks had become, next to Stevie, Whitey's closest associate.

"We need to talk to you," Weeks said, as Whitey looked on. "You got a problem."

Realizing he had no choice in the matter, Stippo motioned

them inside. He had a leg of lamb in the oven. His two baby daughters were ready for bed, running around in snug baby pajamas with padded feet. The three men sat down at the kitchen table, and Whitey began with what was becoming his traditional shakedown refrain, with bar owners, bookies, and real estate agents, among others.

"Listen," he said, "all these other guys want us to kill you." Stippo was stunned. He had thought he'd hit the Lottery when he opened the store. Now, he was being told it could cost him his life.

"You got a problem," Whitey went on. "But we're gonna do something else. We're gonna buy the liquor store."

"It's not for sale," Stippo said.

"You don't understand," Whitey said, pronouncing every syllable slowly, clearly. "We'll just kill you and take it." He stood up, and Weeks did the same. "We'll be back later to talk to you."

About three hours later, Stippo's doorbell rang again. His heart pounding, Stippo buzzed them in. If he didn't, he knew they'd get to him the next time he left the house, or worse, they'd get to his family. When he opened the door this time, he saw three of them—Whitey, Weeks, and now Stevie Flemmi. He led them into the kitchen. Weeks sat directly across from him, Whitey on his right, Stevie on his left. Stevie sat down and pulled a .38-caliber revolver out of his coat and slapped it on the table. Whitey's hands were under the table. Every few seconds, from under the table, Stippo would hear a rapid click-click, followed by a pause. Then again. Click-click.

They went over the same ground. Whitey said they were buying. Click-click. Stippo said I'm not selling. Click-click.

At that point, one-year-old Meredith wandered into the kitchen. Stevie leaned over, picked her up, and put her on his lap. She reached over for the shiny object on the table—the revolver. Stevie smiled down at the little towhead, and then looked sadly over at Stippo.

"It'd be a sin for this child to grow up without a father."

Stevie put Meredith back on the floor, and for the second time the three gangsters filed out of the apartment. Stippo called Julie at the liquor store and told her what had happened.

"We're going to have to do something," she said.

"We'll do nothing," Stippo said. "If we do, they'll come back and kill us. Not me, us."

She wanted to reach out to her uncle, a Boston cop named Joe Lundbohm. Stippo couldn't believe it. He did not trust Uncle Joe, never had.

"No," said Julie. They could trust him. "Uncle Joe is a good man."

The next day, Friday, they received more anonymous death threats at the store. Julie relieved Stippo around four, as always, and when he arrived home, the phone was ringing. It was Kevin Weeks, saying that they "needed" to talk to him. They arrived around 9:30, the same three, and the same scenario was played out again. The only difference was, this time Weeks was carrying a brown paper bag in his hand. As they sat around the kitchen table, Stippo heard the sound again. Click-click. Click-click.

Weeks handed the paper bag to Bulger. Then the baby Meredith came in again. Flemmi picked her up, just as he had twenty-four hours earlier.

"What beautiful blond hair," he said, mussing her locks. "You know what would be a sin—"

"Please," Stippo said, "just put my kid down. Please."

Flemmi stared at Stippo for a moment, then smiled, and lowered Meredith back onto the floor. Whitey pushed the bag across the table.

"Here's for your trouble. It's sixty-seven thousand. Now we own the liquor store."

"Yeah," said Stevie. "Now we own the liquor store."

"And we'll give you another twenty-five thousand," Weeks said.

Stippo called Julie and told her to close the store and come home. When she arrived, Stippo grabbed the paper bag with the $67,000 in cash and met her at the curb where she rolled down the window of the car.

He passed her the bag of cash and told her to take it to her mother's, a few blocks away. He went upstairs and called his father-in-law, a streetwise retiree from Roxbury, who immediately told him not to call the cops.

"Those guys got a line right into the cops," his father-in-law said.

"I just don't wanna get killed," Stippo said.

"Then don't call the cops."

Every morning, Stippo would get a call. Kevin Weeks would tell him to come down to the store, for one thing or another. On Saturday, they just wanted him to "hang out," apparently to reassure any customers who might be taken aback by suddenly seeing local gangsters behind the counter.

On Sunday, with the store closed, Weeks had a different demand. This time he wanted Stippo to bring the "paperwork" down.

Stippo asked Weeks what he meant when he said "paperwork."

"You know, the paperwork."

"You gotta be more specific," Stippo said. "What do you mean, the paperwork?"

"I mean the paperwork."

Then Stippo heard a new voice in the background. It was Kevin O'Neil, the gang's money man, who kept the books for Whitey's semilegitimate enterprises, like Triple O's and the appliance store on West Broadway. Now, apparently, he would also manage Stippo's liquor store.

A few minutes later, as Stippo walked in the front door of his store, he decided it was time to get the $25,000 they still owed him. As soon as Stippo saw Weeks, he told him that he had come for his money.

Weeks pointed over across the store, where Whitey was screaming at the hulking O'Neil about something.

"You want your money?" Weeks whispered to Stippo, pointing at Whitey. "Get it from him."

Stippo decided to forget about the $25,000.

On Monday, the scene was repeated. Whitey was loudly berating O'Neil, this time about the deed. Where was the goddamn deed?

O'Neil spotted Stippo first and told Whitey to ask him. Whitey demanded the deed to the property.

"I don't have a deed," Stippo said. "It's a lease option."

"A lease option? What the fuck is a lease option?"

They had stolen his store, but now they didn't have a clue how to operate it. Stippo drove home, told his wife to take $10,000 from the bag at her mother's and buy a minivan. She came home a couple of hours later with the new vehicle, and Stippo packed everyone into it and started driving. He didn't stop, except to eat and sleep, until he reached Disney World, where he checked into the Polynesian Village, on the monorail. He had no plans to return anytime soon. But on his third day, when he returned from the Magic Kingdom, Stippo had a phone message from Kevin Weeks, asking Stippo to call him in Boston. Stippo ignored the message. The next day, Weeks called the hotel again, and missed Stippo once more. On Weeks's third call to the Polynesian Village, Stippo finally picked up the phone and heard the voice of his old high school classmate.

"You need to come back here," Weeks said.

"Fuck you," Stippo replied, secure enough thirteen hundred miles away from South Boston to finally express his true feelings.

"It's an emergency," Weeks said, ignoring Stippo's anger.

"What's the emergency?"

"You gotta come back 'cause everyone thinks we whacked you. Please. You come back and I'll pay your way."

What choice did he have? Sooner or later they would have to return to South Boston. He left Julie and the kids at Disney World and caught the next plane back to Logan. They'd offered to pick him up, but he wasn't getting into a car with any of them. The next morning, Weeks told him to appear at Dorchester Street and Broadway—the center of Southie—and just stand around.

"You called me back from Florida to hang out?" Stippo asked Weeks.

But he did as he was told and showed up at the corner. He was standing next to Weeks when suddenly he felt someone nudge him.

"Hi, Steve," said Whitey, using his first name for the first time. "How you doin'?"

They stood there for an hour, waving at any cars that went by. If the drivers honked back in recognition, Whitey would motion them over to the side, and they'd double-park long enough for Whitey to introduce them to Steve. By the end of the hour hundreds of witnesses had seen Stippo alive, in the flesh, with his two close friends, Whitey Bulger and Kevin Weeks. The next day, it was the same thing, only they did it in the afternoon, so they could be seen by different drivers. Finally, after about an hour, Weeks pulled an envelope out of his pocket and gave it to Whitey, who then handed it to Stippo.

"Here's the money for your airfare," Whitey said.

Two months later, Julie told her uncle Joe what had happened. She hadn't cleared it with Stippo. Within hours,

Stippo was sitting at home, by himself, when Whitey and Weeks stopped by.

"You think you're smart," Whitey said. "Going to the fuckin' cops?"

"I have no idea what you're talking about."

"Bad fuckin' move," Whitey said, but after a while, they decided he was telling the truth. Someone had obviously told Lundbohm what had gone down, but it wasn't Stippo, and watching him, near tears, shaking, denying everything, Whitey decided he was no threat. And by then it would have been very difficult to eliminate Stippo, with all the rumors circulating, the most colorful of which was that they had hung him upside down off one of the railroad bridges and threatened to drop him into the path of an Amtrak train if he didn't sign the liquor store over to the gang.

They told Stippo to keep his mouth shut, and then they left. A couple of hours later when Julie returned, he asked her if she'd told anyone.

"Only Uncle Joe," she said. "He's going to help us."

"Help us?" he said. "Help us? Bulger and Weeks were just here." He started crying, and he couldn't stop. A few years later, Uncle Joe was convicted in federal court of aiding two illegal gambling businesses and sentenced to six months in prison.

Whitey renamed Stippo's the South Boston Liquor Mart. They sprayed the cinder blocks white, then painted a giant green shamrock over it. In the front window, favored politicians were allowed to place their signs. Peggy Davis Mullen, the city councilor and former Senate aide to Billy, always had one of hers prominently displayed. On warm days, Whitey and Stevie would stand outside, on the sidewalk, right at the rotary, with all the cars circling around them. They didn't have to worry about bugs recording their conversations—there was too much noise. Their friends would honk, and they'd wave back, just like the two days with Stippo. Soon some of the bars in Southie received visits from Whitey's crew. The owners were told in no uncertain terms that they would now have to buy their booze from the Liquor Mart. The fact that retailers were forbidden under Massachusetts state law from selling to bars didn't seem to faze the "salesmen" in the least.

Stippo kept his mouth shut. He even refused to tell the truth about what had happened when he was twice called before grand juries. Eventually he would be convicted of perjury, and sentenced to probation. His wife, Julie, left him, and one of his brothers married one of Kevin Weeks's sisters. It was a nightmare he just couldn't seem to wake up from.

A few months after Whitey grabbed the liquor store, a photographer for the *Globe* was driving by one morning when he noticed a city public works truck in front of the store. The workers were installing guardrails in front of the building. By then it was common knowledge who owned the store, and so the photographer circled behind the store, got out, and quickly snapped a few shots. He was pleased with his work, but it never made the paper, despite the obvious news value—a city work crew, doing a private job for a gangster, whose brother was the most powerful politician in the state. The photographer eventually forgot about his photos until he ran into an FBI agent three years later, in 1987.

The photographer ended up giving the photos to the agent, who showed them to John Morris. As Morris studied them, the blood drained out of his face, and then Morris told the agent to show them to Zip Connolly. Connolly had no reaction, but he did tell the agent that Whitey had provided good information to the bureau in the past.

The agent nodded and put the photos in his desk while he awaited further instructions that never came. A couple of days later, the *Globe* photographer noticed a private work crew tearing up the now three-year-old city-installed guardrails.

That Christmas, agents of the Boston FBI office bought the booze for their annual holiday party at the South Boston Liquor Mart. For the FBI the price was always right.

Not every cop in the city was on Whitey's pad, and one day in the fall of 1985, two straight BPD detectives spotted Whitey and Kevin Weeks outside the Liquor Mart in the parking lot. Weeks had a brown paper bag in his hand. The cops decided to roust the two gangsters, but before they could search them, Weeks had walked over to his car and casually tossed the brown bag onto the front seat.

The cops looked inside the car and saw the bag lying on its side, stuffed full with cash, some of which had fallen out onto the seat.

One of the detectives turned to Whitey and asked, "What's this?"

"That's our money," Whitey said with a smile. "We have the busiest liquor store around."

Stippo soon ran through the $67,000, and he began looking for a job. He'd long since sold his sub shop to raise cash for the liquor store, and now it too was gone. Nothing else looked very promising so, being from Southie, Stippo made what was for him the natural decision, to seek employment at the MBTA.

Stippo went to a guy he knew, not Billy Bulger, but someone who had once been with another Southie politician a long time ago. Some might have thought that, given the circumstances, Stippo would have at least been given a discount when it came time for him to buy his job. But in Southie in those days, Stippo recalled in an interview in 2004, everything was retail.

Stippo's new job at the MBTA cost him $3,000. Cash.

*　　*　　*

Years later, after Whitey had fled Boston, Stippo was sitting in the new federal courthouse on Northern Avenue, talking to one of the prosecutors, when the fed opened a desk drawer and extracted a stiletto—a penlike knife, almost five inches long when closed. The prosecutor held it in his hand, then clicked it open—now it was nine and a half inches long.

The prosecutor then folded the blade back in, and Stippo heard the click again.

"Do that again," he told the fed.

"Do what again?"

"Open it and close it." The fed did. Click-click. Click-click.

"You know whose knife this was?" the prosecutor said.

Stippo shivered. "I know," he said.

CHAPTER 14

By the mid-1980s, the heat over World Jai Alai had died down, and business was booming at the South Boston Liquor Mart. Gerry Angiulo and Larry Baione were in jail, awaiting trial, and Raymond Patriarca was dead. What remained of the local Mafia was leaderless and dispirited, little more than a handful of trigger-happy crews whose main source of income was cocaine. The intelligent tough guys whose absence Gerry Angiulo had bemoaned on the FBI tapes never did materialize.

It was a wonderful time for Whitey, and now he wanted more. He wanted to control everything, and to do so he would have to eliminate every other competing wiseguy in the city.

Once everyone else of any stature was gone, he could demand tribute from any hoodlum who wanted to run any sort of organized criminal enterprise in Boston. As the victims continued to pile up, along with the money, the weapons, and the ruined lives, Whitey found it all quite amusing. He was deep into the cocaine trade himself, first as a protector of local dealers, and then, once he realized the potential profits, as a distributor. And yet, in the *Globe*, he was still lionized by his brother's sycophants as the heart-of-gold, Cagneyesque hood who "kept the drugs out of Southie."

Billy traveled the world with the cardinal, Bernard Law, who spoke eloquently of the plague of drugs that was destroying the youth of his archdiocese, seemingly oblivious to the fact that it was his traveling companion's brother who was actually directing the drug rings wreaking such havoc in Boston. Later, in court, Kevin Weeks was asked how such an incredible situation could be so utterly ignored, or covered up, in America.

"We weren't in America," Weeks replied. "We were in Boston."

Whitey read the papers carefully, keeping track of who said what, if not about him, then about his brother. He shopped in bulk for "his" FBI agents and cops; at Christmas he didn't want to just simply give them an envelope of cash. That would have been just too déclassé. His cops would receive, in addition to the money of course, something more thoughtful—Whitey liked presenting them with collectible figurines, which he bought by the dozen to pass out.

He was always "Whitey" now, the guy in charge, the one who picked up the tab, if anyone dared even hand him a bill. After all the wasted years, he was "the Man," and in his rare introspective moments, Whitey would rationalize what his life had become.

"I never killed anyone," he would say, "who wasn't trying to kill me."

And yet, despite his reign of terror, Whitey remained nearly invisible to the larger world. In the first draft of a report by a presidential commission on organized crime, he was identified as "Jimmy Bolger." When a short-lived political journal published a profile on his brother Billy, he was described, thanks to a typo, as "the dreaded Whitney." Even the *Globe* seemed to have forgotten the entire gang, and the city from which it sprang. When Howie Winter was finally released from prison in 1987, a brief story claimed that the

Winter Hill Gang was named after Winter. Again, no one caught the mistake.

That was fine by Whitey. Out of sight, out of mind.

Extortion, bribery, truck hijackings, gun smuggling—Whitey was game for any racket. But the gang's major source of income was increasingly narcotics. At first Whitey mainly protected marijuana dealers who had taken to storing their loads in abandoned warehouses in Southie.

One of Whitey's earliest sources of drug money was a thirty-seven-year-old smuggler from Charlestown named Joe Murray. In 1983, Murray was running a drug warehouse at 345 D Street in South Boston. Whitey, who at the time was not receiving any protection money from Murray, stopped by one day to check the place out, and then left. As usual, he had been keeping Zip apprised of his rivals—he'd described Murray as a "real sleeper" and "the best kept secret in organized crime." But he wasn't for long. Moments after Whitey left it, the warehouse was raided by DEA agents and cops. Fifteen tons of marijuana were confiscated.

A few days later, Whitey went to Murray and told him his warehouse was bringing down too much federal heat on Southie, and was costing him money. Whitey also told Murray that he could arrange it so that he'd know about any future raids—before they occurred. The service would be expensive, but what choice did Murray have? He paid $80,000 to Whitey and suddenly they were "partners." What that meant was, Murray had to pay Whitey to leave him alone. He had to cut him in on the profits from every deal. Whitey, of course, did none of the actual work of buying and importing and then selling the drugs. Whitey didn't want to break a sweat. He just wanted the cash, in return for which Murray would not be bothered either by Whitey or the cops.

Murray succinctly described the situation later to FBI

agents: "MURRAY said that WHITEY BULGER and STE-
VIE FLEMMI have a machine and the Boston Police and the
FBI have a machine and he cannot survive against these ma-
chines."

As he consolidated his power, Whitey began tying up loose
ends, picking off people who had eluded him for years. One
such person was Arthur "Bucky" Barrett, an associate of Joe
Murray's and a professional burglar who had been arrested in
the raid at the D Street marijuana warehouse. Bucky was a
good earner; in addition to his income from drugs and bur-
glaries, he owned a bar in Quincy Market. He was ripe for a
shakedown.

Whitey had had his eye on Bucky Barrett ever since 1980,
when a bold crew of burglars had tunneled into the Depositors
Trust Bank in Medford over the Memorial Day weekend and
looted hundreds of safe-deposit boxes, many of which belonged
to organized crime figures. Gangsters from both the Mafia and
Winter Hill lost thousands, if not millions of dollars in cash,
jewelry, and negotiable bonds.

The underworld quickly figured out who was behind the
heists, but several of the ringleaders were cops, and thus off-
limits to Mob retribution. But Bucky Barrett, the crew's safe-
cracker, was fair game. He'd gotten at least $175,000 and some
jewelry as his end of the deal.

By now, Whitey and Zip discussed criminal matters as
gangland partners might, strategizing about the best ap-
proaches to use in realizing their objectives. In this case, the
objective was shaking down Bucky, and Whitey and Zip decided that Morris was the man to make the first run at him.
Morris approached Barrett and warned him that Whitey knew
what he'd done and was coming after him. Bucky, though, also
had friends on both sides of the law, and he didn't panic. He
called in his chits, especially with the crooked cops he was

stealing with, and Whitey decided to back off, at least temporarily. But Whitey was patient, and by July 1983 he had a new plan. Kevin Weeks would lure Bucky to the home of another gang member in Southie. Weeks told Bucky he had some stolen diamonds he wanted to fence.

When Bucky arrived at the house, Whitey was waiting for him with a machine gun. Stevie and Kevin Weeks were there too, and they handcuffed Bucky to a chair and then interrogated him ruthlessly about every racket he was mixed up in. They were particularly interested in learning more details about the drug operations of their new partner from Charlestown, Joe Murray, "who was making millions," as Kevin Weeks put it.

They demanded all of Bucky's money. He was allowed to call Joe Murray's brother, Michael, at his liquor store. Bucky told him he'd "been tied up all day" and now needed $2 million cash. Michael Murray asked him if he was crazy, and Bucky threatened to "give him up."

Murray hung up. He never heard from Bucky again.

Barrett then admitted that he had a stash of cash in a strongbox at his house. Whitey ordered him to phone his wife, Elaine, and tell her to clear out. Then Whitey and Stevie drove over and ransacked the house. When they returned to Southie, they sent Weeks over to Bucky's bar, Rascals, to pick up another $10,000 of Bucky's money. Weeks, of course, didn't actually enter the bar himself. He took a cab to Quincy Market, then sent the cabbie in to pick up the cash. That way, there were no witnesses against him. It was an old Winter Hill trick.

When Weeks returned to the house in Southie, Whitey told him that "Bucky was going downstairs [to] lay [*sic*] down for a minute."

As they walked down the stairs, Whitey put the machine gun to the back of Bucky's head and pulled the trigger. But nothing happened.

As Weeks testified later, "[Whitey] took his glasses out and checked the gun, flipped the safety off. At that point, Bucky had walked down a couple more steps and then [Whitey] shot him in the back of the head."

With the body still warm, Stevie took out a pair of pliers and pulled most of Bucky's teeth out of his mouth, to prevent any forensic dental identification. They weren't worried about fingerprints, because one of Stevie's guys had arrived with a couple of bags of lime, to make the body decompose faster. Then Weeks started digging a hole in the basement.

After finishing the burial, they split the take, with everyone getting between $9,000 and $10,000. In 2002, Weeks recounted Whitey's explanation to them of why Bucky had had to go.

"Jim stated Bucky had a big mouth," Weeks testified. "He couldn't trust him. He'd be telling people what happened. Later on I found out that it was more personal. He had tried to shake Bucky down before, and Bucky had ran [sic] to someone, back him off—"

And nobody got away with that. It had taken three years, but Whitey had made his point. If Whitey shook you down, you either took it, or you died.

Bucky wasn't the last of the Barretts to die. His older sons were never the same after his disappearance, and both ended up committing suicide, eleven years apart, in the same gruesome manner, by hurling themselves in front of Red Line subway trains.

Once someone became "partners" with Whitey, there was only one way to dissolve the partnership. This held true for Stevie's domestic partners as well. In early 1985 Deborah Hussey was twenty-six, the same age as Debbie Davis when she'd been murdered. She was the daughter of Marion Hussey, Stevie Flemmi's common-law wife.

When he'd returned from Montreal in 1974, Deborah was fifteen years old. Almost immediately he began having sex with her. He bought her a new car when she turned sixteen, and later he set her up in an apartment in the Back Bay, even as he continued more or less living with her mother in Milton. By age seventeen, she had graduated from waitress in a tough gin mill on Geneva Avenue in Dorchester to stripper in the Combat Zone downtown.

By 1984, Deborah Hussey was out of control, willing to say or do anything. That fall, in front of her mother in the family home on Blue Hill Avenue, Deborah Hussey personally confronted her "stepfather" and accused him of sexually abusing her. Stevie sputtered out a feeble, halfhearted denial, and Marion then threw Stevie out of the house he'd bought for her almost twenty years earlier.

Deborah Hussey had signed her own death warrant.

A few months later, in March 1985, Stevie took Deborah out shopping. Weeks and Whitey waited for them in the same house where Bucky Barrett had been murdered, and then interred in the basement. Weeks was upstairs using the bathroom when Stevie and Deborah arrived.

"As I was coming down," Weeks later testified, "I heard a bang, and I walked down the stairs, and Jim Bulger was strangling her."

This time, Stevie decided to help.

"He at one point put his head on her chest and said she was still alive," Weeks said, "and then he wrapped a rope around her neck and stuck a stick through it and was twisting it."

After she was dead, Stevie straddled her corpse and again used a pair of pliers to remove her teeth. Then he removed her shoes and stockings and used an ax to chop off her toes, after which he then chopped off her fingers.

Then they buried her in the basement, next to Bucky Barrett. In October 1985, the house would go up for sale, and

Weeks would be assigned the grisly task of disinterring the bodies and, after dark on Halloween night, reburying them in a lot across the street from Florian Hall in Dorchester.

Digging up the corpses, Weeks and another gang member wore painters' masks to cut the stench of the rotting flesh, then loaded the bodies into a station wagon they dubbed "the Hearse."

In the vacant lot, the other gangster dumped the remains into predug graves, while Weeks stood guard with a machine gun. At one point, a passing car slowed down, but the driver apparently saw nothing and quickly sped off. Later that evening, when Weeks reported back, Whitey was outraged that his underling hadn't killed the mysterious witness and thrown his body into the makeshift grave with the others.

Years later, when Weeks was on the witness stand, a prosecutor asked him why he had never tried to stop any of the murders.

"Because," he said, "then I would have been going into the hole myself. They would have killed me. They're not used to people saying no to them. I seen firsthand what happens to people that went to law enforcement."

The shakedowns continued. Anything could be used as a pretext for extortion. A real estate developer in Quincy was taken for $200,000 after he advised a neighbor of Kevin Weeks's in a dispute over the location of a fence. The developer, Richard Bucheri, got a call from Stevie Flemmi ordering him to appear at the Flemmis' house in South Boston. When he arrived he saw Whitey sitting at a table, a sawed-off shotgun in front of him.

"Why the fuck did you get involved in that beef over the fence?" Whitey demanded. "Kevin is like a son to me. You should have minded your own fucking business and kept your fucking mouth shut."

He stood up, and pointed the shotgun at Bucheri.

"I oughta fuckin' kill you," he said, before relenting. "I'll let you go, but it's gonna cost you two hundred grand."

Bucheri paid Stevie by check. When the check cleared, Bucheri got a call from Flemmi.

"Jim says you're his friend now," Stevie reported.

Another victim was a South Boston real estate developer named Raymond Slinger. In federal court, Slinger later testified that Kevin O'Neil called him one day and told him that someone wanted to see him at Triple O's. He understood that this was not an invitation he could refuse. He arrived at the bleak tavern and Kevin O'Neil escorted him up the stairs, where Whitey was waiting for him.

"I've been hired to kill you," he told Slinger, using almost the exact same words that had so terrified Stippo Rakes.

Whitey told Slinger that there were alternatives available. He could pay Whitey to kill the other guy, or scare him.

"How much would it cost me to have you tell the other guy to leave me alone?" Slinger testified that he asked Whitey. "A thousand bucks? Two thousand?"

Whitey fixed him with an icy stare. "Are you shitting me? My boots cost more than that. Fifty grand would be more like it."

Once he was back at his office, Slinger called City Councilor Jimmy Kelly. Kelly was a friend of both Bulgers, a former small-time criminal himself who'd done a stretch at the Deer Island House of Correction for illegal possession of a handgun. It was Kelly to whom Whitey turned when Theresa Stanley's son wanted a city job.

Kelly assured Slinger he'd straighten out the matter. But a couple of weeks later, Slinger received a call from Kevin O'Neil.

"The man wants to see you again," he said.

This time, Slinger brought a gun with him. But while frisking him for body wires, Weeks and O'Neil found the gun. Kevin Weeks punched him in the gut and threw him down into a chair. Whitey entered and Weeks handed him Slinger's gun. Finding one bullet inside, Whitey walked over to Slinger and pressed the barrel against the top of his head.

"You know what happens if I shoot you?" Whitey asked. "When the bullet goes in from the top, there's no blood." He glanced over at Weeks. "Go get me a body bag."

At least that was Slinger's recollection. Weeks remembered Whitey saying, "Go get me a bottle of beer."

Slinger paid Whitey $25,000. The shakedowns stopped after two FBI agents visited him at his office. When the feds had left, Slinger called O'Neil to tell him about his visitors. He was petrified that Whitey would think he'd made the call. He'd heard what happened to anyone who called the cops.

The Mafia was on the ropes. By 1986, the Angiulos and Larry Baione had all been convicted and sentenced to lengthy prison terms, and there were no obvious candidates to succeed Gerry and Larry. Whitey wanted the Mafia disarray to continue. It was good for business.

Eventually, a new Mafia crew emerged, led by a cold-blooded 1971 graduate of Boston College named Vinny "the Animal" Ferrara. The crew set up their headquarters, not in the North End this time, but in the Back Bay, at the Prudential Center, in a bakery called Vanessa's. But they made one mistake. They told Stevie Flemmi their plans. Soon the FBI had a wire in the back room of Vanessa's.

The crew was planning the shakedown of Harry "Doc Jasper" Sagansky, an eighty-nine-year-old former dentist who had been running an extensive gambling operation in Boston since the 1930s. When he answered their summons to appear at Vanessa's, they demanded a half-million dollars.

Doc Sagansky's counteroffer was $3,000-a-month "rent"—double what he'd been paying the Angiulos. The Animal stuck to his demand for a half-million. Doc shook his head.

"Kid, I'm eighty-nine years old," Sagansky said to the Animal. "How long am I gonna be in business? How can I go to work and make the kind of money youse talkin' about? Listen, take the business, will you please, and forget about everything."

"Give us the bankroll," the Animal shouted.

"I'm not gonna give you no bankroll," Sagansky replied.

But a day later, he did—$250,000. The money was passed in the lobby of the Park Plaza Hotel, and Vinny the Animal and his men hurried back to Vanessa's to divide the take.

"Those motherfuckers," the Animal said. "This better be real money."

Whitey had nothing to fear from this new Mafia. With every word of the shakedown recorded on tape, it was only a matter of time before the Animal and his crew joined the Angiulos in federal prison.

Whitey had even fewer concerns about his old friends from Somerville. Without Howie Winter to keep them in line, they began shooting one another, sometimes in bars. Others dabbled in cocaine, often with disastrous consequences. Whitey paid them little heed, although sometimes the subject of Howie Winter's old outfit at Marshall Motors did come up in conversation. On one bug that the Drug Enforcement Administration briefly installed in a car in the mid-1980s, Whitey was heard griping about still having to support Johnny Martorano in Florida. After all, he hadn't killed anybody for Whitey in maybe three years. Whitey was also recorded telling Stevie, "There ain't no more Winter Hill Gang," and, for good measure, "Fuck Howie."

After Winter's release from prison, Whitey began feeding Zip derogatory information about his old boss. Whitey described Howie as "strictly a left-fielder," who shook down criminals for protection he didn't provide.

It wasn't all work and no play for Whitey in the mid-1980s. Sometimes he was spotted at Roxbury Latin football games, watching his nephew Chris Bulger, Billy's son, play.

He often socialized with friendly FBI agents. Whitey gave them all nicknames. John Newton, who had served in Vietnam, was "Agent Orange." Nick Gianturco's father had been a physician; he became "Doc" Gianturco. Most Sundays, he and Stevie hosted a dinner at Mrs. Flemmi's house across the courtyard from Billy's house, and Zip sometimes brought by other agents. Occasionally, two FBI agents later testified, Billy would even make a brief appearance, none of which he would be able to recall when he later testified under oath before Congress. Whitey also visited the homes of agents. John Newton had an apartment in Southie, where Whitey liked to meet Zip late at night to strategize. Newton testified that when Whitey arrived, he would take his dogs out for a walk.

But many of the get-togethers with agents were purely social. One evening in 1985, agent Nick Gianturco, invited Whitey and Stevie to dinner at his home, where they met another guest, the famous undercover New York FBI agent Joe Pistone, better known as Donnie Brasco. Gianturco introduced his Mob friends to Pistone as "Jimmy and Stevie."

In the spring of 1985, Zip arranged a dinner party at John Morris's home in Lexington that included himself, Morris, Stevie, Whitey, and, for good measure, Dennis Condon, still working for Governor Dukakis in the Public Safety Department. Condon fled after dinner, and the evening ended with Whitey pressing $5,000 cash into Morris's palm.

When he wasn't hobnobbing with the FBI or dining out with either of his girlfriends, some nights Whitey could be found hanging out at Jacques, the city's original transvestite bar in his old stomping grounds, Bay Village. It was owned by Henry Vara, the cousin of the Martoranos who in the mid-1970s had become Billy's business partner in a Florida radio station.

Whitey often vacationed in Provincetown, the heavily gay resort at the tip of Cape Cod. When John Callahan was murdered in 1982, Zip pointed out that Whitey couldn't have killed him, because he was in Provincetown—"with female companionship," Zip hastened to add in his report.

On another visit to Provincetown, Whitey had a photograph taken of himself wearing a cowboy hat and a leather vest with nothing underneath. In his hands he cradled a long-barreled revolver. When the *Herald* ran the photograph in 2004, it was captioned, "Wanted by the FBI . . . and the Village People."

Occasionally he and Theresa Stanley went to Florida. Her brother had moved there decades earlier, and gone into law enforcement. He had eventually been elected sheriff of a small county near Tampa on the west coast. But the siblings' visits were often short; Whitey and the sheriff, a pro-life Republican, did not get along.

On rare occasions, Whitey showed his sentimental side. His old Alcatraz buddy, Clarence Carnes, the Choctaw Kid, had never been able to make it on the outside, and back in federal prison, he contracted AIDS, died, and was buried in a prison graveyard in Missouri.

Whitey paid to have the Choctaw Kid's body exhumed and sent back to Indian country for a traditional burial. He arrived twenty minutes late for his friend's funeral, after collecting a speeding ticket in his rented Lincoln for doing 110 in a 55 miles-per-hour zone.

At the funeral, Whitey passed out $100 tips to everyone there—the preachers, the singers, even the funeral director, who would later get occasional late night calls from Whitey, in which Whitey mused about how he just wanted to buy a boat and sail around the world.

But Whitey's main recreation was sex, with partners of both genders. He was often seen in the company of Catherine Greig's younger brother, who would eventually die in what was ruled a suicide on Cape Cod. Some of the stories about Whitey's sexual exploits were collected in a book by one of Whitey's cocaine dealers, Edward MacKenzie—Eddie Mac, as he called himself. Entitled *Street Soldier: My Life As an Enforcer for Whitey Bulger and the Boston Irish Mob*, the book recounted how Whitey employed the same techniques on young males as the pedophile priests of the archdiocese of Boston. After seducing them, he would take the boys out for an ice cream cone.

But Whitey went both ways, and like his partner, Stevie Flemmi, he enjoyed the company of underage females, of which there was a ready supply at Cardinal Cushing High School, a now closed parochial school for girls on East Broadway a block or so east of Triple O's.

Eddie Mac says Whitey often paid off the victims' families with trips, or in at least one case, a new set of furniture, which according to one FBI report was the same modus operandi used by Stevie on more than one occasion. At the time, in the late 1980s, Eddie Mac was running a barroom known as Connolly's Corner Café, and he also operated a gymnasium. The gym included a couple of locker rooms, with a Jacuzzi on the women's side, and Eddie Mac quickly set up a lounge of sorts in a storage area next to the women's locker room. Then he put in a two-way mirror that enabled him and his friends to enjoy a full-length view of the women's locker room, where the young girls, often from Cardinal Cushing, went naked into the shower and the Jacuzzi.

They called their peep show setup the Dog Room.

"Whitey . . . loved it," MacKenzie wrote. "Of course there

was no way he was going to sit with us. When he wanted the Dog Room, he got private shows, at 11 or 12 at night, often with high school girls from the projects . . . We were not allowed in the gym when he was there. He usually arranged for this guy named John to perform with women because he had a huge stick . . . But no one ever got to watch Whitey . . . He trusted no one."

In his book, MacKenzie claimed that one night he surreptitiously watched through the two-way mirror as Whitey raped a fifteen-year-old girl that MacKenzie recognized as one of "Whitey's Cardinal Cushing groupies."

"[The] naked girl lay face-down on a plastic tarp on the floor. Whitey, equally naked, kneeled over her. He was spreading different colors of paint all over her body; she looked like a tie-dye T-shirt . . . When he was finished, he turned her over and began having sex with her."

Over the years, rumors have surfaced about amateur pornographic videotapes that were supposedly made by Whitey at the Dog Room. None have surfaced, so far.

Sooner or later, Whitey must have known, he was going to run out of luck. Zip wasn't getting any younger, and eventually Whitey might have to go on the lam again. This time he was determined that it wouldn't be a half-assed, haphazard flight like his trip across the country as a young fugitive in 1955. This time, he would do it right.

As far back as 1977, Whitey had begun assembling his new identity—"Thomas Baxter," of New York. But to make it work, he would need money, and he would need it everywhere. Soon he and Theresa were taking trips, not just to Florida and Oklahoma, but around the world. Often Whitey would use the opportunity to scout out a bank where he could rent a safe-deposit box, which he would then stuff with cash, jewelry, rare coins, and passports.

But their most frequent foreign destination was the country next door—Canada.

On September 8, 1987, Whitey and Theresa arrived at the Delta Airlines terminal to catch a flight to Montreal. Theresa paid cash for two first-class tickets. As they went through security, a guard noticed several bricklike objects in Whitey's carry-on luggage. The guard opened the satchel and saw that it was filled with brand-new $100 bills. The estimates of the amount of cash Whitey was carrying have ranged as high as $100,000, far above the federal limit of $10,000 that is permitted to be taken out of the country without notifying authorities. When the guard told Whitey that he would have to call the State Police, Whitey grabbed the bag and ran, yelling "Kevin!" at an associate who was leaving the terminal.

"Kevin" took the bag from Whitey and escaped through the revolving door. Security guards tried to chase after him, but Whitey blocked the door, giving "Kevin," most likely Kevin Weeks, time to escape.

Billy Johnson, a plainclothes state trooper and Vietnam veteran, was the first to arrive on the scene. As Whitey, scowling, looked on, Johnson asked the security guards to tell him what happened. As the guard began to speak, Whitey pointed at him.

"Shut the fuck up," he said. "You're a liar."

Johnson asked Whitey for his identification, and he came up with a driver's license with a South Boston address. Whitey kept telling the guard to shut the fuck up, and finally Johnson shoved Whitey up against the wall.

"I'll lock you up," he said.

"Is this how you treat citizens?" Whitey yelled.

Johnson checked Theresa Stanley's bag. She was carrying $9,923 in cash, just under the federal limit. Both she and Whitey had skirted the law, and Whitey had behaved very badly indeed, but neither had committed a crime, at least none that an East Boston jury, or magistrate, would consider worthy of a State Police pinch. Johnson reluctantly let them go.

The next day, David Davis, Mike Dukakis's handpicked director of Logan Airport, appeared at the State Police's F Troop barracks and confronted the trooper, demanding the copy of his report on the incident.

Johnson refused to hand it over without getting a receipt. Davis, a longtime Boston political operative, stormed out of the barracks without the report that someone back at the State House had wanted very badly. Soon thereafter, Billy Johnson was transferred out of F Troop to a less desirable barracks. His overtime dried up, it became clear he would never be promoted, and he plunged into a deep depression that didn't lift even after he finally quit the job. In 1998, Johnson committed suicide. He couldn't fight the machine, any more than Joe Murray could.

In 2003, at the congressional hearing, Billy dismissed the story of Johnson's transfer as "tabloid talk show stuff in Boston." His lawyer produced a notarized statement from Davis saying that he had not gone to the barracks at the behest of Billy Bulger. But of course the order wouldn't have come directly from Billy. Davis worked for Michael Dukakis, so the directive would have come from someone who worked for the governor. In his letter, Davis didn't say who told him to pick up the report.

Joe Murray may have been a major drug smuggler, but he was also an Irish nationalist. And in 1984 he'd convinced Whitey to help him put together, for a price, a shipment of arms for the Irish Republican Army—machine guns, rifles, and heavy-caliber pistols, .357s and .44s, seven tons of ordnance in all. The weaponry was driven up to Gloucester and loaded onto a seventy-seven-foot fishing boat called the *Valhalla*. Three Southie gangsters went along, to protect the boss's investment, along with a crew that included another member of Murray's gang, John McIntyre, a small-time thirty-two-year-old criminal and deckhand from Quincy.

McIntyre didn't much care for Whitey's guys. "They got the Adidas jump suits," he later told the Quincy police, "and they ain't got a speck of dirt on them. Every day, they take two, three showers."

Off the west coast of Ireland, the weapons were off-loaded onto an Irish fishing boat, the *Marita Ann*. But someone had informed the Irish navy and the *Marita Ann* was stopped and its weapons seized, along with a number of bulletproof vests, one of which belonged to Stevie Flemmi's younger brother, Boston police officer Mike Flemmi. When the *Valhalla* returned to port in Boston, it too was seized, and the story briefly became big news on both sides of the Atlantic.

McIntyre had observed Whitey long enough to know that someone was going to have to take the fall, and he suspected that he was at the top of their list. In October 1984, shortly after his return, McIntyre was arrested by the Quincy police on an unrelated domestic charge. Soon he was talking, nonstop, about the Bulger gang, even though he refused to use Whitey's name, preferring to refer to him and Stevie as "the two guys who ride around together."

As he told the cops, "I didn't start out in life to end up like this."

McIntyre told them about another drug ship, the *Ramsland*, and it was seized in the harbor, along with thirty-six tons of marijuana. Whitey was furious; in 2005 Stevie testified that he and Whitey had been expecting to be paid "about a million" for their so-called protection of the shipment. Meanwhile, as a departmental courtesy, the DEA let the FBI know who their informant was, and the clock began ticking down on McIntyre. On November 30, 1984, McIntyre left his parents' home in Quincy to meet Pat Nee, Whitey's liaison to the Murray crew, at the same house where Bucky Barrett had already been murdered, and Deb Hussey soon would be. McIntyre thought he was going to a party; he walked into the house carrying a case of beer. But Whitey was waiting for him.

According to Weeks and Flemmi, Whitey briefly discussed sending McIntyre into the grand jury with a script, or perhaps giving him enough money to flee to South America. But they quickly rejected those options.

"Jim decided at the last minute to kill him," Weeks later said.

With McIntyre tied to a chair in the basement, Whitey looped a rope around his neck and began throttling him. But the rope wasn't thick enough, and Whitey couldn't finish him off. He stopped to catch his breath, then went back to work on McIntyre's neck. Still he survived, and finally Whitey gave up and threw the rope aside. Whitey picked up a revolver and released the lock. He looked at McIntyre.

"Do you want me to shoot you in the head?" Whitey asked.

"Yes, please," McIntyre answered.

Whitey fired once into McIntyre's head, and the force of the shot knocked over the chair he was tied to. Stevie bent over and put his ear to McIntyre's chest.

"He's still alive," Stevie announced. So he grabbed a handful of McIntyre's hair and pulled on it, just enough to get his head off the basement floor. Whitey then leaned over, put his revolver directly against McIntyre's temple, and shot him repeatedly, at point-blank range, as Stevie gripped his hair.

Now McIntyre was dead. Stevie went to work with his pliers, and this time, he removed not only McIntyre's teeth, but also ripped out his tongue. It would be another warning to rats, except for one thing. No one was ever supposed to see McIntyre again. Kevin Weeks had another corpse to bury in the basement.

Sixteen months later, Nee and Joe Murray were indicted for

gunrunning. So was the missing John McIntyre. After his conviction in 1987, Murray found himself sitting in the federal prison in Danbury, Connecticut.

He knew who'd killed Brian Halloran, and Bucky Barrett, and he knew the names of the cops who were selling information to Whitey. Joe Murray reached out for Bill Weld, the former U.S. attorney in Boston who was now in Washington as an assistant attorney general in Ed Meese's Justice Department.

Murray couldn't make the calls himself from prison, so he had someone else phone Weld's office. The first call was on January 20, 1988. Murray's friend named John Connolly and a Boston police officer as two cops who sold information to Whitey. Weld's secretary, Judy Woolley, took the dictation.

In the second call, on February 3, 1988, at 3:04 p.m., Murray's friend informed the Justice Department who had murdered Bucky Barrett, and why. A week later, he called again, and this time he told the secretary who murdered Brian Halloran. And Murray's friend included this tantalizing information: "There is a person named John, who claims he talked to Whitey and [another gang member] as they sat in the car waiting for Halloran on Northern Avenue. He sits in a bar and talks about it."

Weld forwarded the information to the U.S. Attorney's Office in Boston, with the handwritten notation that "both [Jeremiah] O'Sullivan and AUSA [assistant U.S. attorney, and future head of the FBI] Bob Mueller are well aware of the history, and the information sounds good."

It was so good, in fact, that the Boston office of the FBI did nothing with it for fifteen months. Finally, in June 1989, Murray was shipped up from Danbury to Boston, and interviewed. He was questioned by two of Zip's best friends in the office.

"In view of the unsubstantial and unspecific allegations," the agents wrote after speaking to him, "and the official relationship between SSA [Supervisory Special Agent] CONNOLLY and the sources, Boston recommends that this inquiry be closed, and no administrative action taken."

In other words, business as usual. Murray was shipped back to prison and his charges ignored for more than a decade. But everything he had said was true—Whitey and the FBI and the Boston police did have their machines, and Murray couldn't survive against them, nor could anyone else. Because it was all one big machine now, and Whitey Bulger called the shots. Like Jimmy Cagney in *White Heat*, he was on top o' the world, Ma, top o' the world.

CHAPTER 15

ST. PATRICK'S DAY 1987. Senate President Billy Bulger was also at the pinnacle of his power, and he was reveling in it. This was his big day of the year—the Sunday of the St. Patrick's Day parade in Southie. Before it began at 1:00 p.m. out of Andrew Square, Billy would host his annual three-hour breakfast at the old German Club, now known as the Bayside Club, on H Street.

Both of next year's major-party candidates for president—Governor Michael Dukakis, who had just been reelected to his third term, and Vice President George Bush—would be there, if not in person, at least on the phone. Since 1980, most presidential candidates felt compelled to pay their respects to the strange little man who had become the de facto governor of Massachusetts, if only because Massachusetts was next door to New Hampshire, where the nation's first presidential primary was held every fourth year.

The ramshackle old hall was, as usual, jammed with people. Unless you were one of the VIPs with a reserved seat at the head table, under the giant banner that said in Gaelic CEAD MILLE FAILTE (A Thousand Greetings), you were expected to arrive early.

When the doors to the main ballroom opened, around 9:30,

the guests entered single-file and squeezed together along either side of one of the tables packed in at 90-degree angles to the raised head table. The rickety folding chairs were then passed out, and everyone sat down. From that point on, for the three-plus hours until the breakfast finally petered out shortly before 1:00 p.m., everyone in the room—judge, clerk, legislator, or nun—was Billy's captive audience.

Most of those who showed up every year were supplicants of one type or another. They were senators who wanted a more powerful chairmanship, or judges seeking more money for their courthouse's line item in the state budget. Even congressmen showed up, at least they did if they knew what was good for them, because Billy could settle scores, or at least try to, during redistricting, as Barney Frank could well attest.

Billy had taken over the roast in the early 1970s, after Sonny McDonough had grown tired of having to return from Marathon, Florida, to host it. By the mid-1980s, with Billy as the master of ceremonies, it had become as stylized and predictable as a Gilbert & Sullivan operetta. Every year it was the same jokes, the same songs, the same tired routines and references to James Michael Curley. Billy haughtily dismissed all criticism.

"Do they complain," he asked, "when Sinatra sings the same words to his old songs?"

In many ways, 1987 would be Billy's last great St. Patrick's Day breakfast. After 1987, with the state economy reeling under the impact of endless tax increases and the payroll padding that came to characterize the final years of the Dukakis era, the event would appear shamelessly self-indulgent, not to mention ossified, and after the collapse of the Democratic monopoly on statewide political power in 1990, the jokes would grow yet more brittle, forced.

But on this late-winter morning in 1987, the breakfast had not quite lost its exotic air, and all was still right in Billy's constricted little world. All the usual hail-fellows-well-met had gathered in their customary places at the head table—Congressman Joe Moakley, state Treasurer Bob Crane, former House Speaker Tommy McGee. Billy was beaming as he made his customary entry into the ballroom, wielding a shillelagh and singing his St. Patrick's Day theme song—"The Wild Colonial Boy," a rollicking Australian ballad about an outlaw Irish immigrant named Jack Duggan.

On this day, Bernard Cardinal Law of the Boston archdiocese had joined the politicians at the head table, along with the visiting bishop of Harrisburg, Pennsylvania. If Dukakis was running for president, His Eminence was running for pope. It was quite a coup to have the cardinal in attendance—he was the shepherd of the flock, after all, and the pederast-priest scandals that would topple him were still fifteen years in the future.

"This is a remarkable gathering," Law piously said in his invocation, as everyone bowed their heads and stared into their beer glasses. "Thank God for places like this. We ask your blessing on our land and on the Emerald Isle that first was land for many of us and our ancestors."

"Isn't it great?" Billy said, trying to give the crowd direction on how to react. "Isn't he great?"

At this point, Billy was still letting everyone settle into their seats. As the plates of corned beef and cabbage were passed down, boardinghouse style, he was warming up the crowd with a few introductions of people he knew well, and who owed him, and who would thus understand when to smile, and when to scrape and bow.

One recurring theme of the breakfast: If anyone who showed up was "great," like the cardinal, then anyone who didn't was not only not great, but was also fair game. Even Mayor Ray Flynn, his longtime neighborhood rival, would stop in for a few moments.

This year, Billy was displeased with one no-show in particular—freshman U.S. senator John Forbes Kerry. He glanced over at the bishop from Harrisburg and asked him if he'd ever seen Senator Kerry on TV.

The bishop shook his head.

"Then you must not have a TV," Billy said. "He's not coming this morning. He's angry Dukakis is running for his job."

Billy, like most State House pols, figured Kerry was more interested in running for president himself one day than in hobnobbing with them. It was Billy who one St. Patrick's Day coined the phrase that would often be repeated in the 2004 presidential campaign: "JFK—Just For Kerry." In another phrase that would resurface in Kerry's failed run for president, Billy said presciently of the junior senator, "He's only Irish every sixth year."

The more prominent guests, who often had other parades or roasts to get to, arrived by climbing up the hall's back fire escape. The fire escape door opened directly into the ballroom, only a few feet from the head table, so the VIPs could arrive and depart without having to endure the indignity of working the crowd of coatholders. Waiting for Dukakis to arrive, Billy continued acknowledging some of the more familiar faces in the crowd, who might appreciate having their names mentioned on statewide TV.

Zip Connolly got a public plug, as did Zip's guest—that year's new special agent in charge of the Boston FBI office. It never hurt for Zip to remind his transient bosses at the bureau about the kind of hometown clout he had behind him.

Whitey, of course, was off-limits, totally. His name would never be mentioned until 1992, after he "won" the Mass Millions lottery.

Joe Kennedy, the new congressman from Brighton, Bobby's oldest son and Teddy's nephew, appeared in the doorway that opened onto the fire escape. Billy looked at the dim young man with the million-dollar smile and asked him how the traffic was coming up from Marshfield, where he had lived until he needed a Boston address for his successful campaign to replace Tip O'Neill.

Joe smiled and tried his one scripted joke of the morning. It was about Washington.

"Down there we've got President Ronald Reagan who can never seem to remember anything and up here we've got President Bulger who can never seem to forget anything."

There was an awkward silence for a moment—Joe, or an aide who'd come up with the joke, had hit a little too close to home. Most of the other pols, who had learned Billy's vindictive ways at the State House over the years, would never have dared say such a thing. But Joe, with no State House background, had just blundered ahead. Billy quickly changed the subject.

"Where's your uncle Teddy this morning?" Billy asked.

"I don't follow Uncle Teddy in the morning." Gasps from the crowd. "After the decisions he's made the night before, I kinda leave him on his own in the morning."

There it was—the first sound bite for the evening TV newscasts.

Other pols came and went. Some handled themselves gracefully; most delivered lame jokes that fell flat. Then came the day's big moment—the call from Vice President George Bush.

Billy picked up the phone, looked down at Dukakis, and said, "Your opponent is here."

"Ask the governor," said Bush, "if he's going to run for president of the United States."

Dukakis looked up at Bulger and said, "He sounds like Frank Hatch." Dukakis was referring to the old Yankee state rep who had lost the governorship to Ed King in 1978. There was a hint of disdain in Dukakis's voice—he was already underestimating the man who would crush him in the presidential election twenty months later.

Bush, well prepped, then told Billy about his problems with the *Globe*. So Billy mentioned that the *Globe*'s new editorial page editor, who had been hanging around up on stage for the last half-hour or so, had just moved to K Street in Southie.

"Well, there goes the neighborhood," said the vice president, and the unscripted line brought the house down. The TV crews had another joke for their evening newscasts.

By the time Vice President Bush bid his farewells, Dukakis had finished eating, so Billy had him stand up and take a microphone so they could do a routine of sorts together. But Billy always remained in charge, and using Dukakis as a straight man, he began introducing the Bulger family.

"There's my sister," Billy said. "Carol McCarthy."

"Sister Carol," Dukakis said.

"Would you believe she's not on a public payroll?"

"I don't believe that for a minute." Dukakis looked directly at sister Carol. "What agency do you work for? What agency did you work for? What agency would you like to work for?"

A few weeks later, she would end up at a state program designed to fight illiteracy. It was run by one of Billy's dimmest, most loyal soldiers—former Senator Gerry D'Amico of Worcester. The previous year, he'd run for lieutenant governor, but his campaign had never recovered from the moment when, after winning the state convention's endorsement, he rashly introduced Billy to the crowd as "the guy I work for."

Billy was still electoral poison, even in a Democratic primary.

But because he controlled the state budget, Billy could always find jobs for his defeated senators, and in return they would still hire his relatives and friends. D'Amico was soon gone from the state payroll after revelations that he had run up hundreds of dollars in parking tickets on his state car while parking outside the Quincy Market office of his political consultant during business hours. But Carol Bulger McCarthy hopped from one state payroll to another for another fifteen years before finally taking advantage of an early-retirement program in 2002.

Most of Billy's siblings—and their spouses—had similar careers. Other than Whitey, none had any interest in the private sector. They had learned from their father—business was cruel, and heartless. Better to go "on the state," or "on the city." Jackie Bulger was typical. He had the courthouse job, and both his son and his son-in-law worked at the MBTA. His daughter was employed at the State House—on Uncle Billy's office payroll.

But you didn't need to be a Bulger to enjoy a no-heavy-lifting job. As long as you played ball, you and your family were taken care of. It was as simple as that. That was the real context of the St. Patrick's Day breakfast. It was the high holy holiday of hacks. It was a celebration of themselves, and their king. Once you were in the family, the king would take care of you, and the king was Billy Bulger. And on this day, all his liegemen and their liegemen were there to pay homage.

By now, Billy was out of both A-list guests and Irish ballads that everyone knew the words to. He was reduced to running out the clock by introducing his friends, and Whitey's friends.

"Representative Jimmy Brett," he said, "no ordinary mortal." He was married to Billy's secretary.

"Dennis Condon is here," he said, referring to Whitey's old handler in the FBI.

"Senator Walsh," he said, referring to Joe Walsh, the old warhorse from Dorchester, the leader of another ancient hack family that included his sister, a member of the School Committee. His son was on the West Roxbury District Court payroll, along with Jackie Bulger's ex-wife. Senator Walsh himself was on both the state and city payrolls. Times were catching up with Walsh, though, and by 1987 he was sixty-six. He'd just survived a serious primary challenge, after a third candidate suddenly jumped into the race, to confuse and split the anti-Walsh vote. Such minor candidates were a Boston tradition. They were known as straws, and after their secret sponsors had been safely reelected, they were usually rewarded with a public job. The previous year, Joe Walsh's straw had been John Tortora, whose brother was a Mafia leg-breaker named Carmen. With John Tortora draining off just enough votes, Walsh had been reelected to another term, and John Tortora had been hired to work at the MBTA.

Finally, just before 1:00 p.m., with Billy totally out of gas, and jokes, the parade's grand marshal arrived via the fire escape. His name was John Hurley—John "Whacko" Hurley, not to be confused with John Hurley, an oldtime Charlestown hood who was trusted by both Joe Murray and Whitey.

When Whacko arrived, it meant it was time for the parade to begin. And it was time for Billy to make one final joke.

"Whacko," he would say. "The name says it all."

Whacko had a job at the MBTA.

CHAPTER 16

In 1988 the Bulger brothers seemed to be at the top of their games. Whitey ran everything in the rackets, not just in Southie, but throughout much of the entire region. Whitey had moved from simply protecting cocaine dealers to actually distributing it himself, with Weeks overseeing a network of four autonomous rings, separately managed by midlevel Southie hoods. All of them, from Whitey on down, were growing rich far beyond anything they could have imagined in the old days of peddling football cards and grabbing cases of razors off the backs of trucks as they left the Gillette factory.

Billy, meanwhile, continued to serve as the de facto, unelected governor of Massachusetts, more powerful than ever. The four-hundred-pound House speaker, George Keverian, was ineffectual, and the nominal governor, Mike Dukakis, was always out on the campaign trail, running for president. Sometimes it seemed as though Dukakis no longer even considered himself the real governor—one day, asked a question somewhere, he began his response by saying, "If I were a sitting governor . . ."

There were a few, minor dark clouds, such as Billy's new nickname: "the Corrupt Midget," which was often shortened to "the CM." It had been bestowed on him by Judge E. George

Daher of the Boston Housing Court, who'd refused to promote Sonny McDonough's son all those years ago. A year earlier, the House had passed a budget that would have restored the Housing Court's funding that Billy had cut back in 1981. But at Billy's behest, Dukakis had vetoed the restoration, and in a newspaper interview Daher had lashed out at the would-be president: "How can he stand up to the Russians if he can't stand up to a corrupt midget?"

But Billy was still the king of the hill—Beacon Hill. In February, on his fifty-fourth birthday, he threw his annual "time"—Boston slang for fund-raiser—at Anthony's Pier 4. More and more, it was Billy's campaign account that paid for his increasingly lavish lifestyle. In 1987, a nonelection year, he had spent $158,000, much of it on hotel and restaurant bills. His tab for gift certificates at Anthony's Pier 4 alone was $5,000, and he had become a regular at Locke-Ober's, still the most expensive restaurant in the city. The Ritz Café, where his old Senate rival Jimmy Kelly had once concocted schemes, was another of his favorite haunts. He even used his campaign account to shower his friends with copies of books he had enjoyed. Tom Wolfe's first novel, *The Bonfire of the Vanities*, was a particular favorite of Billy's; he thought it perfectly captured the modern urban zeitgeist. He dropped $1,415 on honey-baked hams. He privately printed a pamphlet, *The New Terrorism: Historical Development of Press Power in America*, and it behooved any lobbyist who received a copy to ask for an autograph, at least if he didn't want his legislation dispatched to the oblivion of the Committee on Bills in Third Reading.

To keep his war chest full, Billy reached out to everyone who did business on Beacon Hill—a practice he had always disdained others for. Even after a year-long spending spree in 1987, he still had $355,000 on hand on December 31. And after his birthday fund-raiser at Anthony's Pier 4, he was comfortably above a half-million again.

Billy was so flush with campaign money, in fact, that he stopped taking speaking engagements—a profitable sideline that "the new terrorists" in the media used as a bludgeon against him. He spent $160,000 in public funds renovating his office at the State House. It was the only one in the building with a full kitchen. And when the older, but still perfectly serviceable, carpets were pulled up, they were shipped directly to the Roxbury Latin School, where his youngest son, Brendan, was a student. In April, at a town meeting in Dorchester, a taxpayer had the audacity to ask him a question about his new digs.

"Can you see it?" Billy said. "Of course not! It's only for Napoleon."

In the late spring, he went on a campaign swing with Dukakis through, of all places, Texas. But behind the scenes, Billy played a different role, for a different party, at least according to veterans of the 1988 Bush campaign. After the Democratic convention in July 1988, Dukakis had opened a seventeen-point lead in the national polls, and the vice president's prospects looked grim. But at Billy's suggestion, Bush flew into Boston, and toured Boston Harbor in a boat, stressing not only the massive pollution problems, but also the fact that it was costing billions to clean it up, and that Dukakis and his state government had been so lax in addressing the issue that a federal judge had been forced to take over the entire project.

Bush's harbor news conference and photo op was a direct assault on two of Dukakis's perceived strengths: his environmentalism and the "competence" that he never tired of citing out on the campaign trail. After Bush's visit to Boston Harbor, Dukakis's poll numbers began falling, and by Labor Day, the Duke found himself behind by double digits. The Bush family values loyalty, and ever since, they have gone out of their way to help Billy whenever possible. In 2002, George W. Bush's Justice Department stonewalled Congress on release of thousands of FBI documents on Whitey and the Boston FBI office that would have, and eventually did, embarrass Billy. George W. Bush's first attorney general, John Ashcroft, did not relent until the Republican leadership in the House threatened to cite him for contempt of Congress. Ostensibly the dispute was about executive privilege, but the Bush administration seemed strangely determined to protect secrets from a long-ago era in which Democrats dominated both the Congress and the presidency.

Like the Bulgers, the Bushes have long memories.

In the summer of 1988, Billy seemed to be sitting pretty. Whoever was elected president in the fall would owe him, or at least think he did. But one of Billy's earlier schemes was about to come back to haunt him, in the scandal that became known as 75 State Street.

The complex, twisted tale had begun years earlier. Harold Brown was the biggest landlord in Massachusetts, a dodgy loner from Brighton who once had a convicted arsonist on his payroll. Now he was looking to become a major developer, and he had his eye on a city-owned garage at 75 State Street, just south of the booming Quincy Market area.

Brown had bought up most of the land he needed, but the garage remained beyond his grasp, and until he had the final parcel in hand, he could not begin construction of his skyscraper at 75 State. In 1982, the garage had been transferred from the city to the Boston Redevelopment Authority as part of the same legislative deal that had created the Massachusetts Convention Center Authority. Under the legislation, the BRA was required to sell the garage, to whomever its board chose. At the very least, Billy exercised great influence over the members of both the BRA and the MCCA boards, and it was they who would decide who, in addition to Harold Brown, was going to make a lot of money on 75 State Street.

It was the old State House story: nothing on the level, everything a deal, and no deal too small. Selling the garage to Harold Brown was going to become the classic State House deal.

The first operative to come calling on Brown with his hand out was Eddie McCormack, the Bulgers' old neighbor in South Boston, now happily retired from elective politics and prosperously established as a power broker. Through his connections to, most importantly, Mayor Kevin White, he had already taken control of the largest of the five affected city garages, the one at Government Center.

McCormack suggested that Brown needed someone to "protect" his "interests" at City Hall, but his price was too steep. Next to step up was Tom Finnerty, Billy's longtime law partner. At the time, Finnerty was serving on the MCCA board, where he watched over the Bulger family interests.

Brown understood the clout Finnerty brought to the table. He would later charge that Finnerty had made it clear to him that the garage would not be sold to him by the BRA unless "a satisfactory financial arrangement" was made. After stalling for almost two years, Brown in 1985 finally signed a deal with Finnerty to pay him $1.8 million for his so-called monitoring of the sale at City Hall. It was an astounding amount of money for anyone, especially a renowned cheapskate like Harold Brown, to pay for what was, in fact, virtually nothing.

In July 1985, Brown gave Finnerty a first installment of $500,000, and Finnerty established a new bank account for the money. A month later, Billy Bulger and Finnerty each took $225,000 of Brown's money. In October, they split another $30,000. A paper trail had been created—$500,000 taken, $480,000 divided.

Billy's sudden splitting of the Harold Brown fee certainly looked odd, but then, the two lawyers had an extremely unconventional practice—"a curious relationship," state investigators later noted, "in which Bulger appears to provide little or no substantive services in return for approximately one half of all fees generated by the Finnerty law firm."

In 1986, for example, Finnerty's law firm issued more than $350,000 in checks payable directly to Billy.

What made Finnerty's role in the 75 State Street deal so odd is that he had virtually no experience in this sort of real estate development law. Since quitting as district attorney, he had established himself as a drunk-driving lawyer. It was a living— his clients included Sean McDonough, son of Billy's *Globe* crony Will McDonough. But Finnerty, a father of six children, was in the throes of a messy divorce and needed to start making some real money.

As for Billy, he must have been feeling pretty good about himself. He didn't know Brown, but now he had pocketed $240,000 of his money. Not that he'd miss it—that was how Billy looked at it. In his book, he described Brown as "obscenely rich," and claimed that he had once been caught at the Turnpike's Allston tollbooths throwing slugs into an exact-change basket. What was an endearing story when told about Sonny McDonough—how he bragged that his constituents all used slugs in pay phones to call him in Florida—somehow became a character flaw in Harold Brown.

But Harold Brown's tendency to micromanage was about to catch up with him. In another similarity to Sonny McDonough, he didn't trust bagmen. Brown handled his payoffs personally, a shortsighted refusal to delegate authority for a man who had recently been named to the Forbes 400 list of the richest Americans.

In September 1985, two months after he had paid Finnerty the first installment of $500,000, Brown was indicted for lying to a federal grand jury about a $1,000 bribe he'd delivered to a Boston Building Department employee. Brown's perjury indictment didn't seem unmanageable, at least for Billy. In fact,

Finnerty made the second, smaller payout to Billy after Brown's indictment. But then, on November 15, 1985, Billy picked up the paper and read some disturbing news. A superseding indictment against Brown had been issued, and in the new version, Brown was accused of making payments in a doughnut shop to a Boston city councilor, as well as to "other public officials."

As a board member of the MCCA, Finnerty was a public official. The story broke in the Friday papers, and by Sunday, Billy had issued his first repayment check to Finnerty.

The reason, he explained later, was that he hadn't previously known the source of the money.

Brown by now had had enough of Tom Finnerty and federal indictments, so he refused to make the second payment. Negotiations dragged on for more than a year, but finally, in May 1987, Finnerty sued Brown for $426,000. The deal may have looked shady, but Finnerty did have a signed contract, and he had every reason to believe that Brown would want to settle, to prevent his name from being dragged through the mud any more than it already had been.

Instead, Brown stood firm in his determination not to pay. He hired a new attorney, Harvey Silverglate, the very sight of whom drove Billy into near apoplexy. They had tangled in correspondence during the controversy over the ouster of Senator Alan Sisitsky, but probably Silverglate's worst sin in Bulger's eyes was his friendship with Harvard law professor Alan Dershowitz—"the Al Sharpton of Cambridge," as Bulger called him.

In the countersuit that Silverglate filed against Finnerty, Brown claimed the initial $500,000 payment had been extorted from him, and that the "purported contract was a sham device to sell improper political influence and was the product of duress."

All of this might never have become public, except for the

fact that Finnerty continued litigating for the rest of his "fee." As the months wore on, Silverglate discovered more and more about the intricacies of the 75 State Street deal. The only question was, how could he get the story out?

For more than a decade, the Boston office of the FBI had done Whitey Bulger's bidding, and vice versa. The agents Whitey had bribed continued to move up through the ranks, and John Morris was now the head of the public corruption unit.

But he was going mad. By now he had accepted $7,000 in bribes—the final $1,000 coming in the bottom of a case of wine that Zip Connolly handed over to him at the FBI office—and he knew that Whitey owned him. On the shelf of his office, Morris now kept a book that summed up his predicament. It was by Sissela Bok, the wife of the president of Harvard University. Its title: *Lying: Moral Choice in Public and Private Life.*

He was sickened as he watched his fellow agents grovel before Whitey Bulger. He had taken bribes, but other agents were almost as compromised. They dined out with Whitey, they exchanged gifts with him, they hung out in the same neighborhood. One day when Zip stopped by the State House, he appeared in the Senate gallery. Billy, presiding over the Senate, recognized him from the podium, and the obedient senators responded with a standing ovation.

For Zip Connolly.

And yet Morris could do nothing about any of it, because they had the goods on him. He knew Whitey still had that audiotape of the Prince Street Mafia bugging that he'd left at the Colonnade Hotel in 1981 when he was drunk. That alone was proof of his duplicity. When the feds put a wiretap on a phone belonging to a Roxbury bookie controlled by Stevie Flemmi, Morris became frantic that Stevie would be recorded on the wiretap, and that when he was arrested, he would give up his pal Vino.

So Morris told Zip to tell Stevie and Whitey not to call the bookie anymore on the bugged line. But Morris also told Zip to give them a warning: "I don't want another Halloran," he said.

In other words, no more murders. It wasn't much of a line to draw in the sand, but at this point, it was the only one that Morris could still draw. Sixteen years earlier, in 1972, when Morris had been transferred to the Boston office, he had considered himself an honest man, a decent human being. Now, like almost everyone else he knew in Massachusetts, he was a crook and a drunk and a cheat. He had gone native. And there was only one way out. He would have to expose the corrupt marriage of Whitey Bulger and the FBI.

In the spring of 1988, just as Morris was falling apart, the *Globe*'s investigative unit, the Spotlight Team, began work on a new series, about the Bulger brothers, and their simultaneous rise to the pinnacles of their respective trades.

Whitey's name had first begun surfacing again, as he had feared it would, when the Angiulo tapes were played in open court in the mid-1980s. Reporters had mentioned him, and none had been murdered, and the press's willingness to take him on was increasing, albeit at a glacial pace. What particularly intrigued the *Globe* was the remarkable ease with which Whitey had floated above various investigations for so many years.

Gerry O'Neill was the editor of the Spotlight Team, and for many years he had used John Morris as a source. Once the Bulger series was greenlighted, O'Neill called Morris and they agreed to meet for lunch.

According to O'Neill in the book he co-authored with Dick Lehr, *Black Mass*, almost the first thing Morris said to him was, "You have no idea how dangerous he can be."

There was no need for O'Neill to ask who "he" was.

*   *   *

By Labor Day, the *Globe* had nearly completed its series "The Bulger Mystique." The usual suspects at the Boston FBI office were growing frantic—if Whitey was outed as an informant, there was no telling what he might do, but they all knew that he could bring any number of them down if he so chose. Already there were rumors on the street that Whitey had been surreptitiously recording his conversations with FBI agents for years.

The veteran agents in the Boston office decided to take one last run at derailing the series. They would resort to a tried-and-true method: the death threat against a reporter.

Kevin Cullen, an ex-*Herald* reporter, was living in South Boston and working for the Spotlight Team when he took a call one afternoon from another FBI agent, one who had worked the Winter Hill race-fixing case back in 1978.

The *Globe* reporters had been sniffing around again about the circumstances of the unprecedented free ride that Whitey and Stevie had received from the federal prosecutors who cut them out of the indictment at the last moment in 1979. The agent told Cullen that he had just received a call from Fat Tony Ciulla, who had urged him to pass on to the reporter a warning to be careful about making accusations against Whitey Bulger. Ciulla had been in the Witness Protection Program for almost a decade, so it would be impossible for Cullen to verify independently the message that the FBI man was passing on. (The agent later denied making any such call.)

"Specifically," Cullen later recalled, "he claimed that Mr. Ciulla said to him that if we embarrass [Whitey], if we write something that's not true, I believe the words were: He would think nothing of clipping you . . . [He] then added his own opinion, which was: Especially you, Kevin. And he stressed that he was telling me this because he was my friend."

Cullen and his family—a wife and young child—were temporarily relocated outside South Boston. As the days went on, the reporters increasingly dismissed the agent's call as yet another attempt by the FBI to frighten the media into not publishing a damaging story about one of its informants. That suspicion only intensified as time passed and the agent never called again about the threat.

"I would like to think," Cullen testified later, "that if my life was in danger, they would have gotten back to me."

The *Globe's* four-part series "The Bulger Mystique" ran in September 1988, in the middle of the presidential race. The front pages were full of stories about the Dukakis presidential campaign's missteps, but the *Globe* carved out plenty of room for the series. Whitey's "special relationship" with the FBI did figure prominently in one installment. But it was couched vaguely enough that it ultimately had little impact on Whitey's reputation in the underworld. Likewise there also wasn't anything specific enough on any Boston FBI agents to trigger any kind of Internal Affairs investigation, even if the Justice Department had been interested in pursuing a case against its corrupt agents in Boston.

The series dealt a much more severe blow to Billy's image. It recounted, sometimes at great length, his legislative maneuverings over now forgotten bills and his vendettas against politicians who were obscure even then.

Perhaps the most damaging piece was a sidebar that didn't even run on the front page. The *Globe* reporters simply transcribed a taped session in which Billy had answered their questions about Whitey:

Q. How much do you see him?
A. He's always welcome, but he doesn't come exceedingly often . . . Sometimes if he's in a talkative mood, he might come by. Or if he has something like a warm-up jacket for the kids, or something, that he thinks is good, for ex-

ercise, or something. He's interested in that, encourages that.

Q. Is it painful to have this distance with your brother, given your respective positions?

A. I don't create any distance . . .

Q. Do you think your brother admires you?

A. Yeah.

Q. And you he?

A. There is much to admire, and . . .

Q. He's supposed to be just the toughest guy . . . a very, very determined, formidable person.

A. I hope that the fact is that there is no reason for anyone who cares about him to be apprehensive. . . . I just hope that that's the case. That there's no reason to be apprehensive . . . so I am hopeful.

Whitey went ballistic over the series. He knew instinctively who had ratted him out: John Morris. The *Globe* hadn't actually named him in print as an FBI informant. But they had come very close, mentioning the "special relationship" between Whitey and the feds. The *Globe* wouldn't have gone even that far without at least one inside source, and Whitey knew it was neither Zip nor any of the hapless SACs (special agents in charge) who were rotated through Boston every couple of years.

It was Vino, and as Stevie Flemmi later recalled, Whitey was deeply hurt.

"I felt for Mr. Bulger," Flemmi said. "I felt that he was— maybe he was betrayed . . . I mean, he was upset generally for the whole article."

But Morris wasn't through talking to the *Globe* yet. He wanted to take down Billy too.

On November 5, 1988, the last Saturday before the election, Zip was married for the second time, to Elizabeth Moore, another secretary in the FBI office. Among the other agents in attendance: Nick Gianturco, John Cloherty, and Ed Quinn.

John Morris was not invited.

Three days later, on November 8, Dukakis lost forty states to George H. W. Bush. By then the Spotlight Team was deep into research on its next story—75 State Street. During their investigations for the first series, the *Globe* reporters had become suspicious of the sources of Billy's income. In one of his later filings for Brown, Silverglate included as evidence a story in the series, with two highlighted paragraphs about a bulge in Billy's income that he reported in his 1986 filing with the State Ethics Commission.

Whoever sought out whom first, by Thanksgiving Silverglate and the newspaper seemed to be operating on the same wavelength. In early December, as Billy prepared for a vacation in Europe, the *Globe* called with an urgent request for an interview. In Billy's plush, newly redecorated State House chambers, reporters Gerry O'Neill and Dick Lehr asked Billy if he was aware of the $500,000 that Finnerty had been paid by Brown.

"I don't know that, that I am aware of," Billy responded. "Let me double check. I think I would have remembered that. He may have spoken about it in the office, but I think I would remember if he had. I would think."

Billy mentioned his upcoming vacation. Would the *Globe* be so kind as to hold off on publication for two weeks until he and Mrs. Bulger returned from the Continent?

What the *Globe* may not have known is that Morris, the head of the public corruption unit, had reverted to form, closing down the investigation into allegations of bribery by Billy and Finnerty. If a press release announcing that the probe had been ended without indictments could have been rushed out, and given to the entire media, then the *Globe*'s "scoop" would have been virtually meaningless.

And it would have all happened while Billy was in Europe, unavailable for comment.

What had happened to make Morris give up what seemed to be such a promising investigation? For one thing, as he later testified, under a grant of immunity, he wasn't thinking clearly. He had just separated from his wife and moved in with his longtime girlfriend from the office, Debbie Noseworthy. He was drinking more than ever. Morris was, as he later testified, somewhat in awe, if not in fear, of Zip Connolly. And Zip was, as always, lobbying heavily to deep-six any and every investigation against either of the Bulger brothers. Perhaps most importantly, Morris was extremely concerned that Whitey knew where his family still lived in Lexington.

But before the FBI had an opportunity to officially exonerate Billy, the *Globe* rushed the story into print. Billy and Mary were in Brussels when the story broke on Sunday, December 8, in a slow news period after the presidential election. The headline was "The Deal Behind a Skyscraper" and the lead laid it all out: "Senate President William M. Bulger has benefited from a trust bankrolled with money that a Boston real estate magnate claims was extorted from him in 1985 by Bulger's longtime associate in a downtown law practice."

Jack Cloherty was the spokesman for the Boston FBI office. He lived in Southie and liked to brag that his ancestors came from the same village in County Galway as Zip Connolly's. As late as 2005, two of his siblings remained on State House payrolls controlled by Billy's political allies. In a few months, Cloherty would be retiring from the FBI, and the master of ceremonies at his farewell dinner would be Billy Bulger. Cloherty quickly issued a statement totally clearing Billy: "This investigation failed to develop any evidence of a violation within the jurisdiction of the FBI."

The state attorney general, former Congressman James Shannon, also took a pass. But it was too late to put the genie back in the bottle, especially once the Boston media learned that Billy had never even been interviewed by the authorities.

Billy returned from Europe "terribly depressed," as he later wrote. But he issued no public statements; he was confident that in the end, it would all blow over, the way it always did for him and Whitey. And indeed, events did seem to be moving in his direction. Harold Brown suddenly decided to settle out of court with Finnerty for $200,000—$1.1 million less than Finnerty had claimed he was still owed. It has always been assumed that someone, namely Whitey, made Brown the proverbial Godfather-like "offer that he couldn't refuse." Brown has steadfastly denied this, and his then attorney, Harvey Silverglate, has also maintained silence, citing attorney-client privilege.

In a final press release, Silverglate blasted the FBI and the state attorney general for the collapse of Brown's lawsuit, saying that their "extraordinary public announcements . . . seemed calculated toward, or at least had the appearance of, undermining Mr. Brown's position."

It just didn't pay to cross anyone named Bulger.

But 75 State Street wasn't quite over. In late January, the interim U.S. attorney, Jeremiah O'Sullivan, decided, under great pressure from the media, to reopen the case. The investigation was tossed back into Morris's lap. Billy retained R. Robert Popeo, one of the city's top criminal defense attorneys. Zip Connolly went to work immediately for his mentor, Billy.

Even though Zip knew that Morris had leaked Whitey's informant status to the *Globe*, he still sought him out once the federal probe was restarted. Business was business. And as much as Zip liked Whitey, he loved Billy. Zip had no qualms about soliciting Morris's aid on behalf of Billy.

"They've asked him to submit to an interview," Connolly told Morris. "What do you think?"

"He should do it," Morris told him. "The case against him

isn't very strong. I don't think he hurts himself. He does it and that's the end of the uproar."

Just to make sure, Zip sought out one of the assistant U.S. attorneys on the case, Jonathan Chiel. He begged Chiel to join him for lunch at Zip's personal table at the landmark North End restaurant, Joe Tecce's.

As soon as Chiel climbed into Zip's car, Connolly started in on him.

"The Senate president is a great man, a special person," he said. "This is crazy. I don't know what they think they're doing."

The lobbying continued once they arrived at the restaurant, but Zip's entreaties were undercut somewhat when owner Joe Tecce wandered over to greet Zip and made a crude anti-Semitic remark. Chiel was Jewish.

In his book, Billy later told a far-fetched story about how the $240,000 he accepted from Finnerty was a "loan" pending his payment for legal representation in a civil case he had been brought into by Richard McDonough, another of Sonny's sons. McDonough was a former state employee who had quit to become a lobbyist. His clients were two brothers named Quirk, and the case involved a real estate dispute in a town that Billy has variously identified as Maynard or Sudbury. At the time, Billy wrote, he was nearly broke, and when the case was settled quickly, in favor of the Quirks, Billy claimed he dreamed of buying a new car for Mary and getting a new roof.

In fact, he invested the money in the Fidelity Tax-Free Bond Account. Billy Bulger, who liked to brag on St. Patrick's Day that he could slap a tax on a galloping horse, apparently didn't much like paying those taxes himself.

Billy's interview took place February 28, 1989, in Popeo's fortieth-floor office overlooking the harbor. Present, in addition to the assistant U.S. attorneys, was Billy Bulger Jr., who after four years at two different law schools had lately been working at the Plymouth County district attorney's office for Finnerty's handpicked successor.

A memorandum of the interview was written in 1991 by an assistant attorney general, David Burns. According to Burns's report, when asked about his partnership with Finnerty, Bulger was beyond vague, saying that they had an "oral agreement" and that he "could not be any more specific regarding this agreement."

He also said he had "no documentation" to support the fee he charged the Quirk brothers. And he told the investigators that while he had "a sense" that he had other investments with Finnerty, he couldn't actually name any of them.

Burns addressed other questions raised by Billy's tangled financial relationship with Finnerty, and included Billy's responses:

• "Bulger advised that he is still confused on how he paid for his share of ownership in this property [that he owned with Finnerty]."
• "He did not know the source from which the funds originated other than it came from Finnerty's account."
• "He borrowed another $15,000 from Finnerty for an investment opportunity. Bulger could not recall what investment the $15,000 was used for by him."

The interview had been conducted secretly, but the *Globe* heard about it. They needed a second source, and so O'Neill went back to his original FBI source, Morris, who immediately confirmed it for him. It was not, Morris later said, an attempt to discredit Whitey's brother.

It didn't take long for interim U.S. attorney O'Sullivan to announce that there would be no indictment. There was no evidence, O'Sullivan explained. The joke around Boston became, if you want to hide something real good, just stick it in one of Jerry O'Sullivan's law books. Before O'Sullivan made the announcement, Popeo got a heads-up, and Billy vanished from the State House. The *Globe* wanted a photo of him, and Billy was determined not to play ball. He'd cooperated on "The Bulger Mystique," and they'd croaked him, and then again on 75 State Street. He didn't like the *Herald* either, but this time, he would punish the *Globe* by giving its tabloid competitor the photo everyone wanted. A picture of a grinning Billy standing outside his East Third Street home in the dark appeared next morning on the front page of the *Herald*.

Another Bulger had dodged another federal bullet. But the press had tasted blood, and nothing would ever be the same for Billy again.

CHAPTER 17

———

IN FEBRUARY 1989, Michael Dukakis announced he would not seek a fourth term as governor the following year. It was another terrible tactical decision, tipping his hand so far in advance of the 1990 elections. As Sonny McDonough had always said, "Lame duck is my favorite dish." Even before the Duke's announcement, he had already largely lost control of state government.

During the campaign, Billy had been only too happy to move into the vacuum of power, but now he too was wounded, by 75 State Street. Every day the papers—especially the Rupert Murdoch–owned *Herald*, which unlike the *Globe* had no stake in preserving the Democratic hegemony—were full of stories about government mismanagement and patronage run amok. Everything in state government had gone out of control. Howie Winter even returned briefly to the headlines—during his incarceration, the Dukakis administration had paid for his hair-transplant treatments. Suddenly it was open season, not just on Dukakis, but on Billy Bulger. Seemingly overnight, he had gone from Teflon to Velcro. Now everything stuck to him.

Embarrassing stories that would have once rated at most a mention in the papers' Sunday political notes columns became major revelations. His 1968 partnership with Tom Finnerty, among others, to purchase surplus land in Winthrop had gone unnoticed on the public record for more than twenty years. But suddenly the Finnerty connection made Billy's first financial score front-page news. For days the *Herald* front-paged Billy's radio station holdings in a company owned by Henry Vara, the gay-bar owner who was a cousin of the Martorano brothers. Billy tried to adjust to the new reality, "amending" his State Ethics Commission forms to include the investment, more than seven years after he purchased the stock. But Billy's feeble explanations for his partnership rang hollow.

In 1989, as always, copies of invitations to Billy's birthday fund-raiser at Anthony's Pier 4 were slipped to the papers. But reporters now noticed for the first time that the Bulger Committee shared an address and a phone number with Tom Finnerty's law office. The letter was signed, as always, by a mysterious John J. Sullivan, who did not work at Finnerty's firm. The significance of the Finnerty address was unclear, but it gave the press a chance to rehash 75 State Street again.

Dukakis seemed paralyzed, blaming his woes on radio talk show hosts as he demanded again and again that the legislature raise taxes to deal with his increasingly unbalanced state budget. The more Dukakis complained about the press, the harder he was hit, and his complaints in fact became reality. The radio talk shows, along with the *Herald*, soon were dominating the agenda. And after Dukakis himself, no one made a better piñata for the media than Billy Bulger.

Whitey's world too was changing. After serving sixteen years for the bombing of Joe Barboza's lawyer, Frank Salemme was finally out of state prison, and he was looking to make up for lost time. Even though Vinny Ferrara's crew was still operating out of Vanessa's at the Prudential Center, Salemme fancied himself the next Mafia boss of Boston. After all, Salemme fig-

ured, he'd done a lot more for the Mafia back in the 1960s than
Ferrara and his crew of second-stringers from East Boston ever
had. And then he'd kept his mouth shut all those years in
prison. Both the Mafia and the Hill owed him, big time, or so
Salemme thought.

Suddenly Stevie was spending a lot of time with Salemme,
and his son, Frank Jr. Whitey knew that Zip had asked Stevie
to keep an eye on Salemme, but Whitey still didn't appreciate
Stevie's new "special relationship." He ordered Kevin Weeks to
set up several new stashes of weapons in Southie, just in case
Stevie "wasn't around," as he put it to Weeks. It wasn't that
Whitey didn't trust his old friend Stevie; he didn't trust anybody, period.

Whitey also had another looming headache—the DEA. In
1987 District Attorney Newman Flanagan had gone to the
DEA, and offered to cut them in on a new investigation of the
cocaine dealing that was getting out of control in South
Boston. Flanagan had only one condition: They couldn't tell
the FBI, for obvious reasons. Both the local prosecutors and the
DEA recalled the leaks that had just two years earlier doomed
an earlier drug investigation, Operation Beans. During that
period, Zip Connolly was so wired into the probe that once,
when DEA agents pulled Whitey's criminal records, moments
later they received a call from Zip, demanding to know exactly
what they were up to.

Still, despite Zip's interference in Operation Beans, the cops
had actually succeeded in placing a bug inside the front
driver's-side door of Whitey's Chevrolet Caprice. But as always,
Whitey got a tip, and eventually, the DEA agents had to storm
into one of his garages to retrieve their $50,000 worth of state-
of-the-art bugs. As the feds burst into the garage, Whitey was
ripping open the door panel and Weeks was waving an electronic bug detector, trying to find out exactly where the microphone had been placed.

The agents and gangsters stared at one another for a few moments, until Whitey broke the ice.

"We're all good guys," he said. "You're the good good guys. We're the bad good guys."

A few days later, Stevie Flemmi ran into the DEA crew, and he commiserated with the cops who'd worked so hard on Operation Beans, only to come up empty. A month after he and Whitey had garroted Deborah Hussey with a rope, he calmly lectured the DEA on how they should be working with him and "Jim."

"We don't need Miranda," Stevie explained. "We can wrap a rope around anyone's neck."

By February 1989 the second DEA probe was well underway, and for once, it looked as though there hadn't been any leaks. The DEA was well aware that Zip Connolly had both a brother and an ex-roommate who worked for the drug agency. As an FBI supervisor later noted in a memo, the head of the DEA's Boston office "quietly changed the duties of both these DEA special agents so they would not become aware of this matter."

Whatever the status of any investigations, Whitey maintained a strict policy of total insulation from any dealers below Weeks in the hierarchy of the four cocaine distribution rings that now dominated the drug trade in Southie.

Running one of the crews was John "Red" Shea, a fatherless young boxer, born in 1967. In a 2003 essay, after serving a lengthy prison sentence for his crimes, Shea wrote in the third person about how he was personally recruited by Whitey.

"Whitey convinced Red that he was wasting his time with boxing," Shea wrote. "It was for dumb fucking niggers."

One day Shea got a phone call to come down to Rotary Variety, Weeks's convenience store next to the Liquor Mart. In the basement there he found two men pointing Uzis at him. From

a darkened corner, Whitey began screaming at Shea, demanding to know where one of his partners kept his money.

His associate had no money, Shea said. Then he shrugged
and told Whitey to do what he had to do. Whitey stepped out
of the shadows and threw his arm around Red.

"It was just a test," Whitey said. "The last guy I did that to,
he would have told me where Jimmy Hoffa was buried. He shit
his pants."

Red Shea could hold his mud, as Punchy McLaughlin used
to say. Whitey loved Red Shea; he would make a good drug
mule for the gang. Weeks would give him cash and Red could
travel to Miami and do business with the Cubans. Those
treacherous fucks might sell him stepped-on shit every once in
a while, but Whitey never had to worry about Red running off
with his cash. Red was a stand-up guy, which, to Whitey's way
of thinking, made him a complete patsy, especially with the
feds circling around Southie.

Frank Salemme was trying to put the Mafia back together
again, and he sometimes held court on Castle Island, in
Southie. Whitey didn't care that Salemme's mother had been
Irish, or that he knew Billy from the L Street Bathhouse when
they were both kids. About to turn sixty, Whitey just didn't
need the aggravation. If he could eliminate Salemme he was
sure that the next generation of Mafia wannabes to rise up
would be even more inept than the last two.

Zip, of course, had a plan. He would get Salemme's Mafia rivals—namely, Vinny Ferrara's crew—to kill Cadillac Frank before he could muscle in on the hoods Zip still insisted on
calling "my Irish."

On June 19, 1989, the front-page story in the *Herald* was
about Salemme's impending move to wrest control of all the
local Mafia rackets. The story, quoting anonymous federal

sources, predicted that a gang war was about to break out between the rival Mafia factions.

Two days later, as he walked through the parking lot of the
International House of Pancakes in Saugus to a sit-down with
Vinny Ferrara's guys from East Boston, someone in the back
seat of a speeding rented car leaned out the window with a machine gun and opened fire on Cadillac Frank, striking him with
at least four bullets.

Bleeding profusely, Salemme stumbled into the IHOP and
collapsed into a booth as customers began screaming. A frightened waitress screwed up enough courage to approach him.

"Can I do anything for you?"

"Yeah," he said, clutching his stomach. "Could you bring
me some more napkins, please?"

Salemme eventually recovered, but within hours, the two
Mafia factions were shooting at each other in both Massachusetts and Connecticut. As the toll mounted in Zip's own little
gang war, the Mafia bosses of New England decided that there
was only one way to end the bloodshed. They would hold a traditional Mafia initiation, to bury the hatchet between the two
warring factions.

Zip knew about it almost immediately, not from Whitey,
although he would later try to give him credit for the original tip. But Zip immediately understood that if he could bug
the initiation, this would be his big score. His new wife was
pregnant, and he wanted to retire and start making big, private sector money. If he could pull this off, record an actual
Mafia initiation ceremony, then he could fulfill his dream, of
going Hollywood, writing a screenplay about a courageous
FBI agent who single-handedly destroyed the Mafia in his
hometown.

Taping a Mafia induction. It had never been done before.

*　　*　　*

The initiation took place in Medford, on Sunday, October 29, 1989. There was one problem, though, that looked like it might force a postponement: one of the hoodlums to be made, Vinnie Federico, was in state prison, serving a sentence for killing a black guy in a dispute over a parking space in the North End. They had to spring Vinnie, because it was his sister's house they were planning to use.

In the end, Vinnie was able to get a weekend furlough, just as Willie Horton had a few years earlier. Vinnie apparently didn't realize the great import of the moment, because he brought a date, a thirty-year-old woman who worked for Mayor Ray Flynn at City Hall. When she arrived the puzzled Mafia bosses told her to go downstairs and watch TV until it was time to eat.

The house had been wired earlier, and outside the feds were everywhere. They trailed the Rhode Island guys up from Providence in an airplane. Carmen Tortora, the Mafia leg-breaker whose brother had once run for the Senate in Dorchester, spotted some heat at a phone booth in a parking lot. Despite the ominous portents, they went ahead with the ceremony anyway. It was the usual wiseguy stuff—pricked fingers, incinerated Mass cards, mumbo jumbo for the four new inductees about entering the organization alive and leaving it dead.

"Do you want it badly and desperately?" the family boss, Raymond "Rubber Lips" Patriarca, inquired of Tortora, who had most recently gone to prison for leaving death threats on a telephone answering machine. "Your mother's dying in bed, and you have to leave her because we called you. It's an emergency. You have to leave. Would you do that, Carmen?"

"Yes."

After the ceremony, they adjourned to the kitchen to a good square meal, Mafia style. Newly made man Vinnie Federico demurred. He had other plans, back at the state prison in Shirley.

"We got a Greek guy, cooks for us," he told his new brothers. "Tonight it's lobster, shrimp, and then a pineapple upside-down cake."

One of the old-timers who'd been invited from Revere couldn't believe what he was hearing.

"You call that doin' time?" he said.

Afterward, Vinny "the Animal" Ferrara, the head of the clownish Vanessa's crew, cleaned up the house. As he finished, he turned to one of his men and said, proudly, "Only the ghost knows what happened here today, by God."

Two weeks later, they were all arrested, everyone except Vinnie Federico's date, who continued working at Boston City Hall.

Whitey may have relished this latest body blow to the Mafia, but he didn't have long to savor his good fortune. As the new decade began, the DEA, the IRS, and Boston police raided a number of homes and businesses connected in one way or another to Whitey, including the South Boston Liquor Mart and Rotary Variety, as well as Red Shea's home, where they discovered a pistol and a stun gun.

The raids were a preview of what was to come. Most worrisome for Whitey was that the cops had used phone taps to develop a working knowledge of how his cocaine distribution network was managed. They knew that the street dealers all answered to one of four midlevel gangsters who, with the exception of Red Shea, more closely resembled traditional organized crime enforcers and collectors than wholesalers. Whitey of course kept no organizational charts. The only thing that mattered to him was that the street dealers kicked up, through his men, to Whitey himself.

This time the cops appeared serious. They hit the homes of all the ringleaders, in addition to raiding a warehouse on East Second Street where they discovered "miscellaneous drug packing and processing materials, scales, cutting boards, Baggies, razor blades, etc."

Actually, the raids didn't put much of a dent in Whitey's organization—the cops took only $24,000 in cash, some guns, police scanners, marijuana, and a kilo of cocaine. Newspaper reports linked several of the hoodlums whose homes were searched to a series of murders in West Broadway barrooms in 1985–86.

Despite the slowly increasing heat, Whitey continued to operate in the same fashion he always had, adroitly eliminating any other criminal who he perceived as posing even the slightest threat to him.

The next to go was Pat Nee. In 1990, he'd just finished serving four years in federal prison for the IRA gunrunning operation that had ended with John McIntyre's murder. Nee was smart, and still only forty-five, and although Whitey had worked with him for years, he had never forgotten how Nee had once been part of the crew that had hunted him back in the days when he worked for Donnie Killeen.

On parole, Nee was looking for work, and Whitey steered him to a tough crew of armored car robbers headed by a Lower End hood named Jazzbo Joyce. Whitey neglected to mention to Nee that the FBI had planted an informer, one of Whitey's loanshark victims, in the gang, and that Jazzbo's next job, in Abington, would be his last. Instead, Whitey gave Pat Nee a machine gun and wished him well in his new venture.

When the Southie crew arrived in Abington, the FBI was waiting for them. Surrounded by cops, Pat Nee didn't try to use the machine gun; if he had, he'd have been killed, because Whitey had removed its firing pin before giving it to Nee.

What Nee didn't learn until later was that while he had been in prison, Congress had passed a new law—use of a machine gun during the commission of a federal crime was now punishable by an additional thirty years in prison, on and after whatever other sentences were imposed.

Whitey would never again have to worry about Pat Nee. He

was going away for a very long time. (Ultimately, Nee's conviction on the machine gun charge was thrown out; a judge decided that if a weapon had been disabled, it was hardly fair for the government to still refer to it as a machine gun. Whitey had been, as they say at the State House, too cute by half.)

In 1990, Billy would have a serious opponent for the first time since 1970. Republican Dr. John DeJong, a thirty-four-year-old Back Bay veterinarian, quickly got a taste of hardball Boston politics when the president of Tufts University, Dr. Jean Mayer, called him with concerns that DeJong's candidacy would cost the veterinary school, from which DeJong had graduated, its state grants.

DeJong leaked word of the conversation to the press. Billy denied knowing that DeJong was a graduate of the school. Trying to appear nonplussed by the challenge, Billy came up with a new slogan: "The state may be going to the dogs, but this is no time to call in a veterinarian."

But Billy wasn't taking any chances. A straw candidate, Janie DuPass quickly entered the race, to dilute the anti-incumbent vote. Not only did her name sound like DeJong's, but also like that of a Southie political activist named Janie DuWors. DuPass lived on a $501 disability check, in Roxbury, and yet three-quarters of the signatures on the nomination papers she filed to get onto the ballot came from Southie, including eleven from East Third Street, Billy's home street. Her nomination papers were signed by people with such fine Bulger-associated names as Joyce, Flaherty, Nee, and Gill. The signatures had been gathered by Billy's operatives. It was one of the oldest tricks in the urban political playbook, and if the Bulgers could have found another person named John DeJong, no doubt his name would have gone onto the ballot too.

"Something," DeJong understated, "is very fishy here."

*   *   *

Billy knew that someday soon he would retire, and he wanted his oldest son, Billy Jr., to succeed him in the Senate. Eventually, if Billy Jr. didn't succeed Joe Moakley in Congress, Billy's dream was to see his namesake follow in his footsteps by becoming president of the Senate.

But to assure Billy Jr.'s ascension to Senate president, Billy would need a transitional figurehead to serve as president while Billy Jr. learned the ropes. This regentlike figure would have to be someone who would understand that he would be expected to step aside when the time came.

Enter Tom Birmingham, the son of Billy's old friend and client, Jackie Birmingham. Young Birmingham had a well-known name in Chelsea and Charlestown—his uncle, also named Tom Birmingham, was a local gangster who had been shot to death in a rooming house in 1969. A graduate of Harvard Law School, young Tom had unsuccessfully tried to unseat Democratic Senator Franny Doris of Revere in 1988.

When it came time to run for reelection, Doris went out and collected his nomination signatures as if he would be running for another term. No one else filed, except Tom Birmingham, who was left as the only candidate on the ballot when Doris suddenly announced his retirement a few hours before the deadline for filing nomination papers. Then, after his retirement from the Senate, Doris took a high-paying job at the MBTA.

Billy had his heir apparent.

Next Billy needed a candidate for governor. He couldn't afford any loose cannons who actually might think they were running the state. Billy quickly got behind John Silber, the feisty sixty-four-year-old president of Boston University who had become a fixture at the St. Patrick's Day breakfasts. He and Billy formed a two-man admiration society, perhaps because Silber had at least as large a chip on his shoulder as Billy. Born and raised in Texas, Silber too had always felt like the odd man out—a withered right arm had kept him out first out of schoolboy athletics and then World War II. He became an academic, and after being forced out of his job as the dean of the College of Arts and Sciences at the University of Texas because he was "too liberal," Silber had moved north in the early 1970s to take over a moribund Boston University. He'd saved BU almost by himself, but for twenty years he chafed at always having to play second fiddle to the school across the river, Harvard.

After eight years of Mike Dukakis's stifling political correctness, the voters were ready for Silber's brutal candor. Soon after he announced his candidacy, Silber wondered aloud why so many welfare-collecting immigrants had arrived in Lowell "from the tropical climes."

That was the first "Silber shocker." Many more would follow. He would suggest that elderly people who were "ripe" owed it to everyone else to die and get out of the way. He said that any woman over the age of twenty-five was over the hill.

As a candidate for governor, Silber's greatest albatross was his attempt to position himself as the "outsider" in the Democratic field while running with the complete support of Senate President Bulger.

"Billy Bulger is not a crook," Silber would say again and again.

At the Democratic state convention in June, Silber needed to get the votes of 15 percent of the delegates in order to qualify for the September ballot. It was close, but Billy twisted enough arms to get Silber over the 15 percent hurdle and onto the ballot. Billy figured his man was now a shoo-in.

"He'll be inaugurated in January," Billy told friends, "and he'll invade Rhode Island in February."

The DEA and the Boston and State Police started arresting Whitey's cocaine dealers Thursday night, August 9. Earlier that day, Zip Connolly had been apoplectic. He had sought out Jonathan Chiel—the same assistant U.S. attorney he'd taken to lunch when he thought Billy was about to be indicted during the 75 State Street scandal. Now he burst into Chiel's office again, with a similar question.

"Is Whitey Bulger being indicted today?" he asked. There were rumors out there in the Republican campaigns, he said. Chiel hemmed and hawed until Zip finally left, but in fact Whitey had skated again. They'd even gotten a court order to monitor his cell phone, but Whitey had either gotten a tip about the tap or understood enough about the new technology not to incriminate himself.

"The case, we believe, was compromised," Chiel testified later.

Not so lucky were fifty-one of Whitey's dealers. Among the first to be collared was Red Shea, as he stood on the corner in front of the D Street Deli, one of Kevin Weeks's old joints. He made a break for it, screaming, "I'm a working man!"

He was apparently referring to his public sector job at the Boston Housing Authority.

A few hours later, after midnight, the cops grabbed Thomas "T.K." Cahill. He was sleeping through his overnight shift at the city Department of Public Works yard on Frontage Road, and had been expected to report for work the next morning at his other public sector job at the Massachusetts Water Resources Authority, where the personnel director was the wife of a state senator loyal to Billy.

In case anyone still doubted Whitey's involvement in cocaine trafficking in his hometown, the DEA put everything onto the record at an afternoon press conference.

"For years the Bulger organization has told people there's no drugs in Southie," said the DEA assistant special agent in charge, "that Southie boys are not involved in drugs, that we throw drug dealers out of here. These arrests show that that's not true. These arrests show the people have been had by James Whitey Bulger."

The arrested dealers ranged from drug-addled drunks to players just below Weeks in Whitey's hierarchy. At the John W. McCormack Federal Courthouse in Post Office Square, magistrates recorded their vital statistics. A large percentage of them had public patronage jobs. Many of the dealers were either on disability pensions or workmen's comp. In the vernacular of Boston, they were hacks.

Among those arrested was the proprietor of the Dog Room, Eddie MacKenzie. Along with some of the other higher-level dealers, Eddie Mac was shipped off to the federal penitentiary in Danbury where Raymond "Rubber Lips" Patriarca, the boss of the reeling New England Mafia, was awaiting trial on racketeering charges stemming from the Guild Street Mafia inductions ten months earlier. Patriarca called Eddie Mac over, and without even introducing himself, told MacKenzie: "You know why you're here, don't you? . . . You got ratted out by your boy Whitey. He's been snitching for years."

Rubber Lips didn't have the story exactly straight; Whitey had been snitching for years, but he hadn't directly ratted Eddie Mac out. He just hadn't given Eddie Mac any warning about the busts he had to have known were about to come down. In the final days, Eddie Mac claimed to have been paying Whitey, through his collectors, more than $20,000 a week. For that kind of money, Eddie Mac didn't get much protection.

John Silber easily won the primary, just as Billy had predicted he would. In the general election, he would be running against William Weld, the former U.S. attorney who'd put so many of former mayor Kevin White's crew behind bars, and then later, as an assistant attorney general in Washington, became the prosecutor to whom Joe Murray had tried to funnel information on Whitey.

As the leaves began to turn, Weld found himself trailing Silber in all the polls. He had to find an issue, quickly, and since the electorate had apparently become inured to "Silber shockers," Weld decided to concentrate on the two Bulger brothers, specifically, the fact that so many of Whitey's cocaine dealers had public jobs while the state teetered on the edge of bankruptcy.

Whitey and Billy would be the twin symbols of the corruption and profligacy of the last eight years. Billy's thirty years in the legislature were suddenly an afterthought; his only identity was as the brother of "cocaine dealer Whitey Bulger."

The Republican state chairman called a press conference to demand that Billy publicly address the issue of drug trafficking in South Boston.

"He may very well be condoning it," Billy's GOP opponent John DeJong said. "I just think he better open his eyes and answer the questions the people in the district and the state have about what's going on right under his own nose."

The Republicans unleashed a tough series of ads, referring to the "Silber-Bulger" ticket. Another spot highlighted Weld's career as a "corruption fighter," and noted his crackdown on "disability insurance scams," a type of crime now almost exclusively associated with Southie gangsters on public payrolls.

Even the Republican candidate for treasurer, Joe Malone, vowed to "clean up" the Massachusetts Convention Center Authority. The GOP theme was, if you were a Democrat, you were a Bulger Democrat. The short-tempered Silber was particularly incensed about being continually linked to organized crime and cocaine dealing.

"I get fed up with being told that if I know Billy Bulger I must be some sort of crook," Silber said at a meeting with supporters at the World Trade Center in October. "Billy Bulger is not a crook."

Weld hung in, holding his own in the debates against Silber. Still, it appeared his spirited effort would fall short. But then Silber did an interview with the top female TV anchor in Boston, who asked him a standard question about what he considered his weaknesses. Silber lost his temper and began yelling at her.

When the segment aired, Silber immediately collapsed in the polls, and he and Billy were forced to try to soften their hard images in the final hours of the campaign. Billy even took questions from the State House press corps, complaining about his treatment since 75 State Street.

"I've been Willie Horton–ized," he said.

On election night, Billy easily prevailed over DeJong by a 63 to 37 margin; in the end, he hadn't even needed DuPass. Otherwise, it was a Republican night across the commonwealth. Weld won handily enough in the suburbs to overcome Silber's edge in the cities. Massachusetts would have its first Republican governor since 1974. In the treasurer's race, another Republican, Joe Malone, cruised to victory, and would replace Billy's friend Bob Crane, who was retiring after twenty-six years in office.

But most importantly, from Billy's perspective, nine of his incumbent Democratic senators were knocked off, most by Republican novices, one of whom was a Bible salesman. The Taunton incumbent who was ousted by the Bible salesman quipped to reporters: "Tell him he won't sell too many Bibles in the Senate."

The only bright spot for Billy was that the new lieutenant governor would be Paul Cellucci, a Republican state senator from Hudson who had never crossed Billy. But even that was overshadowed by the fact that 75 State Street was once again returning to haunt him. With the future appearing so uncertain, Billy called in one final chit from that lamest of lame ducks, Michael Dukakis. Billy wanted a district court judgeship for his chief aide, Paul Mahoney, an undistinguished career coatholder.

But the long knives were out for Mahoney. Harvey Silverglate, Harold Brown's first lawyer, had never released his findings about Billy's financial records because Brown, his client, had ordered him not to. But now Silverglate had a clean shot at one of Billy's closest associates. Also appalled by Dukakis's final descent into backroom horse-trading was Alan Dershowitz, the Harvard Law School professor who had also briefly worked for Harold Brown.

Silverglate and Dershowitz waged a public campaign in their usual fashion, bombarding the *Globe* with letters and statements and feeding information to Channel 2's *Ten O'Clock News*. Finally, on December 5, 1990, at Paul Mahoney's confirmation hearing, as Silverglate and Dershowitz waited their turn to speak, Billy Bulger pushed his way into the packed hearing room with his entourage—a couple of his sons, diminutive Senate aide Eddie Phillips, and a few lobbyists looking ahead to the future. Billy pointed directly at Dershowitz and Silverglate and shouted: "The two biggest liars in Massachusetts . . . a true, true conniver . . . exceedingly crafty . . . vindictive . . . very manipulative. . . . They are reckless and they are liars and they have no moral constraints upon them." He pointed at them.

"Look at them!" he said. "Look at them! They are beneath contempt." He paused. "Am I making myself clear?" Another pause. "These two are murderers, murderers of reputation. Too many have put up with them for too long."

In the end, the vote to confirm Mahoney was 8–0.

Almost immediately, Billy was accused of blatant anti-Semitism against the two Jewish lawyers. However, Jewish community leaders, perhaps mindful of their agencies' appropriations in future state budgets, were soon trotted out to absolve Billy of the charge of anti-Semitism. No one who was there in the chambers that day took their exoneration seriously.

*   *   *

About a week after the election, Joe Malone, the Republican treasurer-elect, got a call from Zip Connolly. The famous FBI agent wanted to sit down, one-on-one, at Joe Tecce's. Although Malone had, like Weld, run against the Beacon Hill establishment, Billy wanted to co-opt him. As treasurer, Malone would be the chairman of, among other things, the Convention Center Authority, the Lottery Commission, and the Retirement Board. Billy needed to be friends with Joe Malone.

Zip had just announced he was retiring from the FBI to join Boston Edison. It had seemed a hasty decision, but the moment was propitious—Jack Kehoe, the ex-FBI agent who was vice president of security, was about to retire. It was a natural fit for Billy's friend; Boston Edison was a state-regulated utility, and Billy was the state.

Malone, age thirty-five, sat across the table from Zip and watched him pour a glass of red wine. Zip got right to the point. It was his standard what-I-owe-Billy rap.

"If it wasn't for Billy Bulger," he said, "I wouldn't have gotten into BC, I wouldn't have gotten into the FBI, and I wouldn't have my job at the Edison."

Malone took it all in. Billy, of course, would control his budget. He had been wounded in the election, but he still controlled twenty-four of the forty votes in the Senate.

"He can either be a great ally or a bad enemy," Zip said, "and you wouldn't want him to be a bad enemy, trust me."

Just as he hadn't been able to publicly attend his mother's funeral back in 1980, Whitey had to miss Zip Connolly's retirement dinner at Joe Tecce's. Whitey bid Zip farewell in his own fashion—he gave the crooked FBI agent $10,000 cash, as "severance," Stevie Flemmi would testify in 2005. Over the years, Zip had taken more than $200,000 from the Mob, and now he would be feted at Tecce's by the political and law enforcement leaders of Boston. A videotape of the farewell roast would be given to Whitey, so that he could watch the entire event, complete with cutaway shots of Zip's entire family, not just his brother, Jim, the DEA agent, but also his mobbed-up brother-in-law, Arthur Gianelli, sitting at the table directly behind the rostrum, clapping politely as one law enforcement official after another offered fawning tributes to Zip. Connolly's young second wife, Liz, daubed tears from her eyes as she heard her husband described in glowing terms by one colleague after another. She had given birth to a son the previous year, and was now visibly pregnant again, this time with twins.

The master of ceremonies was not Billy, but FBI agent Nick Gianturco, the agent whose life Whitey had "saved" back in the days when he was working undercover as a fence named "Nick Giarro."

Gianturco would later succeed Zip as head of security for Boston Edison, just as Zip was succeeding former agent Jack Kehoe, who was also in attendance.

Gianturco mentioned the Prince Street wiretaps, and how while other agents showed up dressed casually, Zip would appear in "tan slacks, Gucci loafers, velvet velour shirt open at the chest with enough gold showing to be the envy of most members of the Gambino Crime Family."

Gianturco did not mention that Zip's nickname among the younger agents was now "Cannoli," for the very reasons he had just outlined.

The microphone was quickly handed over to Billy Bulger, who treated the occasion, as he did most, at least when he was among friends, as a smaller version of the St. Patrick's Day breakfast, using his numbingly familiar stock one-liners.

Eventually Billy began quoting from the classics, beginning with Aristotle: "Without friends no one would choose to live, though he had all other goods."

"Who's the personification of friendship in our community

other than John Connolly?" he asked. "He's a splendid human being. He's a good pal."

A good pal—Billy's ultimate accolade.

"The Roman philosopher Seneca said 'Loyalty is the holiest good in the human heart.' John Connolly is the personification of loyalty, not only to his old friends and not only to the job that he holds but also to the highest principles. He's never forgotten them."

Diane Kottmyer, the chief of the organized crime strike force and a future Superior Court judge, gave him a gag gift of a bottle of wine and then added: "John, they wanted me to say that that bottle came courtesy of South Boston Liquors, but I won't say that."

At which point Zip, knowing full well that this bizarre gathering was being videotaped for the edification and amusement of his paymaster, leaned in close to the microphone and said, "No finer liquor store in the commonwealth."

One by one the various connected federal and local cops trudged up to the microphone. Jack Cloherty, who had issued the statement clearing Billy in 75 State Street. Dennis Condon. City Councilor Dapper O'Neil, Zip's old roommate Jack Kelly from the DEA, Eddie Walsh from the police department—all paid their respects, one after the other. Then came Dennis O'Callaghan, the number-two agent in the Boston office, who felt compelled to mention his family's roots in County Cork. He read from the letter Boston Special Agent in Charge Thomas Hughes had sent to Boston Edison: "John Connolly's service to the FBI was the essence of its motto: 'Fidelity, Bravery, Integrity,' and he will be missed."

Then O'Callaghan mentioned Zip's "loyalty to his roots in Southie, loyalty to his family and those who he calls friends."

In less than four years, Zip would show his loyalty to those friends by getting O'Callaghan to warn him of Stevie's and Whitey's impending indictments. In the end, O'Callaghan presented him with a chair—"something for you to sit in and rock the children."

Zip picked up the chair and stared at the bottom. It wasn't a rocking chair.

Finally it was time for Zip to say a few words, and he concentrated his remarks on a predictable subject: the greatness of Billy Bulger.

"He is a special, special person," Zip said. "He taught me the value of public service."

He talked about "working" for Billy, and how "proud" he was to call him a friend. Then he decided to dust off one of Billy's favorite Latin quotations, in English of course. This one came from the satirist Juvenal: "Count it the greatest sin to prefer life to honor and for the sake of life to lose what makes life worth having."

Zip chose not to mention what is perhaps Juvenal's most famous saying, which seemed even more appropriate for the gathering of these public officials in the back room of Joe Tecce's.

"Who is to guard the guards themselves?"

CHAPTER 18

It was 1991, and Whitey's criminal career was winding down. He would turn sixty-two in September and his cocaine rings had been busted up. But he was still the king of Southie. Easy rested the head that wore this crown—there was nobody coming up behind him the way he'd come up behind Donnie Killeen. Kevin Weeks was not a threat, nor was Kevin O'Neil, especially now that he'd ballooned to four hundred pounds. As for the rest of them—Red Shea, Eddie Mac, "Polecat" Moore, John Cherry—they hadn't really been gangsters so much as they'd been ex-boxers and barroom brawlers who had become cocaine dealers. And now they were imprisoned cocaine dealers.

Everybody, it seemed, was in the can. Except for Whitey and Stevie.

Whitey hadn't murdered anyone since Deborah Hussey in 1985. Since being released from Leavenworth in March 1965, he'd never gone that long without killing somebody. Now he carried a senior citizen discount card from the MBTA. He loved cable TV—he was a sucker for all those PBS and Discovery Channel specials on World War II. At the end of the episode, the announcer would mention a toll-free number to call if you wanted to order the video, and Whitey always did.

Money was not a problem, to say the least. In the late 1980s, when the cocaine money was flowing, *Boston* magazine estimated his net worth at $50 million.

There had been so much cash coming in that Whitey set up what he called an X fund, to handle payoffs and other emergency expenditures, such as bribes to FBI agents. By the late 1980s, the amount of cash in the X fund never dipped below $100,000.

Whitey had also come up with a way to establish a record of legitimate income, by continually flipping his properties. He'd "buy" one of Weeks's lots or condos for $40,000, say, and then turn around and sell it on the same day to O'Neil, or Stevie's mother, Mary Flemmi, for $400,000. He would give them a "mortgage," and they'd pay off the note, monthly. It was the Bank of Whitey, and no one ever missed a payment. Three years after Whitey went on the lam, Kevin O'Neil was still dutifully depositing $4,600 a month in Whitey's account at the South Boston Savings Bank. Mary Flemmi was particularly useful in Whitey and Stevie's money-laundering schemes—the feds are always reluctant to hound someone's mother, especially if she is over eighty.

O'Neil was important too. As the owner of record of Triple O's, O'Neil was in a great position to launder cash, plus he had the nearby newsstand (with a Lottery license) as well as a number of tenants in the small apartments above the barroom. So if the Internal Revenue Service ever asked O'Neil how he was paying off those mortgages to the Bank of Whitey, he could show them a steady stream of income.

But by 1991, the newspapers had figured out that property-flip scam. Whitey needed a new way to show income.

Pat Linskey had long since moved out of Southie, to Hanover. Most people had forgotten his arrest, along with Kevin O'Neil, for the fatal stabbing of a black man on D Street back in 1968. In a 1970 trial, Linskey was acquitted, as was a third defendant, Tommy Nee, who later became a hitman and was eventually shot to death outside his West Broadway bar in 1986 in a dispute over $10. But Pat Linskey still hung out with Whitey.

The way the story was told later, at Christmas 1990 Linskey bought ten season's tickets to Mass Millions. Nine of them, the losing ones, he gave to various family and friends. But the one that would turn out to be the $14.3 million winner he would later claim he just happened to give to his brother Michael one day when a bunch of the guys were all lounging around Rotary Variety.

And that, he said, was when they came up with the plan to split the dough if they got lucky.

Seven months later, in July 1991, the lucky 8-15-32-35-40-42 ticket hit. Michael Linskey posed for a front-page photo as he claimed his first installment. He took half the prize, and the three friends from Rotary Variety—Whitey, Kevin Weeks, and Michael's brother Pat—split the other half.

Even if he could have taken a lump-sum payout, which wasn't allowed under state Lottery regulations, Whitey would have opted for the twenty years of annual checks—$89,000 every July 1, after taxes. He wanted the paper trail. He could buy a lot of World War II videotapes every year with $89,000 per year, tax-free.

However he arranged it, Whitey ended up with a share of a $14.3 million jackpot. And what made it even sweeter was that it was also a major embarrassment for the new Republican treasurer, Joe Malone, one of whose duties was managing the Lottery Commission.

It also gave Whitey's hagiographers at the *Globe* a chance to burnish the Bulgers' increasingly tarnished reputations. Most of the reporters had long understood what Whitey was, but some columnists refused to concede that perhaps he wasn't quite the Robin Hood they'd always portrayed him as. After he hit the Lottery, the gullible *Globe* columnist Mike Barnicle insisted that Whitey would likely now be handing out money to down-and-outers at St. Augustine's, and then added that Whitey had nothing to do with Billy "other than saying 'Pass the gravy' during occasional Sunday dinners." Another of the Bulger sycophants at the *Globe* recounted the old fable about how Whitey "has delivered . . . beatings to people accused of dealing drugs to Southie youths."

The problem was, after the cocaine busts of 1990, nobody believed such half-baked fiction anymore. And now, by cashing in that winning Mass Millions ticket, Whitey had made himself national news.

He had become, for lack of a better term, a legend in his own time. And as the late crime novelist John D. MacDonald once observed, "People who become legends in their own time usually don't have much time left."

Until 1991, Whitey had always understood his limitations. He had remained in the background, a "squirrel," as Frank Salemme called him. He had never tried to muscle into anything outside his own natural sphere of influence.

To claim his winnings, Whitey had traveled to Lottery headquarters in Braintree, where a surveillance camera scanned the lobby. Suddenly, every news organization in America had access to videotape or stills of him, in a white Red Sox cap, wearing sunglasses. Part of his mystique of menace had always been his inaccessibility. Grainy black-and-white police surveillance photos of him were few and far between. Only those who lived in Southie, or drove by the liquor store, had known what Whitey actually looked like. Now he was suddenly a celebrity.

Brand-new photos of Whitey ran at the top of the front page of *USA Today*. He was perhaps the nation's second-best-known gangster, after John Gotti. Reading about Whitey's Mass Millions score in *GQ* a few months later, Gotti grew so angry that he threw the magazine to the floor of his jail cell.

"That Irish puke," Gotti said. "What the fuck is going on?"

At the Justice Department in Washington, the same question was finally being asked, if in a more decorous fashion. The old wall that had protected Whitey for so many years was finally crumbling.

Two weeks after Whitey won Mass Millions, one of his boxers-turned-cocaine-dealer, Paul "Polecat" Moore, was sentenced to nine years and one month in prison. He had no intention of ratting out his boss. He was from Southie, after all, and he went way back with Whitey's crew. Back in 1974, when Kevin O'Neil had been looking for a bouncer at Triple O's, Polecat was the first guy he'd offered the job to. Polecat turned him down, Kevin Weeks got the job instead, and the rest was history—at least in Southie, which was the only place that mattered to Polecat.

During a recess at his trial, Moore was handed a subpoena to appear a week later before a federal grand jury investigating Whitey.

Polecat planned to keep his mouth shut. That way, Whitey would take care of his family. Or so he'd always been told.

The drug dealers had always been the ones Whitey had worried would flip. But they stood up, at least at first. They were frightened of Whitey—they were younger, by and large, and they'd grown up in Southie listening to the stories about how anyone who crossed Whitey disappeared, even women. The dealers didn't have enough money to run away for long, and they were certainly savvy enough not to trust the cops.

But Whitey never figured he'd have a problem with the Jewish bookies. In the early 1990s, though, they started going down hard. A lot of them were laundering money through a bar in Chelsea under the Tobin Bridge. It was known as Heller's Café. First the U.S. Attorney's Office, working with the State Police rather than the FBI, went after the bookies, some of whom were paying Whitey and Stevie as much as $3,000 a month for protection. The feds raided their bank safe-deposit boxes, and in November 1992 eight of the Heller's Café bookies were indicted on money-laundering charges. Several decided to cut deals and go into the Witness Protection Program, in return for which they had to spell out for a new federal grand jury how much "rent" they'd had to pay Whitey and Stevie over the years. A few of the bookies balked at rolling over, at least at first, but then the feds began denying them bail on the money-laundering charges, claiming they were in danger, which in fact they probably were. Speaking with them, Flemmi always mentioned the name "Barney Bloom"—a bookie whose murder in the 1970s remained unsolved.

After a few months at Allenwood, they'd be brought back to Boston and given a choice: answer the grand jury's questions or have another eighteen months tacked on, even before their trials, for contempt.

"The government is turning everyone into rats," one bookie said in open court. "It'll become Russia."

A few weeks later, he flipped. In the end, they would all testify.

Next, extortion victims started coming forward. The feds found a bar owner who had been threatened by Whitey in the back room of Rotary Variety, for not coming through with a promised bank loan. Once he got the bar owner behind closed doors, Whitey pulled his trusty knife out of his boot.

"You fuckster!" Whitey screamed at him, stabbing empty cardboard boxes with the knife before finally putting it to the bar owner's throat. "You fuckster!"

The bar owner was shaken down for $35,000 cash before he'd had enough. He went, not to the FBI, but the U.S. Attorney's Office. Two straight FBI agents were assigned to wire the bar owner and send him back to the store. Suddenly, Whitey

refused to meet, or speak with him. As usual, he'd gotten a
heads-up, from the FBI.

Stories began appearing in both newspapers about the grand
jury's ongoing probe. And yet, this time, unlike just a few
years earlier, none of the witnesses vanished, unless it was into
the Witness Protection Program. John Morris was belatedly
getting his wish: There would apparently be no more Brian
Hallorans, or John McIntyres, or Richie Castuccis. Either
Whitey no longer had the juice out on the street, or he just
didn't care enough to kill anybody anymore.

Finally, the drug dealers started turning on Whitey. Polecat
Moore was the first to roll. When the bank foreclosed on his
family's home and no one stepped forward with the cash to save
it, Polecat was treed. He followed the Jewish bookies into the
Witness Protection Program.

By 1994, Whitey had become concerned about the grand jury
and the dangerous drift events were taking. Under the Racketeer Influenced and Corrupt Organizations Act, the feds didn't
need a lot to put an organized crime figure behind bars for
good. All they had to do was prove a couple of recent crimes—
"predicate acts"—and that would be enough to establish what
was called a "pattern of racketeering." And to prove the pattern
they could bring up any crime that the criminal had ever committed. Gerry Angiulo, the Mafia underboss, had always ful-
minated against RICO, but it had been used to put him away
for keeps. The annual attempt by local police to get a Massachusetts version of the RICO statute on the books was always
blocked in the legislature.

But with Zip in retirement, the feds finally appeared serious
about taking Whitey and Stevie down. Stevie, though, seemed
strangely unconcerned about the ongoing probe. Whitey had
been on the lam before, and had been pinched after only a
month or so. Stevie, on the other hand, had had no problems

during his four years as a fugitive, but then, he'd been protected by both the Mafia and the FBI. Stevie appeared to have no understanding of how much the world had changed in twenty-five years. As far as Stevie was concerned, it was business as usual. He had a teenage girlfriend who was pregnant, and he also traveled with a slightly older Asian companion by the name of Jian Fen Hu. One of his two sons by Marion Hussey was about to open a restaurant on High Street, Schooner's, an enterprise in which Stevie was taking a great deal of interest.

In the summer of 1994, Stevie took his annual summer vacation to Montreal, to visit old friends. Whitey hit the road too, but unlike Stevie, he was a man on a mission. With Theresa Stanley in tow, he made the Grand Tour of Europe, often stopping off at banks to open a safe-deposit box. In London, he listed his brother Billy as the person to notify in case of a problem, giving the bank Billy's home address and telephone number. Filling out the forms, Whitey used his own name. His alias, "Thomas Baxter," was a seventeen-year work in progress, and he didn't want to tip anybody to it if he didn't have to.

Whitey had been in jams like this before, but somehow he'd always managed to wriggle out of them. The difference was that, in the past, he'd always been able to give the feds someone higher up on the Mob totem pole—from Howie Winter and Gerry Angiulo all the way to Frank Salemme.

Now, though, Whitey was at the top of the heap. The Mafia was finished, and there was nobody of consequence left in Somerville or Charlestown either. Whitey was now the Man, Mr. Big. There was nobody left to rat out. It was, finally, Whitey's turn to take the fall.

CHAPTER 19

BILLY HIT IT OFF ALMOST immediately with the new Republican governor, William Floyd Weld. It was not a friendship anyone would have predicted, but as 1991 began, Billy needed friends. The 1990 elections had been as much a referendum on him as on Dukakis, and he had been drubbed, his Senate majority decimated in the wake of the 75 State Street scandal and the revelations about his brother's cocaine dealing.

His St. Patrick's Day breakfast that March was a disaster. It was still televised statewide, but the no-shows included both U.S. senators, the new House speaker, and the new attorney general. Mayor Ray Flynn stopped by for all of eight minutes. Every missing politician was needled, of course. On the subject of the just concluded first Gulf War, Billy said, "It was touch-and-go for a while. John Kerry didn't know which side he was going to go with."

Weld made an appearance, though, and even wore a green button that said, in white letters, "I'm a friend of President Bulger." As Weld arrived, Billy looked like a drowning man who'd just been tossed a life preserver.

Unlike Joe Malone or John Kerry, Weld treated Billy with respect. Weld even read an item from the paper, that *The New Yorker* had commissioned a profile on William M. Bulger. Billy beamed; it was something he couldn't have mentioned himself on the television audience, lest he be accused of patting himself on the back.

Once Weld departed, though, the breakfast disintegrated. Billy had no proper foils left. All he could do was sing obscure, sad Irish ballads, and soon enough, the atmosphere in the hall had become as self-pitying and morose as the host.

At 12:36, Billy said, "This is awful." Then he told a joke about gondolas.

"You've heard it before?" he said. "Well, you'd better laugh anyway." At 12:39, as flop sweat formed on his brow, he threw up another prayer of a joke, and it clanged off the rim.

"Oh God," he said, "why am I doing this?"

Even in that grim winter of 1991, Billy was again scheming to restore the old balance of power, that is, the balance where he had all the power. Fortunately for Billy, Weld didn't seem to grasp how rare, and important, it was for the Senate to have sixteen Republican members. If Weld could maintain any party discipline, and he could, he could sustain any veto. That meant that, with his line item veto, Weld could control the $15 billion state budget. And that made Bill Weld, not Billy Bulger, the real governor.

Billy now seemed resigned to his public fate—he would forever be known as a mere "legislative leader," the Corrupt Midget, brother of a gangster. Perhaps as time went on, he could somewhat restore his reputation, at least in some quarters. But most people outside the State House, he understood, would never accept him, nor would the media, which had increasingly turned against him after 75 State Street. Striking a reformer's pose at this late date was simply too absurd to consider. So Billy went back to some of his old ways. He again began openly taking honoraria. What did he have to lose by grabbing, say, $5,021 from Pfizer for an appearance?

At home, in Southie, he struck a more combative pose. Billy's campaign chairman, John J. Sullivan, would write his customary letter exhorting Billy's friends to attend his annual birthday party (his fifty-seventh) at Anthony's Pier 4 and celebrate his victory . . . over John DeJong.

"Against the thundering editorialists and their media accomplices," wrote Sullivan, in a tone not unlike Billy's own, "the voices of his neighbors and supporters were heard with emphatic clarity. . . . Hence, our celebration will be especially gratifying this year as we assemble to honor Senator Bulger."

And for Billy, there was still the occasional punishment to be meted out. Congressman Chester Atkins, Billy's former Ways and Means chairman, had turned against him in the wake of 75 State Street. Now it was time again for a congressional redistricting, and for Massachusetts to lose a seat. Atkins was in deep trouble. He'd been humiliated when he was publicly identified in the House banking scandal as one of the top check-kiters in Congress. And his former Senate aide Mark Ferber was headed to federal prison in a massive kickback scheme he'd masterminded as a private-sector adviser to several state agencies. If he had to run against an incumbent, Atkins wanted a shot at another weak check-bouncing incumbent, Joe Early of Worcester.

Atkins wanted to rid himself of most of his own district— namely, the Merrimack Valley, and annex Worcester. Through intermediaries he extended the olive branch to his old boss. But Billy made it clear that he was through being the fall guy for every crude power play on Beacon Hill. Billy insisted that before he could even consider gerrymandering the two districts into one, he would need Chester to publicly ask for it. Billy was baiting a trap for Chester, and Atkins was desperate enough to fall right into it.

Chester dutifully claimed that he felt more kinship with Worcester than with the Merrimack Valley, and those were the insincere words Billy had been waiting to hear. Billy immediately announced that no matter what changes in the map were required by the congressional redistricting, the "integrity" of the Valley would be maintained. Chester was shocked at his former boss's move; most other politicians were amused that Atkins hadn't realized that he was being set up.

In the Democratic primary the next year, Chester would be crushed two to one by a young assistant district attorney from Lowell making his first bid for public office, Marty Meehan.

The next foe of Billy's to be taken down a notch was Christopher Lydon, the former *New York Times* reporter who was now the anchor of *The 10 O'Clock News* on the local public TV station, WGBH. Lydon and one of his reporters, David Boeri, had been relentless on the subject of 75 State Street, and Lydon had gone out of his way to humiliate Dukakis in a live interview after the lame-duck governor nominated Paul Mahoney for his judgeship in 1990.

Every year, Channel 2 sponsored a popular imported wine tasting for its well-heeled audience. For the tasting, Channel 2 needed a one-day liquor license, and all such licenses had to be approved by the legislature.

In 1991, the legislature initially balked at rubber-stamping WGBH's liquor license, the way it would have for almost any other home-rule petition that came before it.

In the spring of 1991, *The 10 O'Clock News* was canceled. The one-day liquor license for Channel 2 was then approved.

As he had promised during the 1990 campaign, the new attorney general, Luther Scott Harshbarger, did undertake a new investigation of 75 State Street. The results of his office's probe were released in September 1991, and the material, if not enough for an indictment, was still damning.

The investigators pointed out that "notwithstanding Bulger's assertion that he repaid" the entire $240,000 to Finnerty, "substantially all of those funds were later returned from that trust to Bulger over the next 12 months." As an example, they cited a $61,000 check issued by the St. Botolph Trust, to which Billy had repaid his supposed loan, on June 6, 1986. The check was made out to Thomas Finnerty, P.C. Three days later, Finnerty issued a check for $61,000 payable to "William Bulger." And Billy then deposited the money in the same Fidelity municipal bond account "which 10 months earlier had been used to accept the original St. Botolph checks which Bulger later repaid."

The investigators also looked into other transactions between Finnerty, Bulger, and Richard McDonough. In addition to their work for the Quirk brothers, Sonny's son and Billy also "received over $50,000 from a firm in California known as Herbalife reportedly for out of state 'consulting' activities by McDonough and Bulger on behalf of that firm."

In the last four months of 1985, Billy took more than $50,000 out of the Finnerty firm. In 1986, the firm issued him checks worth more than $350,000.

There was no follow-up to the report. There would be no indictments.

The story about Billy ran in *The New Yorker* in the October 28, 1991, issue. The writer, Richard Brookhiser, tipped his hand when an interviewer asked him his opinion of Billy.

"I think," Brookhiser said, "he is an admirable man in many ways."

Billy, of course, had said much the same thing about his brother less than three years earlier.

In his gushing profile, Brookhiser ignored the recent report from the attorney general on 75 State Street. Billy's patronage empire was brushed aside as the occasional procurement of "a job for a deserving acquaintance." No mention was made of the ongoing cocaine trials in the federal court, in which the wiretaps included repeated references to the poor quality of the "snow" that "Whitey" was peddling. Franny Joyce of the Convention Center Authority surfaced as a "former Bulger aide," but not as his tin whistle player, or the guy who hired both Whitey's stepdaughter and hitman Johnny Martorano's daughter.

A *Herald* columnist noted that after such an obsequious puff piece, Brookhiser "must be at the top of the waiting list for the next elevator operator's job at the Suffolk County courthouse."

Few people in Boston may have read the *New Yorker* article, but it was studied with great interest at CBS News headquarters in New York, and soon Billy would have his greatest moment in the media sun, on *60 Minutes*.

On St. Patrick's Day 1992, the CBS camera crew was rolling tape at the Bayside Club. Once again Governor Weld was the guest of honor, and this time he brought with him a song written by the former treasurer, Bob Crane. It concluded with a reference to Whitey:

"And now Bill this bonus is on me / Your winning ticket to the Lottery. / You're going to be a millionaire, there is no doubt / For I had your brother pick these numbers out."

Billy was beside himself with glee. "He's a great sport, isn't he?" he told the crowd.

Six months later, on September 17, more than twenty million Americans watched Morley Safer's *60 Minutes* piece on Billy. It made *The New Yorker* story look like hard-hitting journalism.

"In this age of gray, faceless men, it's just plain fun to have a leader with blood in his veins," the elderly Canadian correspondent intoned. "Billy Bulger almost defines Boston Irish. His district is South Boston, the home of the legendary boss politician, James Michael Curley, whose spirit is alive and well in Bulger."

Except that Curley was from Roxbury, not Southie.

Whitey's name was ever so briefly invoked, so that Billy could say, "He's my brother. I care about him. I encourage him to come by all the time."

Safer fell back on the oldest of clichés, the good brother and the bad, the good one "always with a song in his heart and on his lips, and, yet true or not, a shadow of menace."

Menace, from Billy? It was clear Morley Safer was having none of it, and that was the message he conveyed to the viewers. The ogre of the 1990 campaign had almost totally reinvented himself, for a national, if not local, audience, as a lovable leprechaun.

Billy basked in his national exposure. And election night 1992 would be even sweeter, almost as much of a vindication as 1990 had been a repudiation. Bill Clinton's victory in the presidential election meant little to Billy. What did matter was that five Republican state senators were defeated, and Governor Weld lost his power to sustain a veto. The 1990 Senate Republicans were reformers, and as Billy always said, reformers never came back. The Senate once again belonged to Billy Bulger.

By 1993, it had become clear to the junior members of the Senate that, in his fifteenth year as president, Billy was staying put. The old saying was "Up or out," but until there was an "up" for Billy, there would be no "out."

Once again, Billy was trying to expand his influence. When Mayor Ray Flynn quit City Hall to become ambassador to the Vatican, a special election was scheduled to replace him. Billy quickly mobilized his troops behind Representative Jimmy Brett of Dorchester, the husband of his longtime secretary, Patricia Brett.

Brett made it to the runoff, but in the final couldn't overcome Tom Menino, who as the president of the City Council had become acting mayor after Flynn's departure. But the fact that Billy had been able to muscle his lightweight candidate into the final meant that he wasn't quite dead yet.

Many younger Democratic politicians were growing concerned that with the governorship gone, and the two U.S. senators less than attentive to state politics, the face of the Democratic Party in Massachusetts had become William M. Bulger.

Any Democrat who ran for governor from now on could—and would—be portrayed as a tool, not just of Bulger, but of "the Bulgers," which was to say, organized crime. The Democrats would remain in control of the legislature, but the Corner Office seemed out of reach until someone could rid them of that diminutive ward-heeler, Billy Bulger. For the good of them all, someone would have to wrest the Senate presidency away from him.

That thankless task would eventually fall to Senator Bill Keating of Sharon. Keating was not someone anyone would have picked as a future rival of the Senate president. But it was 1993, and the natives were restless. Billy understood that any legislative leader who wishes to survive must preserve at least an illusion of upward mobility for his members. If the rank-and-file legislator sees no future for himself in the status quo, he is more likely to willingly participate in any uprising against the leadership.

Everyone in the Senate now knew that Billy had nowhere to go, and that until he found himself a parachute, preferably of the golden variety, he wasn't leaving. To survive, Billy would have to start easing out his more ambitious members, among them Bill Keating. Billy had passed him over for the chairmanship of Ways and Means, picking instead Tom Birmingham, Billy's obvious heir apparent. Soon after Birmingham got Ways and Means, a court officer approached Keating and told him "the president" wished to see him in his office. Keating dutifully appeared.

"How'd you like to be a judge?" Billy asked him.

"I'm too young to be a judge," Keating said.

"I don't think so."

After turning down the judgeship, Keating knew he was finished in Billy's Senate, which gave him a new freedom. One day in the spring of 1993, in the Senate chamber in front of the podium, he goaded Billy. He began talking about his old pal from the House, Mayor Ray Flynn, who was about to be confirmed by the U.S. Senate as the next ambassador to the Vatican. Keating went on, in loud terms, about what a great guy Hizzoner was. Finally Billy handed the gavel to one of his underlings and stalked off the rostrum, steaming. A few minutes later, a court officer told Keating the president wanted to see him.

Keating was ushered into Billy's office. This time, Morley Safer wouldn't have recognized "the little Irishman from South Boston." Billy was pacing the floor of his exquisitely carpeted office. Finally he looked up at Keating.

"That Flynn is not a good person, you know."

"I know Ray a long time," Keating said, using the present tense, relishing the chance to give Billy the needle. "I know him since before I was even a state rep. You know where I first met him?"

Billy inhaled and looked at Keating truculently. He had no interest in how or where Keating and Flynn met, and Keating knew it.

"I met him at this bar in Savin Hill," he said. "Maybe you heard of it—the Bulldog Tavern."

Of course Billy had heard of the Bulldog Tavern. It was in his district.

"Yeah," Keating continued, "I'm in the Bulldog, and so's Ray, and this guy I know, he introduces us. You know who that guy was?"

Billy must have known by now where this story was going,

but it still seemed inconceivable that someone would dare trifle with him like this.

"It was Eddie Connors." The same Eddie Connors that Whitey and Stevie had machine-gunned in the phone booth on Morrissey Boulevard in 1975. Eddie Connors, partner of Suitcase Fidler, for whom Tom Birmingham's father had committed welfare fraud. Billy knew very well who Eddie Connors was. It was verboten to mention Whitey or his crimes in Billy's presence, and Keating had done it, in a backhanded way no less, with a smirk on his face. Bill Keating paused a beat to let it all sink in.

"Yeah, Mr. President," he said. "It was poor Eddie Connors introduced me to Ray Flynn. You remember Eddie Connors, Mr. President?"

Now it was war.

The "insurrection," as Billy called it, began October 26, a week or so before Tom Menino crushed Bulger's man Jim Brett in the mayoral race. To run his campaign, Keating hired Michael Goldman, who'd handled George Keverian's successful insurgency against House Speaker Tommy McGee in 1984.

The rap on Keating's challenge was that he had no real rationale for his campaign other than his desire to take control of the Senate. But what was never articulated quite so bluntly was that Billy had no real rationale for wanting to maintain control, other than the fact that he had nowhere else to go.

Keating rented a room down the hill at the Parker House for his announcement, and if he needed an indication of how the battle would be waged, he immediately got it. Fifteen minutes before his scheduled announcement, someone phoned in a bomb threat to the hotel.

The eleven-month battle for the Senate presidency never quite developed into a major statewide campaign, but as it began, no one could know it would be a nonstarter. Tension was palpable in the State House corridors. At one point in the fall of 1993, a Bulger senator, Bob Durand of Marlboro, confronted one of Keating's band.

"Why?" Durand reportedly said. "Why? Why did you have to make this a Bulger-Keating thing?"

The Keating guy was puzzled. "What's wrong with that?"

"Don't you understand?" Durand said. "I'm with Bulger!"

There were advantages, though, to being with Bulger. Now that the redistricting of the congressional seats was done, it was time for the legislative redistricting. All of Billy's supporters in the Democratic caucus ended up in impregnable districts, while Keating's supporters suddenly found themselves representing much more problematical constituencies.

The most blatant gerrymandering was of Keating's own district. He lost two of the towns where he was best known—Norwood and Canton—and several GOP communities were added to his district, to weaken him and to strengthen the pro-Bulger Democratic senator who was shedding them. GOP Senate leader Brian Lees told Keating he now represented the most Republican Senate district in Massachusetts. It slithered south to the Rhode Island border—to get to Norton, Keating actually had to drive through Rhode Island.

Keating quickly came to believe that he was under surveillance at all times. A new trash pickup crew appeared at the State House. One night, just to test his suspicions, he scrawled the name of a former state rep on a pink While-U-Were-Out telephone message sheet, then wrote under his name, "WILL RUN!" Keating then tossed the slip into his office wastebasket and left for the evening. The next day, the relatives of the state rep called Keating, asking why they were getting calls about their father, who, as Keating well knew, had been dead for several years.

He also assumed his phone was tapped. As the months wore on, the tapped phones became a running joke in Keating's campaign. One day, he and his campaign manager Goldman decided to send them on a wild-goose chase. They began discussing how they hoped Bulger would never find out about "that case" out in Hampden Probate Court. Was it public record? Goldman inquired, in a whisper. Yes, said Keating, that was what made it so potentially damaging. All somebody had to do was drive out to Springfield and dig through the records and they'd find—here he made up a name—and that would be the end of his campaign. Keating always assumed someone had been ordered to make a pointless two-hour trip out to Springfield.

At one point, the dissidents scheduled a bus tour of various newspaper editorial boards in the hinterlands. At 5:30 a.m., just before they left, Senator Lois Pines of Newton remembered something she had left behind in her office. She turned the key and opened the door and found a young man going through her desk. He said he was there to work on the "plumbing," and then quickly ran out the door.

One day, Keating got a telephone call from a reporter who said "unnamed sources" had told him that Keating's son had been arrested for beating his wife. At the time, Keating's son was three years old.

Billy and his allies did a masterful job of keeping Keating off balance. They hit him everywhere, even on the op-ed page of the *Globe*. Two of the most ardent pro-Bulger columnists were former President George H. W. Bush's nephew, and a black writer who in one piece quoted at length from a black "community leader," without mentioning that the leader worked for Jackie Bulger in the Juvenile Court, making almost $1,000 a week.

Inside the building, Bulger and his allies harassed Keating whichever way he turned. He would come under withering personal fire in the Senate's Democratic caucus, which was closed to the press, and supposedly off the record. Calls would be made to all the Democratic members in the morning, and they would "caucus" in Bulger's office before the regular, open session began. One or another of the Bulger regulars would tee off on Keating, for something that had appeared in a suburban newspaper, or an offhand comment made on a radio talk show.

Bulger would listen impassively, as though he were an independent arbiter. Finally, as the Bulger loyalist sat back down, he would turn to Keating and demand: "Well, what do you say to that?"

One morning, Keating stood up and yelled at the tormentor, "Don't you understand—I'm not the threat to you." He pointed at Bulger. "He is. He's the one who's going to cost you your seat."

As the fight went on, Bulger spent more time with his undersized aide Eddie Phillips, a licensed private detective. Phillips was one of the few people anywhere who could understand Billy's obsession with his height, which seemed to bother him more than ever during the "insurrection." One day, Billy bumped into the owner of a local talk radio station. Billy asked about one of the station's hosts, who continually described him as "sixty-five inches tall" and insisted on referring to him as the Corrupt Midget.

"I don't mind corrupt," Billy said, "but can't you make him stop calling me a midget?"

In addition to pummeling Keating, the Bulger forces also went after his campaign manager, Michael Goldman. The usual code words were trotted out once more. By various senators across the state, Goldman was described as "a master manipulator . . . mercenary . . . greedy . . . voice from the shadows." He had a "profit-making agenda." In one newspaper, a senator referred to him as "an ambitious puppeteer manipulating reform senators who have chosen to surrender their votes and consciences to Goldman's control."

By the summer of 1994, it was clear that Keating's challenge was doomed, and Billy began to relax. The surest sign that it was all over came in Milton a week before the primary election, when he joked about Whitey in a speech sponsored by the Milton Town Club.

"Next month," he said, "no one play the Lottery. I hear my brother is going to win again."

On primary day 1994, Billy voted early at St. Brigid's, then met former mayor Kevin White for a walk around the Public Garden. That evening, he dined at Amrhein's on West Broadway with his son Billy Jr.—two years from now, God willing, it would be a different William M. Bulger running unopposed in the First Suffolk District.

By ten, the results were in. Not a single one of Keating's challengers had ousted a Bulger loyalist. Billy Bulger was the once and future Senate president.

Two months later on election day 1994, Bill Keating just wanted to hang on to his own Senate seat, not that he would have much trouble with Chris Lane, the former one-term Republican senator who had been personally recruited by Governor Weld to run against Keating. Still, Keating felt he had to show the flag in the Republican-leaning towns of his new district.

Everywhere Keating drove, he and his aide, a Southie native, saw members of the old Bulger crowd from City Point and the Lower End. They were all holding signs for the Republican Lane, even Andy Donovan, the legendary talk show caller who always defended Billy on the radio airwaves, invariably describing himself as a "first-time caller."

Late in the day, Keating and one of his aides pulled their car into the parking lot at Norton High School, not far from the Rhode Island border. It was dusk, and few voters were in evidence, but Keating and his aide saw two men holding Lane signs. One was older, but Keating quickly recognized the younger man as a member of Billy's inner circle. At least nominally, Billy was still a Democrat, and yet here was one of his own holding a sign for a GOP candidate, in violation of Democratic State Committee rules.

"Get the camera," Keating told his aide.

But when the younger man and his older partner saw Keating and the aide walking toward them, they moved the signs up over their faces so they couldn't be seen.

"You're a fucking asshole," the older man yelled at Keating. "You are a fucking asshole."

Keating laughed. It was the end of a long, miserable campaign, and the Bulgers had beaten him, badly, but now, at least, he had a couple of them back on their heels, worried about being photographed as they held a Republican's signs.

"We're not leaving," Keating's aide said. "You can keep those Lane signs over your faces all night, but when you put them down, we'll be here to take your pictures."

The two men with the signs just stood there a few seconds longer. Then Keating heard the older man say to the younger man: "Put down the sign and go over there and let them take your picture."

The young man obeyed instantly. Keating relished his mini-victory, as his aide snapped the pictures they could now at least threaten to send to the Democratic State Committee—or the newspapers. Meanwhile, the older man kept his Lane-for-Senate sign over his face, to prevent any pictures from being taken of himself. Finally Keating and his aide gave up and got back in their car.

It wasn't until he was headed home toward Sharon that Keating suddenly realized why the younger man had so meekly followed the orders of the older man, and why the older man had never lowered the sign that covered his face. Miles away now from Norton High School, with the polls closed and all the sign holders scattered, Keating finally understood who the older man really was. It was Whitey Bulger.

CHAPTER 20

SEVEN WEEKS AFTER THE election, on December 23, 1994, Whitey vanished, ahead of the indictments he knew were coming down. As 1994 turned into 1995, it took a while for the cops even to grasp the fact that Whitey was gone for good.

For one thing, the indictment he was facing didn't seem that serious. Taken as a whole, it was little more than a racketeering case, and its centerpiece was the extortion of some elderly bookies. How excited was a Massachusetts jury going to get about a gambling case?

Plus, Whitey had been away so often in the last couple of years that this latest absence didn't seem particularly noteworthy. It was Christmas, after all, and then it was New Year's, after which they assumed he'd be back, and they'd grab him. If Stevie was still in town, and he was, then obviously he and Whitey hadn't heard about the pending indictments.

Certainly Stevie didn't anticipate any major problems. After he was arrested outside his son's restaurant near Quincy Market, he was taken to the federal courthouse, where he ran into Ed Quinn, one of the FBI agents who'd worked on both the Prince Street bugging and the Joe Murray case. Quinn was one of the agents Gerry Angiulo had always described as "a piece of shit Irish cop." He was a friend of Zip's. "Can you help me out here?" Stevie asked.

Quinn offered to get him a Coke.

After seventeen years as a fugitive, Johnny Martorano was arrested in Boca Raton. His brother, Jimmy, was collared in Boston. Frank Salemme stayed on the lam until August 1995, when he was picked up in West Palm Beach. Two other defendants—Frank Salemme Jr. and George Kaufman—died soon after their arrests. Only Whitey remained a free man.

As late as March 1995, Whitey's flight was still regarded as little more than a lighthearted lark. On St. Patrick's Day that year, Governor Weld journeyed to the Bayside Club to belt out a song about Whitey. The tune was taken from "M.T.A.," the famous 1959 Kingston Trio song about the straphanger stuck on the Boston subway system. Except that the lyrics had been rewritten so that "Charlie" was now Whitey on the MTA.

"Will he ever return? No, he'll never return. No he'll never come back this way. I just got a call from the Kendall Square Station. He's with Charlie on the MTA!"

It was the hit of the day. Billy especially enjoyed it.

"Isn't he great?" said Billy.

The FBI didn't seem terribly concerned about Whitey's flight either when they handed the investigation over to agent Charlie Gianturco. His brother Nick had just retired from the bureau, and had succeeded Zip as director of security for Boston Edison when Zip was promoted to vice president. When Stevie was arrested at Quincy Market, he had been told he could make one phone call.

"Get me Charlie Gianturco," he said.

The indictments were handed up on Thursday, January 5. With Whitey nowhere to be found, on Monday morning, January 9, 1995, FBI agents John Gamel and Joe Harrigan dropped by the State House to speak to the Senate president.

"We cooled our heels for about fifteen minutes," Gamel recalled. "Finally one of his aides came out and said he was pretty busy with legislative stuff and didn't have time to talk."

Gamel asked the aide to have Billy give him a call, and then both agents returned to their offices at the JFK Building in Government Center. Early that afternoon, Billy phoned and told Gamel without preamble: "I don't expect to hear from my brother," he said.

Gamel got the distinct impression that Billy did not want to be talking to the FBI. Gamel told Billy that if he did hear from Whitey, he should urge Whitey to call Gamel, so that a surrender could be arranged.

"I'll consider it," said Billy.

Later that month Billy and Whitey did speak, on the phone, at Eddie Phillips's house. Gamel did not receive a call from Billy.

Whitey and Catherine Greig arrived in Grand Isle, Louisiana, in late January 1995. They were driving a new 1994 Mercury Grand Marquis that Whitey had bought on Long Island with a $13,000 bank check.

Twice in 1995, local police became suspicious of Bulger's car, once when it was parked outside a Veterans Administration hospital in Wyoming, and later when a cop in Long Beach, Mississippi, decided to run the Massachusetts plates on the Marquis with the National Criminal Information Center. But in both cases, the car came back registered to a "Thomas Baxter," who had no outstanding warrants. Not only was "Thomas Baxter" not arrested, he wasn't even pulled over.

By early fall 1995 Whitey would be back on Long Island. And in October, he returned to South Boston. From a pay phone in a waterfront freight terminal, he called John Morris, who was wrapping up his FBI career at the agency's training center in Quantico, Virginia.

The caller identified himself to Morris's secretary as "Mr. White," and said he urgently needed to speak to Mr. Morris. Morris took the call, and began taking notes. He knew he would have to prepare an incident report, a 302, if only because he suspected that Whitey was taping the call. Whitey demanded that Morris get a retraction from the *Globe* of their seven-year-old story that he was an FBI informant.

"He wanted me to use my Machiavellian mind to go to people at the *Globe* in order to get them to print a story which he in essence said that the prior information was . . . given to the *Globe* in an effort to discredit him or to remove him from a position of power."

Whitey also mentioned something about Morris "ruining him and his family," as Morris later recalled. Then he hung up, and Morris began writing his 302 incident report.

Whitey, meanwhile, called Kevin Weeks to tell him he'd gotten through to his nemesis. Again Whitey used the phrase "Machiavellian mind." Apparently Whitey had been rereading *The Prince.*

"Basically," Weeks said, "he told Morris that if he went down, he was taking him with him, that he blamed this whole thing on Morris, that Morris started this whole thing and for him to use his Machiavellian mind to try to straighten this out. He blamed Morris for the *Globe* articles that started back in '88. He figured it was the beginning of his problems."

Later that evening, Morris's secretary-turned-wife picked him up at the FBI training center.

"Remember that thousand dollars that John Connolly gave to you, to go to Glencoe?" he asked. "It came from Bulger and Flemmi."

By this time he had decided to get it all off his chest.

"He told me that he asked for it," Debbie Noseworthy Morris said under oath. "He told me that Mr. Bulger and Mr. Flemmi really liked him, and that if there was anything he ever wanted or needed that they would help him out, and this was something that he chose to ask for."

Then Morris told her about the other two payoffs from Whitey.

"He told me that there was another thousand dollars in the bottom of the case of wine and $5,000 that he was given some other way."

That night, soon after they arrived at their suburban tract home in northern Virginia, Morris suffered a massive heart attack that nearly killed him. Ten weeks later, on December 31, 1995, Morris retired from the FBI.

Billy had other things on his mind. He was writing his memoirs, a book that would appear under the title *While the Music Lasts*. Published in early 1996, the book received respectful, if not rave, reviews. It was published before the full extent of Whitey's criminality became public knowledge, and so Billy felt free to write how his older sibling "abhorred addictive drugs," and that much of the evidence against him was "purchased."

"From everything I could see," he wrote of Whitey, "he appeared to have taken enormous steps to separate himself from the environment that led to his early misbehavior. . . . I know some of the allegations and much of the innuendo to be absolutely false. Other matters I cannot be sure about, one way or the other."

A recurring theme of the book was how much Southie loathed informers, as they're described on page 4, and snitching, as it's called on page 8, and spies, as they are referred to on page 171. In what seemed to be an unconscious description of his own travails since 75 State Street, Billy wrote of the hero of his youth, James Michael Curley: "It was said he accepted graft, but that was never proved."

*   *   *

The state colleges and universities of Massachusetts have long been dumping grounds for politicians with nowhere else to go, a description that certainly fit Billy. He had to get out of the legislature. He had overcome the "insurrection," so it could never be said that he had been pushed out. But his time was over, and he didn't want to end up like deposed House speaker Tommy McGee, a pathetic shadow from the past, trying to hang on for a few more years to increase his pension before finally decamping for Florida.

Billy probably would have preferred an appointment to the Supreme Judicial Court, but between Whitey and 75 State Street, that was not in the cards. But the presidency of the University of Massachusetts was open. And it had several distinct advantages over the SJC. First, it paid a lot more, and the higher his salary, the larger Billy's pension would be when he finally retired. And UMass would provide him with yet another patronage pit. He could bring everybody over from the State House. And power would be easy to hold, because his board of trustees would be appointed by his good friend, Governor William F. Weld.

On November 28, 1995, the UMass board of trustees voted to hire Billy Bulger as the new president of UMass. His starting salary was $189,000.

Billy had two final tasks to accomplish before leaving the Senate. The first was to see that Tom Birmingham, the nephew of an Irish gangster, secured the votes to succeed Billy Bulger, the brother of an Irish gangster, as president of the Massachusetts State Senate.

The second was to make sure Billy Bulger Jr. succeeded him in the First Suffolk District seat that Billy had held for twenty-five years. Running against Billy Jr. would be Pat Loftus, the candidate Whitey had considered killing back in 1970, and state Representative Steve Lynch. Lynch, an up-from-the-bootstraps ironworker who had gone to night law school, appeared formidable, and Billy tried to stall the date of the election, until after the filing deadline for the September primaries. That way Lynch would have to risk his House seat for a dicey fight. But Bill Galvin, another of Billy's old enemies from the State House, was now secretary of state, and he saw through Billy's ploy. The primary would take place in the spring, and for Lynch, it would be a free shot—if he lost to Junior, he could still run for his House seat in the fall.

Billy had tried his best to bring Billy Jr. along, but the undistinguished thirty-four-year-old lawyer proved to be a hopeless candidate. In most of the newspaper photographs of the abbreviated campaign, Billy is almost always seen with his son, and he is the one talking. At subway stops, Billy would invariably be the one out front. The signs said "William M. Bulger" with a tiny "Jr." next to the "r" in Bulger. Most of Lynch's workers, if not Lynch himself, called the boy "Junior."

As the campaign wound down, Billy was surprised by the fissures in his own now creaking political machine. Mike Flaherty, the former state rep and longtime co-host of the St. Patrick's Day breakfast who nurtured dreams of political success for his own son and namesake, endorsed Lynch, and Billy never forgave him.

Billy wanted an old-style Bulger campaign, but the edge was gone. Billy's people had gotten old. They had moved to the suburbs, many of them, or they were retired, collecting their monthly "kiss in the mail" from the city or state. It had been so long since the Bulgers had been in a real fight in Southie that they'd forgotten how to conduct a street-level campaign. For Junior, there would be no polling, no targeting of voters, no computers. Once, when a reporter asked Billy why none of the modern methods were being utilized, he smiled and said, "We don't do that here, lad."

The only real effort to generate any kind of buzz came at

what turned out to be Billy's final St. Patrick's Day breakfast. All the politicians seen on the TV newscasts that night, and in the next morning's papers, were wearing Junior's campaign buttons. Even Senator John Kerry, who showed up in an election year with his new wife, Teresa Heinz, pinned one on his lapel.

But the race was over even before the polls opened on election day, and Billy knew it. Lynch had always been respectful, and just before the election, one of the Bulgers reached out to tell him, "Even though we're on different sides, if you win, don't worry, you don't have a problem."

On March 28, 1996, Junior managed barely 35 percent of the vote, while Loftus couldn't even break into double figures. Lynch even carried the Bulgers' home precinct, 332–296. Only in Chinatown did the Bulgers hang on, thanks to Billy's old army buddy, Frank Chin, the precinct captain. But even a four-to-one majority in Chinatown's precinct 3-8 wasn't nearly enough. It was the first election in South Boston since 1964 in which Whitey had not been lurking in the shadows, and it was the first time a Bulger had ever been defeated, let alone crushed. No Bulger would run for any elective office again.

Whitey and Catherine Greig, "Tom and Helen from New York," as they called themselves, returned to Grand Isle in November 1995. They holed up in a motel for a while, then rented a duplex on the beach called It's Our Dream, and soon met and befriended a financially struggling Cajun family, the Gautreauxs.

The Gautreauxs quickly benefited from the largess of "Tom and Helen." "Tom" bought them a stove, refrigerator, and freezer, paying $1,900 in new $100 bills. According to a later story in the *Globe*, when Whitey reached into his pouch for the cash, the clerk at the hardware store noticed that he also had a pearl-handled knife inside.

In that newspaper account, the fugitives were portrayed as Good Samaritans, pining, apparently, for their two poodles, Gigi and Nikki, back in Southie. Whitey kept a bag of dog biscuits in the trunk of his car for strays. When Penny's husband had to put down a puppy by shooting it, Whitey wept.

But as time passed, Whitey reverted to his old, overbearing self. He lectured Penny's husband, Glenn, on the value of a work ethic, telling him: "Get off your lazy butt. You need to make something out of your life."

Sometimes, "Tom and Helen" would drive to the Wal-Mart superstore in Galliano, forty miles away. It was open twenty-four hours a day, and it had a pay phone, which Whitey used to reach out to at least five of his fellow former Alcatraz inmates, most of them ex–bank robbers like himself. He asked most of them for assistance in getting new identification. As always, he was planning ahead.

"Tom and Helen" hit the road again in the winter of 1996. Grand Isle was basically a resort community, and in the winter, the population dwindled a little too much for Whitey's liking. They stayed on the road until May 1996, when they rented a two-bedroom house near the Gautreauxs. Whitey paid his new landlord with the usual $100 bills, and always passed on his monthly issue of *Soldier of Fortune* magazine.

But things had changed at the Gautreaux household since "Tom and Helen" had last visited. Glenn's ex-father-in-law, Thomas Rudolph, had moved in, and he and Whitey didn't get along. Rudolph didn't like his bragging in front of "Helen" that "I have control of my woman." The two old men also argued over the value of work.

"I worked every day of my life since I was fifteen," Rudolph told him.

"I never had to work," Whitey said. "I had people working for me."

* * *

In July 1996, Tom and Helen left Grand Isle. In Boston, the FBI had, finally, interviewed Theresa Stanley, and she had given up Whitey's "Thomas Baxter" alias. Kevin Weeks soon learned what she had done, and he immediately called Whitey in Louisiana. Whitey drove north and ditched his car in a nondescript commercial district in Yonkers, New York. The feds soon had it staked out, but Whitey never returned for it. When it was finally impounded, the FBI discovered that "Tom and Helen" had put 65,000 miles on the car in the eighteen months since he'd vanished. In the glove compartment, they found receipts for businesses in Grand Isle.

Meanwhile, back in Boston, Fred Wyshak, the federal prosecutor who had cobbled together the indictment against Whitey, got a call from a local forger.

The forger said he had been approached by Kevin Weeks, who was in dire need of new IDs. The forger said Weeks told him that he would provide him with mug shots and blank Massachusetts driver's licenses, and the forger would be expected to fashion everything together into passable IDs.

Wyshak handed the tip-off to the combined DEA–State Police task force, and they met the forger in a local hotel (as two FBI agents, one of whom was Charlie Gianturco, sat in the lobby downstairs).

The State Police decided the forger was not a reliable source, and sent him on his way. Weeks, in the meantime, had posed Whitey's younger brother Jackie for a series of mug shots in which he wore a false mustache. Weeks then delivered the mug shots and blank driver's licenses to the forger, who, before returning the finished products to Weeks, showed them to the State Police.

Incredibly, the State Police task force did not recognize Jackie Bulger. They did, however, put Weeks under surveillance, but he quickly slipped his tail and flew to Chicago, where he delivered the new IDs to Whitey. Whitey was so unhappy with the photos that he ordered Weeks to get a new Polaroid camera and retake the pictures—this time of Whitey himself. Weeks flew back to Boston with the snapshots while Whitey remained in Chicago, where he felt safe, thanks to the assistance he was getting from his old bank-robbing pal from Alcatraz, Barney "Dirty Shirt" Grogan, who now had a shaved head and a job with an Outfit-connected union.

Back in Boston, Weeks went straight to the forger. He said Whitey now wanted a Massachusetts driver's license with the name "Mark Shapeton," as well as three more, with names that could be backed up with birth certificates. It was the sort of research that was simple enough to do, either through searching birth notices on old newspaper microfilm available at most public libraries, or by visiting the state's Bureau of Vital Statistics. That was how Whitey, in 1977, had come across "Thomas Baxter," a Woburn man born in 1929, the same year as Whitey.

But now the heat was too much, so Weeks instructed the forger to come up with the new aliases himself, and the birth certificates. The forger once more called the State Police, showed them the new photos of Whitey, and asked what he should do about the other names.

For reasons that still remain inexplicable, the State Police decided they would select the new aliases for Whitey, and sent a trooper over to the Bureau of Vital Statistics to pick them out. He selected the names Evers, Boudreau, and Henson. They were then turned over to the forger, who produced the counterfeit driver's licenses and turned them over to Kevin Weeks for $10,000 cash.

The State Police again put a tail on Weeks, but then, astonishingly, broke it off. That left Weeks free to rendezvous with Whitey for the last time, in New York, where he provided him with bogus identification produced with an assist, unbeknownst to either Whitey or Weeks, from the State Police.

With all the new IDs in hand, Whitey quickly returned to Chicago, picked up Catherine Greig, and then left with her on a commercial flight out of O'Hare Airport to New York. It was September 1996. There has not been a confirmed sighting of Whitey Bulger in the United States since.

According to court records filed in the Jackie Bulger perjury case, an unidentified Southie man received at least two telephone calls from Whitey in 1996, shortly after he left the country.

Whitey said he was fine, asked how his two brothers were doing, and told the friend that if he saw Billy he should tell him he was all right. A few weeks later, the man ran into Jackie and passed on the message.

"I'm relieved to hear that," Jackie said.

Back in Louisiana, the feds used the receipts they found in the glove compartment of Whitey's car to track down the Gautreauxs. They were twice subpoenaed to appear before a federal grand jury in Boston. Penny Gautreaux was unrepentant about her friendship with the man she knew as "Tom Baxter."

"How could you not love him?" she said.

Awaiting trial at the Plymouth County House of Correction, Stevie Flemmi was losing it. He may have been a big man out on the street, but he'd never done time. Now he was waiting impatiently for Zip and Whitey to ride to the rescue before his racketeering trial began.

Kevin Weeks began visiting Stevie regularly. They discussed the "other guy," Whitey, and both agreed they hoped he never came back. Stevie used Weeks to reach out to Zip. The conversations between Weeks and Zip became more and more involved. With Whitey gone, everything seemed much more complicated. There were so many issues—how to get money from the X fund to Johnny Martorano, and what to do about the arsenal that was still stashed on Mrs. Flemmi's sun porch.

And then there was the problem of the Italian hoods who had taken to slowly cruising through Kevin's neighborhood in Quincy. They also had to speak frequently to Stevie's lawyer, Kenny Fishman.

Stevie had believed he had protection—not immunity, but protection. But as 1995 faded into 1996, it began to dawn on Stevie that no one was going to bail him out, figuratively or literally. Stevie took up with a Jehovah's Witness, a burglar. The other guys would walk by his cell, and Stevie would be moaning, clad only in his underwear, as the burglar massaged his feet with oil.

When he wasn't attending Jehovah's Witness services, Stevie began spilling his and Whitey's secrets to his fellow inmates and co-defendants—Frank Salemme, the Martorano brothers, Johnny and Jimmy, and Rhode Island mobster Robert DeLuca.

Silent for decades, Stevie now couldn't stop talking. Stevie claimed Whitey had worn a wire for many of his meetings with various FBI agents, and bitterly added that he was now kicking himself for not obtaining his own copies of the tapes. If he had the tapes, Stevie said, he could cut his own deal to get out.

Stevie told them how Zip was like a son to Billy, and how Billy joined them "plenty of times" at the Sunday afternoon get-togethers at Mrs. Flemmi's house, allegations Billy would deny at the congressional hearing years later. Stevie told them that all the stories about Whitey taking LSD were "bullshit," and that it was FBI agent H. Paul Rico who had arranged for him to get good-behavior credits to reduce his sentence. He said the FBI had its own "hit squad," although he never mentioned any specific murders they'd committed.

Stevie took to covering his bed with pictures of the saints. And all the while, he watched his back. Many of the local inmates were from Southie; they knew the girls he and Whitey had raped, and now some of them were looking for payback.

*   *   *

The pretrial hearings continued for Whitey's five co-defendants, but one concern continued to nag at Judge Mark Wolf, Bill Weld's former top assistant in the U.S. Attorney's Office. More than once Wolf asked federal prosecutor Fred Wyshak and his top deputy, Brian Kelly, if the government knew anything else about Whitey that they weren't sharing with the court and the defendants. Wyshak and Kelly always said no, and Wolf would warn them that he would hate to start the trial and have Whitey suddenly pop up and take the stand and send everything back to square one.

Eventually, the other defendants realized what Wolf was getting at, without actually coming out and asking the question: Were Whitey and Stevie federal informants?

In all of his rants, Stevie had never directly admitted it, but most of his co-defendants had concluded early on that Stevie and Whitey were both snitches for the FBI. Soon, as they went over every detail of the case with their lawyers, it dawned on the other hoods that if they could prove that two of their co-defendants had been working for the government while they were all committing crimes together, they might have a shot at getting their own indictments thrown out. After all, how could the government permit some people to commit crimes, while prosecuting other participants in the same conspiracy? Their lawyers may have brought the Fourteenth Amendment to their attention first, but soon the hoods themselves were asking one another, what about our rights under the equal-protection clause?

Tony Cardinale was the lawyer for both Frank Salemme and Robert DeLuca. In March 1997 Cardinale filed a motion asking the government to reveal the names of all the informants, including the defendants, that it had used in building the case. Among those he suspected of being informers, Cardinale named Whitey, but not Stevie. Cardinale was afraid Stevie would flip and screw Frank one final time by testifying against him.

A few weeks after Cardinale filed his motion, Wolf asked the defendants if they were just interested in only the potential informants they'd listed in their motion, or in all the informants?

In other words, in addition to Whitey, did they want Flemmi too?

The answer was, yes.

A couple of weeks later, at the end of another hearing, Wolf called Stevie into the judge's lobby and told him that he had received more FBI documents, and that he now knew that Stevie was an informer. Stevie shrugged. A federal prosecutor came in and told Flemmi it was time for him to flip. Flemmi just shook his head.

That afternoon, Flemmi was not on the bus back to Plymouth with the others. His co-defendants figured he was gone, permanently. Their gambit had failed, and now there would be yet another witness against them—Stevie Flemmi. But around 7:30, Flemmi reappeared in the cell block and said he had an announcement to make to everyone. All the remaining defendants—Flemmi, Salemme, DeLuca, and the Martorano brothers—filed into a small room next to the visitors' area.

"I was an informant for over thirty years," Stevie said. "And so wasn't Whitey. Wolf's going to tell you that in court. But I wanted you to know, it's not what you think it is. Me and Whitey gave them shit and got back gold in return."

The others would always remember that last line, because they knew what Stevie meant by the "shit" he'd given the feds. He was talking about them, his co-defendants.

After he finished he turned and walked hurriedly out of the room.

"The only one that looked surprised," said someone who was there, "was Frank."

*　　*　　*

Once Stevie announced that he was an informant for the FBI, Wolf granted the defendants' motion for open, pretrial hearings. He had little choice; the issues raised by the indictment of an informant who was providing intelligence about his codefendants needed to be publicly addressed, and dealt with, before any trials could begin. The only question now was just how much of the FBI's dirty laundry would be aired.

Almost immediately, on May 22, 1997, the feds admitted that Whitey too had been an informant—something they had adamantly denied for almost a decade. Such admissions weren't everyday occurrences, the federal prosecutors conceded. This one involved "unique and rare circumstances."

The hearings began with a parade of current and former FBI agents. But the fed who would have been the star of the show—Zip Connolly—refused to testify without a grant of immunity, a deal the government would not consider. As his lawyer he retained R. Robert Popeo, who had represented Billy Bulger in the later stages of the 75 State Street probe.

When Zip was finally called to the stand, he took the Fifth. Outside the courtroom, as one FBI agent after another tore into him, Zip held press conferences, called reporters, and issued any number of denials—for example, the front-page story that he had received free stoves and refrigerators from Kevin O'Neil's appliance store on West Broadway was "an abject lie," as he put it. He went on friendly radio talk shows to rebut everything and everybody, especially Morris, who, unlike Zip, had been granted immunity. Zip described his old friend as "the most corrupt agent in FBI history." Zip mounted some of his most eloquent defenses on the weekend radio talk show hosted by Andy Moes, a former freelance narcotics agent from Cape Cod who had sold marijuana to a couple of Kennedy cousins while working undercover as a taxi driver.

Meanwhile, as thousands of previously classified FBI documents were made public, Stevie's history of treachery over the decades began to emerge in graphic detail. Johnny Martorano now read that in the mid-1960s, Stevie had dismissed him as a "pimp." A report from another informant described how Stevie had planned to murder Larry Baione and then frame Johnny for the hit.

One morning in Plymouth, during a lull in the hearings, Johnny walked into Robert DeLuca's cell in H3.

"Robert," said Johnny, "I am going out that door before Stevie does. I am going to destroy him before he destroys me."

He had made the decision to become an informant. The next morning Johnny was gone from the jail. Zip realized the immense danger that Johnny's defection posed to him. It was Johnny who had procured the diamond ring back in 1976 that Whitey had given to Zip—his first payoff from the mobsters. Johnny had been around all those afternoons in the Marshall Street garage when Whitey was bragging about his close ties to Zip—or so Johnny would soon be testifying.

Within days, one of the most loyal Bulger sycophants in the press, Mike Barnicle of the *Globe*, turned in one of his trademark concoctions of factual errors mixed with outright fiction. Barnicle wrote that Martorano had murdered three young black women in a car in 1968—it apparently wasn't enough that he had shot three African-Americans, one of whom had happened to be female. Then Barnicle quoted one of Connolly's closest friends in the Boston Police Department, Eddie Walsh, as saying Martorano used blacks in Roxbury for "target practice," a statement so inflammatory that the U.S. attorney later felt obliged to denounce it as "madness" and "fantasy."

In a strange coincidence, Barnicle's half-baked attempt to protect Zip by trashing Martorano turned out to be his final regular column for the *Globe*. A quarter-century of journalistic abuses had finally caught up with him and he was forced out in disgrace over other, earlier transgressions unrelated to the final Martorano column. After Barnicle's departure, the paper had to run one last lengthy correction cataloguing the errors in that final piece. And the Bulgers had one fewer lackey they could rely on in the media.

Stevie was, of course, the hearing's star witness. He was the gangster who'd been protected by the FBI, and telling all was the only way he was ever going to see the light of day again. If he could prove, through the testimony of himself and others, that he had indeed had protection from the FBI, then Judge Wolf would have no choice but to throw out the entire indictment.

But Stevie's problem was that he couldn't really come clean. Without immunity, he couldn't admit to killings he hadn't been charged with. And by the time Stevie took the stand, in August 1998, Johnny Martorano had already started outlining the details of almost twenty murders he'd committed. Many of his hits had been done at the direction of Whitey and Stevie, who had paid him more than $1 million during his years on the lam between 1978 and 1995. With notes from Martorano's ongoing debriefings in front of him, Fred Wyshak would pepper Flemmi with questions about, say, the murder of Tommy King, or Eddie Connors, or James Sousa.

"Assert the Fifth on that," Flemmi would say over and over again.

Wyshak hammered him repeatedly on how much he and Whitey benefited from the destruction of the Mafia in Boston.

Flemmi: "I'm not saying I didn't capitalize on it in some way."

Wyshak: "And you capitalized on eliminating your competition from the picture, isn't that true?"

Flemmi: "In the course of our involvement with the FBI, that's what was happening. The LCN [La Cosa

Nostra] was getting decimated. That's what the goal was of the FBI."

Wyshak: "And that was your goal too?"

Flemmi: "It goes with the territory . . ."

Wyshak: "And that made you a wealthy man, didn't it?"

Flemmi: "I'll assert the Fifth on that."

Wyshak: "Do you think, Mr. Flemmi, that you and Mr. Bulger single-handedly took the LCN down?"

Flemmi: "I'll tell you something, Mr. Wyshak. We did a hell of a job."

Stevie's lawyer, Ken Fishman, was in constant contact with Zip, who was trying his best to protect, not only himself, but also Billy. When Morris testified that he too had seen Billy at one of the Sunday dinners with the gangsters, Stevie brought up the testimony himself, to deny that it ever happened.

"Just wanted to clarify that," he said.

Stevie also tried to insulate Zip from taking the fall for tipping him to the pending indictment back in 1994. He told Wyshak he got the message from Whitey "by telephone" at his mother's house.

Wyshak: "Where was Mr. Bulger?"

Flemmi: "He didn't say."

Wyshak: "Did you ask him?"

Flemmi: "No, I just took the message."

It was a hearing, rather than a trial, which meant there was no jury in the courtroom, so the marshals seated the two remaining defendants—Salemme and Rhode Island mobster Robert DeLuca—in the jury box. Salemme sat directly across the courtroom from his old friend on the witness stand, and watched in increasing disbelief as Flemmi continued to lie. Stevie was jeopardizing all their cases to protect a crooked FBI agent.

During the next break, when they were all back in the courthouse holding pen, Salemme grabbed Flemmi and screamed: "You piece of shit! You fucked me all my life, and now you're screwing everyone around you. Fucking scum!"

By now, Johnny Martorano had told the prosecutors that Stevie believed Whitey had tape-recorded many, if not most, of his conversations with FBI agents. Whitey had just considered it prudent to have evidence of the "protection" that he'd been promised over the years. Judge Wolf asked Stevie if he really believed Whitey had tape-recorded his meetings with the feds.

"Knowing Mr. Bulger, Your Honor, it's very possible. . . . Anything is possible."

Judge Wolf asked him if he'd ever seen any such tape recordings.

"I've seen his tape recorder. It was a pretty good one, a small tape recorder, and he had other electronic equipment."

The prosecutor Wyshak tried to draw Stevie out, by asking him if he felt betrayed by Zip Connolly. Stevie admitted that he'd expected Zip to get him out of this terrible predicament. Through intermediaries, he'd asked Zip to help him out.

> Wyshak: "And did you receive an answer?"
> Flemmi: "He didn't testify in my behalf."
> Wyshak: "Did you receive an answer?"
> Flemmi: "That was my answer. He didn't testify in my behalf."

Zip had let him down, the feds had let him down, everyone had betrayed Stevie. And then there was Whitey.

Wyshak: "At some point, I guess, you realized Mr. Bulger
    wasn't going to come to the rescue, is that right?"
Flemmi: "I can't say that."
Wyshak: "You can't say that? Well, he hasn't rescued you so
    far, has he?"
Flemmi: "He must be working on it."

As president of the University of Massachusetts, Billy tried to
ignore the circus unfolding down in Post Office Square. Usually when his name was mentioned, his spokesmen—two former State House reporters—haughtily responded that "the
president" had no comment. On occasion, he had to respond.
Eventually, former FBI supervisor James Ring took the stand
and placed Billy at that dinner with Whitey and Stevie at Mrs.
Flemmi's house next door to his. Billy was asked to comment
on Ring's sworn testimony.

"I never met the man," Billy said. "It never took place, but
the business of denying such things is to make it appear as if
something sinister had happened."

Billy remained secure in his UMass sinecure, even after the
departure of Governor Bill Weld, who had lost whatever little
interest he still had in the governorship once he was defeated
by Senator John Kerry in the 1996 U.S. Senate race. In 1997,
Weld resigned and was replaced by Lieutenant Governor Paul
Cellucci, that good friend of Billy's whose primary political
handicap was a $700,000 debt that he couldn't quite explain.

Despite those lingering questions, in 1998 Cellucci eliminated two more of Billy's longtime foes. In the GOP primary
for governor, Cellucci crushed state Treasurer Joe Malone. And
in the general election, Cellucci edged the attorney general,
Luther Scott Harshbarger, who had issued the final not-
exactly-exculpatory report on 75 State Street.

Still, election night 1998 was perhaps the last time that
Billy could tell himself that nothing had really changed. Cel-

lucci's victory meant four more years of business as usual, and what pleased Billy even more was that Cellucci had picked as his running mate yet another malleable ex-Republican state senator, Jane Swift, a member of the Senate's GOP Class of 1990.

Billy could relax for a while now. Even if Cellucci moved on, Billy would continue to have a close friend, a former senator, in the Corner Office. And that was what counted, because the governor appointed the members of the UMass board of trustees. And Billy quickly discovered that it was even easier to control the board than it had been the state Senate. Just as he'd renovated his own office at the State House, now he moved the president's office to a much plusher location, at One Beacon Street. From the twenty-sixth floor, he could look down, literally, on the State House.

He now controlled thirty thousand square feet of prime office space, which he filled with the same crew of yes-men who'd subsisted for years, if not decades, on his Beacon Hill payroll. Paul Mahoney was gone, and in his place was Paul Mahoney Jr. Billy also continued the old State House tradition of "taking hostages"—hiring relatives of the politicians who controlled his budget. One of his new vice presidents was the wife of his handpicked replacement as Senate president, Tom Birmingham. Mrs. Birmingham made $148,000 a year.

Others were hired simply because they were longtime lackeys Billy felt comfortable with. Just as he surrounded himself with aides of questionable talent, so did his underlings. His new $168,000-a-year chancellor of UMass Dartmouth appointed as her $140,000-a-year associate chancellor a woman who didn't even have a bachelor's degree. The pair of State House reporters Billy had hired to issue his "no comments" to reporters were both soon making over $100,000 a year.

As his trustees, Billy sought out yet more of his "friends." Andy Moes, the rotund ex-narc-turned-weekend-talk-show-host who had been so obsequious to Zip—his wife was a lawyer, and she was quickly appointed a trustee.

Once the board was stacked with similar rubber stamps and nonentities, Billy decided it was time to renegotiate his own contract. The $189,000 had seemed like a decent wage when he first engineered his own hiring, but since then, he'd been to conferences with other college presidents, and he'd also brushed up on the various foundations' annual salary reports. Billy now felt he deserved a salary more befitting a man of his . . . caliber. The negotiations were handled by Bobby Karam, a businessman from Bristol County and a friend of Senator Biff MacLean's, one of Billy's oldest cronies on Beacon Hill, whose career had ended with his payment of a $512,000 fine for conflict of interest in the awarding of state insurance contracts.

Billy's salary skyrocketed to $359,000, including perks. State employees began talking about just how huge Billy's pension would be, should he ever retire. Soon the husband of Karam's cousin was hired by Billy's handpicked UMass Dartmouth chancellor for a $120,000-a-year job at the school. Billy and his friends then tried to buy a nearby unaccredited law school for UMass Dartmouth, even though less than a quarter of its recent graduates had been able to pass the Massachusetts bar exam. But even Billy couldn't close that deal; faced with a need to spend perhaps as much as $40 million to win accreditation for a school the state didn't even need, the Board of Higher Education nixed the purchase. Billy's clout was starting to slip, if just a bit.

As Senate president, Billy had long chafed at the fact that reporters could find out how much he was paying, say, his niece, or his sister, or his son-in-law. So as soon as he was able to manage it, he had all the university payrolls transferred from the state comptroller to his own office. If any "savages" from the press now wanted to scour his schools' payrolls, they'd first have to get his permission, and that would happen at about the same time he "deemed it appropriate," as he once put it, to explain 75 State Street, namely, never.

Zip Connolly was living on borrowed time. In the wake of Judge Wolf's hearings, a new prosecutor, John Durham, had been appointed to investigate FBI corruption in Boston. He worked out of Worcester, rather than Boston, but his imported, out-of-town FBI agents soon raided Zip's offices at Boston Edison. They seized his computer, and on its hard drive, along with early drafts of his unsold screenplay, they found a copy of an anonymous letter that had been sent, on Boston Police Department stationery, to Judge Wolf two years earlier, alleging misconduct by the FBI, the DEA, and the Massachusetts State Police.

It was purportedly written by three BPD detectives, but now it was obvious Zip had composed it. Also in his office, the agents found stacks of blank stationery from both the BPD and the *Globe*. They had also located witnesses, acquaintances of Zip's, who were willing to testify that he had shown them early drafts of the letter, before he had mailed the final version to the judge. With incontrovertible evidence that Zip had written the letter to Wolf, the feds had Zip cold on an obstruction-of-justice count. Now the only question was how much more they could pin on him, and who he could take with him if he rolled.

Nineteen ninety-nine was a terrible year all around for the old gang. In September, Judge Wolf issued a 661-page opinion castigating the FBI, in which he concluded that "someone" in the FBI had leaked the information to Whitey about Brian Halloran's overtures to the FBI. Two weeks later, Martorano pleaded guilty to ten murders, including Roger Wheeler's in Oklahoma. Tulsa now had at least one witness against Whitey, if he were ever captured. In December, Frank Salemme pleaded guilty to racketeering, loansharking, and extortion, in exchange for the dropping of the murder charges. He would now be a witness against Zip.

Meanwhile, Stevie's mother finally died, and two of his illegitimate sons by Marion Hussey decided to case the gang's old "clubhouse" on East Third Street. They found $500,000 in cash, which they blew through in a six-month spending spree, as one of them later testified.

Of course, not everything had changed in the world. Four years after Whitey had vanished, the FBI belatedly put pen registers on his two brothers' phones, which allowed the feds to trace the origin of all incoming calls.

But then a female telephone company employee told her father, a bookie, about the wiretaps, and he immediately told Kevin Weeks, who told Jackie Bulger. The pen registers provided no usable leads.

That was to be Kevin Weeks's final service to the Bulgers. He couldn't handle this new, post-Whitey world. When he tried to shake down drug dealers in Somerville they told him to go fuck himself. He was roughed up in Southie bars. His mother, Peggy, was dying. His only relaxation came when he took off for paintball tournaments, but whenever he left, he would be trailed by FBI agents who thought he was delivering cash, or still more IDs, to Whitey. He tried to keep up appearances, of course—when the premiere party for the Boston movie *Good Will Hunting* was held at his favorite local watering hole, the L Street Tavern, Weeks showed up wearing a tuxedo. Also in attendance that evening was a local Teamster official who'd had a cameo role in the film as a judge. It was Jimmy Flynn, who had been tried, and acquitted, of the murder of Brian Halloran in 1982.

But time was running out for Weeks. In 1999, the feds found the man they needed in order to reel him in. Kevin

Hayes was a City Hall hack who had a cushy job as the custodian of the voting machines of the city of Boston. He was also
a bookie, and Weeks had kidnapped him in the early 1990s for
not paying "rent." Now, in deep trouble over his "job" at City
Hall, the feds subpoenaed him to testify about Weeks under a
grant of immunity.

On November 17, 1999, Kevin Weeks and Mob money-
launderer Kevin O'Neil were both arrested. The next day,
Weeks's mother died. The papers began speculating which of
the Kevins would flip first—O'Neil or Weeks. They were
shipped out to Central Falls, Rhode Island, away from Flemmi
and what was left of the gang down in Plymouth. In cell block
H3, Robert DeLuca took pen to paper to commemorate the
end of what was left of the Bulger gang with a poem that recalled Catherine's Greig's abandoned poodles, Nikki and Gigi.
When she went on the lam in 1995, Catherine Greig had left
the dogs with her twin sister, Margaret McCusker. But
McCusker herself had been indicted earlier in 1999 for perjury
after she lied about receiving telephone calls from her twin.
After being sentenced to six months of house arrest, McCusker
had both poodles put down. But DeLuca nonetheless entitled
his poem "Who's Minding the Puppies?"

Who's keeping tabs on Broadway,
Now that Weeksie's landed in court?
Who's gonna clean the rifles?
Who's gonna put out the hits?
Who's gonna pull the trigger
Now that Stevie's hit the pits?
Who's shaking down the bookies,
And who's gonna deal the drugs?
Who's gonna sell the hot stuff
From TV's to Persian rugs?
Who's gonna travel the whole world

Disguised as a couple of yuppies?
And while Whitey's with the Greig girl,
Who's taking care of the puppies?

The feds asked Kevin Weeks how old his kids were—sixteen and fourteen. If you go down on these charges, they told him, your oldest son will be your age, forty-three, before you get out. You'll be seventy. Weeks cut a deal, and his nickname instantly became "Two," as in Two Weeks, which was about how long he'd held out.

On December 12, 1999, Zip was indicted on racketeering and obstruction-of-justice charges. By then, it was common knowledge that Weeks had flipped, and in mid-January, the State Police began unearthing the first death pit, at Florian Hall in Dorchester.

When he pleaded guilty, Weeks read a statement to the judge about how both of his brothers had gone to Harvard, while he had never gotten beyond South Boston High. Yet, Weeks said, his late father, an ex-boxer, had been prouder of him than either of his Harvard-educated brothers, one of whom had been elected a selectman in a suburban town, while the other had become a trusted aide to Governor Michael Dukakis.

Kevin Weeks said his father had always bragged about him, not his brothers, Bill and Jack. The thing his father was proudest of, Kevin Weeks said, was the fact that his youngest son worked for Whitey Bulger. In his father's eyes, Kevin Weeks said, that made him a big man in Southie.

Despite everything, Billy was able to land one prestigious event for the University of Massachusetts.

Presidential debates are always haggled over and arranged at the highest levels, and Billy knew that in this election year, he had both sides covered. On the Democratic side, there was Ted

Kennedy, his old foe, now a friend. Soon Billy would be negotiating with the senior senator to turn his papers over to
UMass. And UMass Boston was next door to the JFK Library
in Dorchester. Any debate in Boston, especially the first one,
would entail a week of media genuflection at the memorial to
Teddy's slain older brother.

On the other side, the Bush family still felt warmly about
Billy, and his surreptitious tips during the 1988 presidential
campaign against Dukakis. And so the first debate of the 2000
campaign took place at UMass Boston, and Billy enjoyed a
brief moment in the national spotlight as he welcomed everyone both to his city and his school.

Unbeknownst to Billy, however, Kevin Weeks had just told
his law enforcement handlers about another of the death pits,
and as George W. Bush and Al Gore flew to Boston to debate
the great issues of the day, just south of the campus on Columbia Point, within easy view of the candidates and the national press corps, the State Police were exhuming the remains
of Catherine Greig's late brother-in-law, Paulie McGonagle,
whom Whitey had murdered a quarter-century earlier, with
help from Tommy King, whose murder Whitey had ordered a
year or so later, after which he was buried next to McGonagle.

In early 2001, Billy was subpoenaed to testify before the
Boston grand jury. Once Weeks flipped, it had been only a
matter of time. It was Weeks who in January 1995 had
arranged Whitey's phone call to Billy at the Quincy home of
his longtime employee (and driver), Eddie Phillips, whose son
was now on Billy's UMass payroll.

Billy admitted taking the call, but acknowledged little else.

"I don't feel an obligation to help everyone catch him," he
said. "I do have an honest loyalty to my brother, and I care
about him, and I know that's not welcome news, but it's my
hope that I'm never helpful to anyone against him."

Did he urge Whitey to surrender?

"I doubt that I did because I don't think it would be in his best interest to do so."

It would have been devastating to Billy's career if his testimony had been made public and the taxpayers had learned that the highest paid employee of the Commonwealth of Massachusetts, not to mention an officer of the court, felt no compunction to assist the authorities in capturing a serial killer and cocaine dealer. But Billy made his admissions in the secret proceedings of the grand jury, and they did not leak, at least immediately.

In Tulsa, the investigation into the 1981 murder of World Jai Alai owner Roger Wheeler remained open, even after Johnny Martorano pleaded guilty to being the hitman. The lead detective remained Mike Huff, who would occasionally fly in to Boston to pursue his latest leads.

Once, shortly before Zip's indictment, he had dropped in on the crooked ex-agent in his Boston Edison office in the Prudential Center. Zip spent much of his time toiling on his screenplay about the 1989 bugging of the Mafia initiation in Medford. The working title: "Only the Ghost Knows." Zip's secretary typed and retyped draft after draft, as she later resentfully explained at his racketeering trial.

Zip ushered Huff into his plush inner office. Huff sat down and immediately hit Zip with the $64 question.

"What do you know about Bulger and Flemmi?"

Zip ignored the question. "Do you know HBO is going to make a movie about me?"

"I know they set it up," Huff continued. "But nobody here will help me."

"Do you understand what I did?" Zip said. "I mean, do you really understand? I took down LCN. I took down twenty-eight guys, man, I'm proud of what I did. You guys, you just don't know what it's like. That's why I have to write the screen-play. I'm the only one who can do it."

Finally, in 2002, Huff had had enough of the runarounds. He put out a wanted poster of Whitey, describing him as a man with "extreme bad breath" who "may be found in homosexual communities/resorts or nudist facilities."

With the case heating up again, *America's Most Wanted* ran three segments on Whitey in 2002—on January 29, March 11, and September 23. That made seven in all, so far.

Next it was Congress's turn to make a run at the Bulgers. Con-gressman Dan Burton was the chairman of the House Com-mittee on Government Reform, and what in the federal government could possibly need more reforming than the Boston FBI office?

The committee members had been following the develop-ments in Boston as far back as 1997, when Governor Weld pardoned Joe "the Horse" Salvati, one of the four innocent men convicted in 1968 of the murder of Teddy Deegan on the per-jury of FBI informant Joe Barboza.

As the FBI began releasing documents from the files of Stevie Flemmi, it became clear that the FBI had known the identities of the real killers hours after Deegan's murder in 1965, and had in fact known before his slaying that he was about to be killed.

Burton subpoenaed still more FBI documents, but the Justice Department balked. When Burton threatened to cite Justice De-partment officials for contempt of Congress, the administration quickly folded, and turned over yet more previously classified re-ports. In May 2001, in Washington, Congressman Burton's com-mittee held its first hearings into the thirty-year pattern of FBI corruption in Boston. Joe the Horse was a particularly compelling witness, as was his wife, Marie. Soon they would be featured on *60 Minutes*, like Billy Bulger before them.

Nothing in the Deegan case directly involved Whitey, but any even moderately thorough investigation of the Boston FBI office could only lead directly to him.

Perhaps the most damning testimony in that first hearing came from former agent H. Paul Rico. Surly, monosyllabic, claiming memory loss, the seventy-six-year-old Rico practically snarled his way through a brief appearance. Asked about Salvati's thirty years in prison for a crime Rico had known he didn't commit, the old fed shrugged.

"What do you want from me?" Rico asked Burton. "Tears?"

The Bulgers' old neighbor, Congressman Joe Moakley, died on Memorial Day 2001. During one emotional interview, Billy recalled how an ailing Moakley had made a point of sitting with him in a public place during some of the worst of the revelations about Whitey, as a way of showing his continued support for the Bulgers.

Another linchpin had been knocked out from under Billy's base of support.

Had Moakley lived, the congressional hearings might not have gone quite so badly for Billy. Moakley was well liked on both sides of the aisle, and although he couldn't have halted the hearings, he might have at least been able to . . . guide the membership with some relatively gentle questioning of his old pal.

But now that was impossible. In a special 2001 election, five state senators—four Democrats, one Republican—squared off to succeed Moakley. The winner was Steve Lynch, of South Boston.

Zip Connolly had expected to be represented at trial by R. Robert Popeo, who had successfully defended a number of local politicians, including Billy Bulger. But Popeo didn't like losing, especially when he wasn't being paid much. Zip's dwindling band of cronies had organized a Friends of John Connolly group to raise money for his defense, but the dollars dried up as one death pit after another was excavated. Popeo handed off the case to one of his lesser partners.

In the courtroom, a parade of witnesses exposed Zip not only as a scheming gangster, but also as an utterly inept crook. For instance, when calling Steve Flemmi's lawyer, Ken Fishman, to strategize on Flemmi's defense, Zip would use a pay phone near his house on the Cape. But after taking the precaution of leaving his own home in order to avoid having his calls traced, he would then charge the calls to his Boston Edison credit card, thereby creating the paper trail that he was using the pay phone to avoid. The prosecutors even produced a former FBI staff assistant who testified that once, when she'd opened the top drawer of Zip's desk, she had seen "at least ten" uncashed pay checks. When Whitey was taking care of you, who needed a paltry government paycheck?

Kevin Weeks and John Martorano also testified against him. Weeks's most memorable moment came when he quoted Whitey's words as he'd counted out cash for his annual holiday payoffs to the local constabulary: "Christmas is for cops and kids."

Martorano's testimony at the Connolly trial devastated Billy. Martorano recalled Whitey telling him how Billy had instructed Zip to take care of Whitey. Now Chairman Burton had a reason to call Billy as a witness.

After Martorano testified about the two-carat diamond ring that Zip had taken from Whitey in 1976, Connolly's ex-wife was called to confirm that she had indeed received a two-carat diamond ring as a gift from Zip that year. Liz, Zip's second wife, twenty years his junior, watched in stony silence as the ex-wife testified, and the media duly noted that if Zip hadn't dumped her for Liz, she would have been precluded from testifying against him.

Also offered as evidence was an FBI training video from 1983, in which the future defendant intoned, "It's my belief that you should never pay informants."

He did not say whether he thought informants should pay FBI agents. And in what might have been his epitaph, Zip solemnly lectured the young agents-in-training: "Never try to out-gangster a gangster."

As the trial wound down, the papers speculated that perhaps Zip's low friends in high places had managed to slip a ringer onto the jury, "a Hibernian highwayman," as one columnist put it. If Zip could get a mistrial, the theory went, despite the overwhelming evidence against him, perhaps he could finagle a plea bargain, which he had angrily rejected before the trial began.

But it was not to be. Zip was found guilty on several serious charges, including obstruction of justice and racketeering, although he was not convicted of setting up any of the three FBI informants that Whitey murdered. Zip was sentenced to ten years in prison. If he is not convicted of any other crimes, he will be eligible for parole on June 15, 2011.

As 2002 began, despite the controversy that now enveloped him, Billy still felt he could hang on a few more years. Even if the next governor was a foe, it would take him years to gain a majority on the UMass board, and if the next governor was a friend, Billy would be able to survive indefinitely.

But Billy's luck finally failed him. Jane Swift had succeeded Paul Cellucci as governor a year earlier, when President Bush appointed his longtime supporter ambassador to Canada.

But Swift had been buffeted by a series of minor scandals, and it was obvious she could not be reelected. Enter Mitt Romney, a wealthy Republican businessman from Belmont, a graduate of both Harvard Law and Harvard Business Schools. In March 2002, a poll showed Romney leading Jane Swift among

Republican voters by a margin of 72–11, and three days later Swift dropped out of the race for reelection.

Billy was backing state Treasurer Shannon O'Brien, a former state senator and the daughter of a governor's councilor who had served with Sonny McDonough. Shannon had an impeccable hack pedigree, but she ran a surprisingly inept campaign. She sealed her fate in the final debate against Romney when she tried to make a joke about, of all things, parental consent for teenage abortions. Wearing an all-black outfit that accentuated her weight problem, Shannon suddenly flashed a weird grin at debate moderator Tim Russert and said, leeringly, "Want to see my tattoo, Tim?"

Mitt Romney won convincingly, and it couldn't have come at a worse time for Billy.

Billy went to work on the new governor-elect immediately. He had co-opted the last four governors, so he had no reason to believe that Romney couldn't be brought around with a little blarney and bluster. But just in case he couldn't work his magic one more time, Billy wanted to make sure his pals were taken care of. Lame duck Governor Swift found a Superior Court judgeship for Stevie Flemmi's lawyer, Ken Fishman. Billy's $175,000-a-year top aide, Jim Julian, had a younger brother named John who worked as an assistant district attorney in Boston. Swift appointed John Julian to an open district court judgeship on Nantucket.

But even as judgeships for his loyal retainers were being arranged, the U.S. House Committee on Government Reform was painting a target on Billy's chest. Chairman Burton would be holding his next series of hearings in Boston, and a couple of weeks after Romney's election, the committee issued a subpoena for Billy. Billy had researched the situation, and he knew that under the new rules of the House, Burton was term-limited as a chairman. Come January, he would be replaced as chairman by Tom Davis of Virginia, an Amherst College graduate who Billy was certain would be amenable to working something out privately.

So Billy decided to duck the appearance. He made no such pronouncements himself, of course, but his minions put out the word. Burton was nothing more than a "habitual headline fiend," as one of Billy's lickspittles in the press put it. But then someone asked Governor-elect Romney what he thought of the impending Bulger no-show.

"I believe," he said, "that President Bulger has a responsibility, as all citizens do, to respect Congress by responding to their subpoena."

That changed everything. Billy couldn't afford to alienate the man who would be appointing the trustees to the UMass board for at least the next four years.

Then Billy suffered a staggering setback, when transcripts of his 2001 testimony before the grand jury suddenly appeared on the front page of the *Globe*. All the devastating quotes about not wanting Whitey captured were suddenly on the public record.

On Friday, December 5, Billy appeared at the old McCormack Courthouse in Post Office Square. The press, including some of his most severe critics, sat in the jury box, just a few feet away. With C-SPAN broadcasting the hearing live, Burton began by reading a quotation from Edmund Burke: "The only thing necessary for the triumph of evil is for good men to do nothing."

Billy stared straight ahead. He was usually the one who quoted Edmund Burke to great effect. Present that morning were two Republicans, Burton and Chris Shays, from Connecticut, and three Democrats, all from Massachusetts—John Tierney, Marty Meehan, and Bill Delahunt, the former district attorney of Norfolk County, whom Whitey had long ago disparaged in Zip's FBI reports. Neither Meehan nor Delahunt were members of the committee, but would be allowed to ask questions. The other Massachusetts congressman who served on the committee, Steve Lynch of South Boston, the Bulgers' recent nemesis, was running late.

Burton, a graduate of the Cincinnati Bible Seminary, looked down at Billy and asked him if he had anything to say for himself before the committee began questioning him.

"I believe," Billy said haltingly, "my attorney if it, if it, uh, if it, uh, is acceptable would like to make a statement."

Burton smiled wanly. "You may confer with your attorney, but we want to hear from you, so could you pull the mike close to you, sir?"

Then Billy read from some notes, citing Rule 11k(5), which allowed the committee to proceed in closed session if the hearing "may tend to defame or ridicule the witness."

In other words, Billy wanted the press expelled, so that he could take the Fifth behind closed doors. Burton smiled again. The hearing was not going to be closed. Burton ran his committee hearings much the same way Billy had run his state Senate deliberations—everything had been hashed out beforehand, behind closed doors. When the congressmen appeared in public, at least at these sorts of regional hearings, everyone was on the same page. The vote by the committee members not to close the hearing was 4–0, with the tardy Steve Lynch arriving just in time to join the two Republicans and John Tierney to make it unanimous.

Burton immediately asked Billy if he knew where James Bulger was.

"On advice of counsel," Billy said, "I am unable to answer any questions today. This position is based among other things on privacy and due-process rights and the right against being compelled to provide evidence that may tend to incriminate oneself, all of which are found in the Bill of Rights."

Burton adjourned the hearing, and Billy rushed for the

courtroom door, several of his sons behind him blocking the reporters tumbling out of the jury box in pursuit. Accompanied by a flying wedge of beefy state court officers, Billy scurried down the back stairs of the courthouse toward a double-parked sedan out on Devonshire Street, like so many just indicted State House pols before him.

In the hallway outside the courtroom, Billy's attorney told UMass students watching on television that their president's refusal to testify in a congressional probe of organized crime was merely "a lesson in civics . . . [that] this constitutional protection exists to protect the innocent."

Meanwhile, on the other side of the hall, Burton addressed his comments directly to the oldest Bulger brother.

"If Whitey [is] paying attention today," he said, "he could have done his brother a real service by turning himself in. I'm sure taking the Fifth Amendment is going to cause Mr. Bulger a great deal of concern."

Billy had always been lucky. With a couple of exceptions like 75 State Street, everything had always broken right for him. Now nothing did. Every few weeks, it seemed, new lawsuits were filed by survivors of one or another of the victims of Whitey and Stevie. The families of John McIntyre, Deb Davis, Brian Halloran, and both Wimpy and Walter Bennett all filed civil suits against the U.S. government, claiming that the FBI's protection of Whitey and/or Stevie had resulted in the murders of their loved ones. In almost every news story, Billy Bulger's name would be mentioned along with his brother's. But Billy had gotten used to that.

Then, in February, Will McDonough, Billy's childhood friend and 1960 campaign manager, died suddenly while watching *ESPN SportsCenter*. For Billy, McDonough's death was a crushing blow. Will was a contemporary, and, like Joe Moakley, he had always stood by the Bulgers, in good times and bad.

At the funeral Mass at St. Augustine's, Billy collapsed and had to be wheeled out on a stretcher. Moments after the videotape appeared on TV, cynical talk radio callers began suggesting that "the Corrupt Midget" was setting himself up for a 72 percent tax-free disability pension—"white man's welfare," as Billy's constituents always called it.

Billy and Mary flew to Florida. Ostensibly Billy was "fundraising" for UMass, but it appears that after forty years of taxpayer-funded junkets, he was enjoying one last "trade mission." He spent days holed up in the finest hotel in Palm Beach, The Breakers, where sixty years earlier James Michael Curley and Joseph P. Kennedy had been turned away as undesirables. Times, and standards, had obviously changed.

Back in Boston, Romney was laying waste to whatever little reputation Billy had created for himself as a university administrator. The UMass payrolls were leaked to the *Herald*, and soon they were posted on the Internet, available for perusal by faculty members who had gone years without a pay raise. The UMass payrolls had been larded almost beyond belief. There was layer upon layer of bureaucracy—entire new levels of Bulgerite hackocracy had been created in less than seven years. Everyone in both academia and politics, it appeared, had been allowed to hire or promote whomever they wanted. The husband of the state rep from Amherst, a history professor, was being paid $128,000 a year. An obscure former state rep was making $125,000 as an "associate chancellor." There were new provosts, chancellors, and deans by the dozen, all making more than $100,000.

In February 2003 came word of the first confirmed Whitey sighting in six years. On September 10, 2002, a British man walking in Piccadilly Square had spotted an American gentleman he'd made the acquaintance of back in 1994, when the American was staying at a local hotel and working out daily at a neighborhood health club.

The British man recognized his old friend, who was tanned

and now sporting a goatee, and asked him how he'd been. The American, shocked at being recognized, told the Brit he had the wrong man, and then set off quickly in the opposite direction. The Brit thought no more of it until a few months later, when he was watching the movie *Hannibal*. When he noticed a brief shot of Whitey as the FBI's Ten Most Wanted List appeared on the screen, the Brit decided to tell Scotland Yard of their brief meeting.

Weeks later, the FBI discovered a safe-deposit box registered to James Bulger at a Barclays branch bank in Mayfair. Inside the safe-deposit box, police found more than $50,000 in various currencies and a key to another safe-deposit box, in Dublin. Then word leaked that Theresa Stanley had told the FBI about the Barclays box in 1996.

"I find that interesting," Congressman Burton commented on this latest example of FBI ineptitude. "There was either some sloppy work done or they didn't want to do it."

America's Most Wanted put Whitey back in the spotlight, running segments on him February 22 and again on May 3.

Whitey's photo appeared in the British media, and soon there was another sighting, this time in a military memorabilia shop in Manchester, where he was reported to have been buying Nazi memorabilia. It turned out not to be Whitey, but that news wasn't announced to the media until months later.

Unable to keep his brother's name out of the headlines, Billy continued trying to negotiate a deal with Davis, who had succeeded Burton as chairman of the Government Reform Committee. But under heavy pressure from both Republicans and Democrats on his committee, Davis was forced to schedule a public hearing in Washington on June 19.

Meanwhile, on April 10, Jackie Bulger pleaded guilty in federal court to two counts of perjury. He admitted lying in 1996 when asked about whether he'd ever visited yet another of Whitey's safe-deposit boxes, this one in Clearwater, Florida.

He also admitted lying in 1998 about his attempts to provide Whitey with new ID photos. Just before his indictment, Jackie had resigned from his beloved clerkship in an attempt to preserve his $3,778-a-month pension.

The only break Jackie caught was that the federal judge in his case, George O'Toole, was married to a woman who had contributed hundreds of dollars over the years to Jimmy Brett, the state rep who was married to Billy's personal secretary. The feds asked for a fourteen-month sentence; O'Toole handed Jackie a four-month wrist slap. Asked by a reporter whether he should have recused himself from the case, given his family ties to the Bulgers, Judge O'Toole said he'd considered bowing out, then decided not to.

In January 2003, Stevie Flemmi's brother Michael, now a retired Boston cop, also pleaded guilty to selling a load of his brother Stevie's stolen jewelry for $40,000. The major witness against him was his nephew, William St. Croix, formerly known as William Hussey, Stevie's bastard son by Marion Hussey. St. Croix had turned against his father after learning that Stevie and Whitey had strangled his half-sister, Deborah Hussey.

Franny Joyce, handpicked executive director of the Massachusetts Convention Center Authority, was forced out with a golden parachute that included $72,000 for thirty-eight weeks of unused vacation, an $80,000 bonus, and a retroactive $24,000 pay raise, to $150,000, which also raised his annual pension to $75,000.

Bernard Cardinal Law was the next friend of Billy's to go, after more than a year of newspaper accounts of pedophile priests running amok in his archdiocese. Law was "reassigned," first to Maryland, then to Rome.

Billy had lost yet another person with whom he could commiserate over the decline of morality in American society. Fortunately for Billy, John Silber, nearing eighty, still endured at

Boston University. He urged Billy to hang in as president of UMass, that it was his "destiny" to lead.

Negotiating with the Congressional committee, the most Billy's lawyer could arrange was a grant of immunity from prosecution for his sworn public testimony. That meant that Billy could not be prosecuted for anything he admitted to under oath. But if he lied, he could be charged with perjury. The stakes were high as Billy reached Washington on June 19, 2003, to testify about an organized crime faction that had for all practical purposes ceased to exist.

Billy's position, he knew, was untenable. He had been summoned to Washington to be pummeled, humiliated. And if he lied, he would be indicted for perjury, like his brother Jackie.

He had prepared to some degree. His attorney provided a number of produced affidavits for the committee and the press. Harold Brown said no one, i.e. Whitey, had threatened him in the 75 State Street scandal. Mike Barnicle, the disgraced former journalist and longtime apologist for the Bulgers, said Billy had never told him that Whitey taped his conversations with FBI agents. An executive from Boston Edison, now known as NSTAR, wrote that Billy had never intervened to get Zip Connolly a job. And on it went.

The congressmen, though, seemed more interested in that morning's front-page story in the *Herald*, headlined "Club Whitey," in which it was reported that two perpetually destitute South Boston hangers-on had somehow scraped up the cash to purchase a ramshackle inn in the Caribbean. One of the buyers admitted knowing Whitey, whom he called Seamus, which is Gaelic for James. His name was Concannon, and his brother worked in the probation office, with Billy's son Chris. The other buyer was a Boston police officer who had recently returned to active duty after twenty-nine years on disability.

Workers at the club said that soon after the place was purchased by the Southie men, a strange-acting priest took up
residence.

"He was wearing a collar, but he didn't act like a priest," the
bartender said of the strange, Whitey Bulger–like cleric. "He
had a foul mouth and a bad temper."

Billy's lack of memory did not play well with either the congressmen or the public. The Massachusetts congressmen stuck
mainly with specific lines of questioning—Lynch, for instance,
questioned Billy at length about which FBI agents he had
known, and took pains to point out the well-paying jobs they
had landed upon their retirement.

Chairman Burton, meanwhile, worked the broader themes,
as in this exchange.

> Burton: "There are people who say Whitey came up to
> them and said, 'Do you know who I am and if you
> don't leave my brother alone you'll regret it.' You
> don't know anything about that?"
>
> Billy, after a pause: "I don't know much about it, no."
>
> Burton: "Do you know who the people were who were
> threatened?"
>
> Billy: "No."
>
> Burton: "You had no connection or relation—"
>
> Billy: "I can assure you, I would never never authorize or
> ask for such a madcap kind of conduct on his part
> or anyone's part."

At other times, Burton did inquire about specific incidents,
such as a rider anonymously attached to the 1982 state budget
that would have forced the retirement of several high-ranking
members of the State Police, one of whom was Lieutenant
Colonel Jack O'Donovan, Whitey's sworn enemy who had
blamed the FBI for the blown Lancaster Street garage bugging

operation. After word of the budgetary attack on O'Donovan got out, Governor King had immediately vetoed the outside section. At one point during the hearing, Billy suggested that perhaps a State Police union had managed to insert the rider. Later that year, congressional investigators would be dispatched to Massachusetts to pore over the ancient budgetary records and to interview the legislative leaders of the time. But no fingerprints—of anyone—were ever found.

Still, Burton questioned Billy relentlessly about the surreptitious attempt by someone to sack a cop who was hot on the trail of Whitey Bulger.

Burton: "You had nothing to do with it and you don't remember?"

Billy: "Well, the premise is not true that such people were penalized."

Burton: "Well, what did the amendment do?"

Billy: "I'm uncertain of that."

Burton: "To say it wasn't penalizing you must know what it did."

Billy: "But it never became law, Congressman."

Burton: "If you don't remember it, how do you recall it didn't take effect?"

Billy: "Because subsequent to that, it's been written about."

Burton: "Oh, I see. You picked it up from the newspaper."

At the end of his disastrous day in the District, only one or two new-breed *Globe* sycophants were willing to deny the obvious: that Billy had damaged himself beyond repair. Of course, he still had his handpicked university trustees behind him. After the hearing ended in mid-afternoon, Grace Fey, the chairman of the UMass board, issued a statement saying she had "never been prouder" of Billy.

Both Republican Governor Romney and Democratic Attorney General Tom Reilly, a longtime Bulger ally who had once taken a $100 campaign contribution from Zip Connolly, expressed their disbelief that Billy would try to stonewall a congressional committee. Romney, moreover, decided to do something about it. Fey's husband had at least one contract with the university, so the Republican State Committee quickly filed a complaint with the State Ethics Commission, charging her with a conflict of interest. Embarrassing headlines appeared in both newspapers, and it would cost her thousands of dollars in legal fees to contest the charges. Billy had deliberately picked trustees who could be controlled, like the state senators he'd once dominated. With his shot across Fey's bow, Romney had made it clear that he was not averse to trashing the trustees' reputations or their bank accounts, if they were unwilling to vote to fire Billy.

When, on June 26, the trustees again gave Billy another ringing endorsement, the Romney forces decided to go a different route. They would pack the board with Billy's "foes."

Three vacancies were opening up in September. Romney's operatives began talking up three people: Alan Dershowitz, Judge E. George Daher, and a *Herald* columnist—the author of this book—who had sat behind Bulger at the hearings. All expressed willingness, indeed eagerness, to join the board.

One Sunday night in late July, Billy and his wife, Mary, dined at Baxter's in Hyannis, enjoying the same treat they'd shared on their first date, almost a half-century earlier, fried clams. When Billy spotted a former UMass trustee and his wife, he invited them over to his table, and talk quickly turned to the ongoing struggle with Romney.

"I think it's pretty well blown over," said Billy. "Don't you?"

"I don't think so," said the former trustee. He then named the three men Romney planned to appoint.

"He wouldn't dare," Billy said.

Two weeks later, in Lowell, Billy resigned as president of UMass. Ted Kennedy issued a statement saying that he was "saddened" by the news. Bill Clinton, who had phoned Billy at a couple of the later St. Patrick's Day breakfasts, called from Chappaqua with his condolences. The settlement of the deal the trustees had negotiated with him cost Massachusetts taxpayers more than $960,000.

And Billy got a pension too. He took the survivor's option, which assured that Mary would continue to receive the kiss in the mail even if Billy predeceased her. After taxes, his monthly check from the commonwealth came to $11,312.29 a month.

But even that wasn't enough for Billy. In his final hours on the job, he ordered one of his lackeys to send over more documents to the State Retirement Board, claiming that his "housing allowance" and his annuities, which amounted to another $40,000 or so a year, should also be included in calculating his pension, thus adding another $32,000 a year to what was already by far the largest public pension in state history.

The *Herald* led its next edition with the story—and a photo of a grinning Bulger next to the headline, "Back for More."

One of the few anti-Bulger trustees on the board told the newspapers, "[He's] going out the door, grabbing everything but the pictures on the walls. It's supposed to be public service, not self-service."

It was a concept the Bulgers never did grasp.

EPILOGUE

In October 2003, Stevie Flemmi pleaded guilty in U.S. District Court in Boston to ten counts of murder. He made the decision as part of a deal to reduce the sentence for his brother Michael, the former Boston cop, who was not scheduled to be released from prison until 2010. In open court, prosecutor Fred Wyshak read aloud Flemmi's agreed-upon statement, and as Wyshak reached the paragraph about the 1981 murder of Debra Davis, one of her brothers stood up in court and screamed at Stevie, "Fuck you, you fucking piece of shit!"

At a single hearing, the State Retirement Board heard the appeals of both Billy and Jackie Bulger. Billy's attorney argued that his client's pension should be increased by another $32,000 a year. Jackie's lawyer contended that his client's $44,000-a-year pension should be restored, because although Jackie did commit multiple felonies while a public employee, he'd resigned from his job and applied for a pension before he was indicted.

On separate 5–0 votes, the board turned down both Bulgers.

In November, Frank Salemme led police to the Hopkinton Sportsmen's Club, where he said he and Stevie had buried the bodies of Wimpy and Walter Bennett in 1967. After days of digging, the police abandoned the search, claiming that the topography of the area had been changed by the dumping of millions of tons of dirt from the Big Dig, the $15 billion public works boondoggle in downtown Boston that was now the subject of multiple federal and state corruption investigations.

In December 2003 the city of Somerville began foreclosure proceedings on the old Marshall Street garage out of which the Winter Hill Gang once operated. According to city officials, Howie Winter, now seventy-four and living in Millbury, owed more than $11,000 in back property taxes.

In December 2003, former FBI agent H. Paul Rico answered a knock at his front door in Miami and admitted several police officers to his house. When they told him they were there to arrest him on a murder warrant from Oklahoma, he asked them if they were joking. When he realized they were serious, and that he was going to be taken away to jail, Rico defecated in his trousers.

In January 2004 Rico was extradited from Florida to Oklahoma to stand trial on charges of arranging the 1981 murder of his boss, World Jai Alai owner Roger Wheeler. From a wheelchair, Rico pleaded not guilty at his arraignment at the county jail.

On January 16, 2004, H. Paul Rico died in a Tulsa hospital room, as armed jail guards stood outside his door. He was alone when he died.

In January, federal agents arrested a Winthrop man named Graham Bulger for allegedly burglarizing a telephone company building in Waltham a month earlier. In its press release, the Secret Service said Bulger was a relative of Whitey Bulger's. The headline in the *Herald* the next day read: "Bulger Kin Charged in Thefts of Equipment."

Graham Bulger's sister fired off an e-mail, denying that she and her brother were related to any other Bulgers. She said her family was a victim of "Unjust Surname Profiling."

In February, on the day of the New Hampshire primary,

when few reporters were in Boston, Billy appeared in a charcoal-gray business suit and topcoat at the Social Security office at the Tip O'Neill Building in the West End and filed his application for Social Security.

In March, the Boston Public Library hosted a black-tie "Celebration of Service and Leadership 70th Birthday Tribute to William M. Bulger." The master of ceremonies was former Governor William F. Weld.

In the spring of 2004, the family of Billy Bulger was again questioned by federal investigators, this time about a call that was placed to their home on East Third Street by Barclays Bank in 1997 when the branch where Whitey had stashed $50,000 and the key to another safe-deposit box in Dublin was moved. According to bank records, a woman answered the phone and was asked if she knew where the bank could reach James Bulger.

"His current whereabouts are unknown," the bank recorded the woman as replying.

On April 1, Jackie Bulger was released from the minimum-security federal prison in Ayer, Massachusetts, after serving four months with, among others, Mafia underboss Gerry Angiulo.

On April 17, 2004, *America's Most Wanted* ran its twelfth segment on Whitey Bulger. None of the tips Fox received after the show's airing proved of worth to investigators.

In May 2004 imprisoned ex-FBI agent Zip Connolly was transported from a federal penitentiary in North Carolina to testify before the federal grand jury in Worcester that was continuing its investigation of FBI corruption and organized crime in Boston. In prison, without benefit of dye, Zip's black hair had turned gray. During the interrogation, he guzzled glass after glass of ice water. Whenever a difficult question was asked of him, he would look up at the prosecutor and ask, "Can I go to the little boys' room?"

In May, one of Billy's toadies at UMass Boston wrote a letter to the editor of a weekly newspaper in Dorchester suggesting that the new campus center at UMass Boston be named for Billy Bulger "because of his unparalleled career in service to the Commonwealth in general and to students and the people of Boston in particular."

The building was not named after Billy.

Working out of the Coast Guard Building on Northern Avenue, the Violent Fugitive Task Force in Boston continued running down leads on the whereabouts of Whitey. Sightings were reported in, among other places, a remote town in Thailand best known for its male brothels, in Portugal, in Maine, and in Ohio, where two uniformed cops reported that they believed they had released him after a routine traffic stop. None of the leads panned out.

The new state treasurer of Massachusetts sought an appraisal of the Hynes Convention Center, the building on which Billy had spared no expense when he created the Massachusetts Convention Center Authority. Including debt service on the bonds, the MCCA admitted that the building on Boylston Street had cost taxpayers at least $450 million. With a new state-funded convention center about to open in South Boston, the treasurer decided that the center was no longer viable as a commercial property, if indeed it ever had been. He asked that the appraisal be based on the land's worth if the Hynes were torn down and replaced with housing units. Using those parameters, the appraisers decided that the Hynes's true current value was $35 million.

In July at the Democratic National Convention in Boston's Fleet Center, Senator John F. Kerry—"Just For Kerry," as Billy had called him—was nominated as his party's presidential candidate. Billy did not attend, but his old rival from Southie, former mayor Ray Flynn, made the rounds, offering comments to reporters on any subject except his refusal to appoint Zip Connolly as the Boston police commissioner twenty years earlier.

"It's a Southie thing," Flynn said with a smile, shaking his head. "You've got Billy under oath on it, right? What more do you need?"

Letting bygones be bygones, Flynn added, "Whatever Billy said, that's what happened."

In August, Bulger loyalist Grace Fey resigned as chairman of the UMass board of trustees. In a newspaper interview, she described what it was like to be associated with Billy Bulger in his final days as president of the university.

"I realized I was in trouble," she said, "the day I got a call from someone at *The New York Times* who said he was a crime reporter. A crime reporter!"

At Johnny Martorano's final sentencing, Judge Wolf tacked another two years onto the almost ten years he had already served. Wolf complained that a twelve-year sentence for nineteen murders still didn't seem nearly long enough.

A local gangster who survived a 1973 machine-gunning on Morrissey Boulevard by Johnny and Whitey sent a letter from prison to Judge Wolf that was read into the record.

"I expect to see most people involved in this case in hell someday," said Ralph DeMasi, sixty-eight. "I hope you all get there before me. Don't worry, the drinks will be on me."

Zip Connolly's screenplay, *Only the Ghost Knows*, about a crusading FBI agent who brings down the Mafia in his hometown, remains unsold in Hollywood.

Kevin O'Neil, former owner of Triple O's, onetime law client of Billy Bulger's, and veteran money-launderer for Whitey, was sentenced to time served—eleven months. He was described as a cooperating witness and his lawyer claimed that the gangster, who had trimmed down to 320 pounds, was in danger from a "psychotic killer"—Whitey. An unnamed observer was quoted in the *Herald* the next day as saying that Twinkies and Ho-Ho's posed a greater threat to Kevin O'Neil's health than Whitey. As O'Neil's lawyer described his "economic hardships," his two daughters wept. After the sentencing, they left the J. Joseph Moakley Courthouse in a Lexus SUV.

The same day O'Neil was sentenced in Boston, in Tulsa Stevie Flemmi pleaded guilty in state court to conspiring to murder World Jai Alai owner Roger Wheeler in 1981. He apologized to the Wheeler family and offered any assistance he could in bringing the last killer—Whitey Bulger—to justice.

Boston mayor Thomas Menino confirmed that Billy would remain on the board of the Boston Public Library.

"He's an avid reader," the mayor said.

In October, a district court judge best known for singing Irish ballads at public occasions restored Jackie Bulger's $3,778-a-month pension, saying that the felonies he was convicted of, including perjury, had nothing to do with his job as a court clerk. The state treasurer announced he would appeal.

In November, an administrative law judge overruled the State Retirement Board and ordered that Billy Bulger's pension be increased by another $29,000 a year, raising his annual post-retirement take to $208,365. The state treasurer announced he would appeal.

In November 2004, Frank Salemme, age seventy-one, was arrested in Virginia after his indictment on charges of lying to federal agents about a 1993 murder. The main witness against him once again: Stevie Flemmi.

In December 2004, Zip Connolly's brother-in-law, Arthur Gianelli, was indicted by a federal grand jury and charged with attempted arson.

That same month, Zip Connolly was revealed as having served as an informant in federal prison against a Louisville crack dealer. In an interview with the *Globe*, Zip said he just wanted to help law enforcement.

"Once an FBI agent, always an FBI agent," he said. "I have never forgotten my oath."

In April 2005, Stevie Flemmi was deposed in New York by a group of lawyers representing the families of his and Whitey's victims who are now suing the federal government.

Among other things, Stevie testified that he and Whitey had been paying off six FBI agents in the Boston office. Those who could be reached for comment issued denials. Flemmi also named Pat Nee as the other shooter, along with Whitey, in the 1982 murders of Brian Halloran and Michael Donahue. Nee responded in the *Globe* by calling Flemmi a "punk."

"He should shut up and do his time like the rest of us," Nee said.

Stevie was also questioned at length about the 1985 murder of his step-daughter, Deborah Hussey.

"How could you, Mr. Flemmi?" the Hussey family attorney asked. "How could you?"

"You need not answer that," Flemmi's court-appointed lawyer told him.

In May 2005, Zip Connolly was indicted on first-degree murder charges in Florida for the 1982 shooting of World Jai Alai executive John Callahan. If convicted, Zip could spend the rest of his life in prison.

In June 2005, ex-House Speaker Tom Finneran, who became the most powerful legislative leader in Massachusetts after Billy's retirement in 1996, was indicted by a federal grand jury on three counts of perjury relating to his testimony in a civil lawsuit over legislative redistricting.

Finneran, a fixture at Billy's St. Patrick's Day breakfasts who first described the MBTA as "Mr. Bulger's Transportation Authority," hired as his attorney the same lawyer who defended Jimmy Flynn when Whitey attempted to frame him for the murder of Brian Halloran in 1982.

Finneran was succeeded as speaker by Majority Leader Sal DiMasi of the North End, whose name and phone number had been found in Vinny "the Animal" Ferrara's address book a decade earlier. DiMasi said he was the Mafia captain's divorce lawyer.

After serving sixteen years in prison, Vinny the Animal was released from prison. Now fifty-six, Ferrara swore that he would not "revisit" his past.

"To do so," he told Judge Mark Wolf, "would be to qualify myself for the Hall of Idiots."

In July 2005, the FBI sent agents to Uruguay on yet another fruitless search for Whitey. A Montevideo newspaper ran a story about Whitey under the headline "Million Dollar Baby."

"Alias Whitey," the article began in an Internet translation, "is a dark personage, in spite of his present face of a defenseless grandfather. Always is he armed with a knife. Bulger had friendship with superior agents of the FBI during the time in which he collaborated with them to catch the enemy number 1, the Italian Mafia. Later, as usually it happens, its own ally became the enemy to follow—the bin Laden syndrome."

In August 2005, Billy and Mary Bulger spent a week in Israel on a junket for "community leaders." Other guests included the new House Speaker, Sal DiMasi.

Also in the summer of 2005, from his jail cell in Miami, Zip Connolly filed motions seeking a new trial on the racketeering charges. In one brief, he accused his old friend, former federal prosecutor Jeremiah O'Sullivan, of telling investigators conflicting stories about his knowledge of Whitey Bulger's crimes for "dishonorable self-serving reasons."

Connolly also released a sealed 1997 FBI interview in which O'Sullivan described Zip as a "disruptive" agent who "wanted nothing to do with police corruption cases."

In addition, the bitter Connolly filed a 2004 FBI interview of a minor organized crime figure who had been imprisoned with Frank Salemme, who had been a witness against Zip in 2002. The informant quoted Salemme as saying that he believed Billy Bulger "was still in contact" with Whitey and "had sent him money."

Reached for comment, ex-con Kevin Weeks scoffed at the informant's claims, saying that "Jimmy" would never "put his brother in that position."

Besides, Weeks added, Whitey "has money stashed all over. He didn't need his brother to send him money."

On September 3, 2005, Whitey turned seventy-six. The search continues.

INDEX